The Lusiad by Luís de Camões

or The Discovery of India, an Epic Poem

PART II: Books VI – X

Luís Vaz de Camões, without doubt, remains to this day the Portuguese language's foremost poet and has mentored many with his work through the centuries and wherever the Portuguese Empire or its Sailors reached, or its language spoken – from Brazil and Africa, through Portugal itself to India and the Far East. During his lifetime the Portuguese Empire, grew rapidly and this was, perhaps, a Golden Age for Portugal in many areas.

His lyrical poetry showed such mastery that, for many, his talents are the equal of Shakespeare, Homer or Dante. With lines as encompassing and truthful as "em várias flamas variamente ardia" ("I burnt myself at many flames") it is hard to argue against.

Probably born in 1524 it is unknown as to where. There is a statue dedicated to him in Constanzia which together with Lisbon, Coimbra or Alenquer also rival as his birthplace.

What is known is that he was an only child from a fading family of the old Aristocracy. His father went to India to pursue his fortune and died in Goa. His mother later remarried and for Camões early life was financially comfortable.

He was educated within the Catholic church and then attended the University of Coimbra giving him access to a wide range of classical and contemporary literature. Aside from his native Portuguese he read in Latin and Italian and wrote poetry in Spanish. What can be acknowledged from his work was that Camões was a man of great learning and widely read. He was able to use that knowledge and influence to write beautiful and lasting poetry.

Camões was a romantic, and it was rumoured, fell in love with a lady in waiting to the Queen and also Princess Maria. Possibly due to indiscretions surrounding these love affairs, he was exiled from Lisbon and enlisted in the overseas militia where he lost the sight in his right eye and eventually returned to Lisbon.

He now led a bohemian lifestyle and a fracas resulted in him injuring a member of the royal stables. He was imprisoned but his mother successfully pleaded for his release which involved paying a large fine and serving three years in militia in the Orient after which he took up a post in Macau.

During this time he was shipwrecked and some romantics claim that he swam ashore whilst holding aloft the manuscript of his unfinished epic; Os Lusíadas , the poetical tale of how Vasco da Gama discovered India.

When finally back in Lisbon, in 1570, he finished and then published two years later, 'Os Lusiadas', the masterpiece for which his poetic talent has deservedly been recognised.

In July of that year he was granted a royal pension, probably in recompense for both his service in India and his having written Os Lusíadas.

Luis Vaz de Camões died in 1580 on 10th June, coincidentally Portugal's national day, and is buried in the Jeronimos Monastery in Lisbon.

Index of Contents

DISSERTATION ON THE FICTION OF THE ISLAND OF VENUS
BOOK X
FOOTNOTES

THE ORIGINAL DEDICATION, 1776

TO THE DUKE OF BUCCLEUGH.

MY LORD,

The first idea of offering my LUSIAD to some distinguished personage, inspired the earnest wish, that it might be accepted by the illustrious representative of that family under which my father, for many years, discharged the duties of a clergyman.

Both the late Duke of BUCCLEUGH, and the Earl of DALKEITH, distinguished him by particular marks of their favour; and I must have forgotten him, if I could have wished to offer the first Dedication of my literary labours to any other than the Duke of BUCCLEUGH.

I am, with the greatest respect, My Lord,
Your Grace's most devoted
And most obedient humble servant,

WILLIAM JULIUS MICKLE.

EDITOR'S PREFACE

In undertaking, at the publishers' request, the function of editor of Mickle's Lusiad, I have compared the translation with the original, and, in some places, where another translation seemed preferable to, or more literal than, Mickle's, I have, in addition, given that rendering in a foot-note. Moreover, I have supplied the arguments to the several cantos, given a few more explanatory notes, and added a table of contents.

"The late ingenious translator of the Lusiad," says Lord Strangford,[1] "has portrayed the character, and narrated the misfortunes of our poet, in a manner more honourable to his feelings as a man than to his accuracy in point of biographical detail. It is with diffidence that the present writer essays to correct his errors; but, as the real circumstances of the life of Camoëns are mostly to be found in his own minor compositions, with which Mr. Mickle was unacquainted, he trusts that certain information will atone for his presumption."

As Lord Strangford professes to have better and more recent sources of information regarding the illustrious, but unfortunate, bard of Portugal, I make no apology for presenting to the reader an abstract of his lordship's memoir. Much further information will be found, however, in an able article contained in No. 53 of the Quarterly Review for July, 1822, from the pen, I believe, of the poet Southey. "The family of Camoëns was illustrious," says Lord Strangford, "and originally Spanish. They were long settled at Cadmon, a castle in Galicia, from which they probably derived their patronymic appellation. However, there are some who maintain that their name alluded to a certain wonderful bird,[2] whose mischievous sagacity discovered and punished the smallest deviation from conjugal fidelity. A lady of the house of Cadmon, whose conduct had been rather indiscreet, demanded to be tried by this extraordinary judge. Her innocence was proved, and, in gratitude to the being who had restored him to matrimonial felicity, the contented husband adopted his name." It would appear that in a dispute between the families of Cadmon and De Castera, a cavalier of the latter family was slain. This happened in the fourteenth century. A long train of persecution followed, to escape which, Ruy de Camoëns, having embraced the cause of Ferdinand, removed with his family into Portugal, about A.D. 1370. His son, Vasco de Camoëns, was highly distinguished by royal favour, and had the honour of being the ancestor of our poet, who descended from him in the fourth generation. Luia de Camoëns, the author of the Lusiad, was born at Lisbon about A.D. 1524. His misfortunes began with his birth—he never saw a father's smile—for Simon Vasco de Camoëns perished by shipwreck in the very year which gave being to his illustrious son. The future poet was sent to the university of Coimbra—then at the height of its fame,—"and maintained there by the provident care of his surviving parent."

"Love," says Lord Strangford, "is very nearly allied to devotion, and it was in the exercise of the latter, that Camoëns was introduced to the knowledge of the former. In the Church of Christ's Wounds at Lisbon, on 11th April, 1542, Camoëns first beheld Doña Caterina de Atayde, the object of his purest and earliest attachment ... and it was not long before Camoëns enjoyed an opportunity of declaring his affection, with all the romantic ardour of eighteen and of a poet." The peculiar situation of the lady, as one of the maids of honour to the queen, imposed a restraint upon her admirer which soon became intolerable; and he, for having violated the sanctity of the royal precincts, was in consequence banished from the court. Whatever may have been the nature of his offence, "it furnished a pretext to the young lady's relations for terminating an intercourse which worldly considerations rendered highly imprudent."

But Love consoled his votary: his mistress, on the morning of his departure, confessed the secret of her long-concealed affection, and the sighs of grief were soon lost in those of mutual delight. The hour of parting was, perhaps, the sweetest of our poet's existence.

Camoëns removed to Santarem, but speedily returned to Lisbon, was a second time detected, and again driven into exile.[3]

The voice of Love inspired our poet "with the glorious resolution of conquering the obstacles which fortune had placed between him and felicity." He obtained permission, therefore, to accompany King John III. in an expedition then fitting out against the Moors in Africa. In one of the engagements with the enemy our hero had the misfortune to lose "his right eye, by some splinters from the deck of the vessel in which he was stationed. Many of his most pathetic compositions were written during this campaign, and the toils of a martial life were sweetened by the recollection of her for whose sake they were endured. His heroic conduct at length procured his recall to court," but to find, alas, that his mistress was no more.

Disappointed in his hope of obtaining any recognition of his valiant deeds, he now resolved, under the burning sun of India, to seek that independence which his own country denied. "The last words I uttered," says Camoëns, "on board the vessel before leaving, were those of Scipio: 'Ungrateful country! thou shalt not even possess my bones.'" "Some," says Lord Strangford, "attribute his departure to a very different cause, and assert that he quitted his native shores on account of an intrigue in which he was detected with the beautiful wife of a Portuguese gentleman. Perhaps," says Lord Strangford, "this story may not be wholly unfounded." On his arrival in India he contributed by his bravery to the success of an expedition carried on by the King of Cochin, and his allies, the Portuguese, against the Pimento Islands; and in the following year (1555) he accompanied Manuel de Vasconcelos in an expedition to the Red Sea. Here he explored the wild regions of East Africa, and stored his mind with ideas of scenery, which afterwards formed some of the most finished pictures of the Lusiad.

On his return to Goa, Camoëns devoted his whole attention to the completion of his poem; but an unfortunate satire which, under the title of Disparates na India, or Follies in India, he wrote against the vices and corruptions of the Portuguese authorities in Goa, so roused the indignation of the viceroy that the poet was banished to China.

Of his adventures in China, and the temporary prosperity he enjoyed there, while he held the somewhat uncongenial office of Provedor dos defuntos, i.e., Trustee for deceased persons, Mickle has given an ample account in the introduction to the Lusiad. During those years Camoëns completed his poem, about half of which was written before he left Europe. According to a tradition, not improbable in itself, he composed great part of it in a natural grotto which commands a splendid view of the city and harbour of Macao. An engraving of it may be seen in Onseley's Oriental Collections, and another will be found in Sir G. Staunton's Account of the Embassy to China.

A little temple, in the Chinese style, has been erected upon the rock, and the ground around it has been ornamented by Mr. Fitzhugh, one of our countrymen, from respect to the memory of the poet. The years that he passed in Macao were probably the happiest of his life. Of his departure for Europe, and his unfortunate shipwreck at the mouth of the river Meekhaun,[4] in Cochin China, Mickle has also given a sufficient account.

Lord Strangford has related, on the authority of Sousa, that while our poet was languishing in poverty at Lisbon, "a cavalier, named Ruy de Camera, called on him one day, asking him to finish for him a poetical version of the seven penitential psalms. Raising his head from his wretched pallet, and pointing to his faithful Javanese attendant, he exclaimed, 'Alas, when I was a poet, I was young, and happy, and blest with the love of ladies; but now I am a forlorn, deserted wretch. See—there stands my poor Antonio, vainly supplicating fourpence to purchase a little coals—I have them not to give him.' The cavalier, as Sousa relates, closed both his heart and his purse, and quitted the room. Such were the grandees of Portugal." Camoëns sank under the pressure of penury and disease, and died in an alms-house, early in 1579, and was buried in the church of Sta. Anna of the Franciscan Friars. Over his grave Gonzalo Coutinho placed the following inscription:—

"HERE LIES LUIS DE CAMOËNS. HE EXCELLED ALL THE POETS OF HIS TIME. HE LIVED POOR AND MISERABLE, AND HE DIED SO. MDLXXIX."

The translator of the Lusiad was born, in 1734, at Langholm, in Dumfriesshire, where his father, a good French scholar, was the Presbyterian minister. At the age of sixteen William Julius Mickle was removed, to his great dislike, from school, and sent into the counting-house of a relation of his mother's, a brewer, where, against his inclination, he remained five years. He subsequently, for family reasons, became the head of the firm, and carried on the business. It is not to be wondered at, however, that with his dislike to business in general and to this one in particular, he did not succeed; and it is quite reasonable to suppose that the cause of his failure, and subsequent pecuniary embarrassments, arose from his having devoted those hours to his poetical studies which should have been dedicated to business. Mickle obtained afterwards the appointment of corrector of the Clarendon Press in Oxford, and died at Wheatly, in Oxfordshire, in 1789.

Southey speaks of Mickle (Quarterly Review, liii. p. 29) as a man of genius who had ventured upon the chance of living by his literary labours, and says that he "did not over-rate the powers which he was conscious of possessing, knew that he could rely upon himself for their due exertion, and had sufficient worldly prudence to look out for a subject which was likely to obtain notice and patronage." His other poems, Pollio, Sir Martyn, etc., with the exception of his Cumnor Hall, are not held in high estimation.

Describing the several poetic versions of the Lusiad, Mr. Musgrave says,[5] of Fanshaw's version, that "its language is antiquated, and in many instances it travesties the original, and seldom long sustains the tone of epic gravity suited to the poem. It is, however," says he, "more faithful than the translation of Mickle, but it would be ungenerous," he adds, "to dwell on the paraphrastic licences which abound in Mickle's performance, and on its many interpolations and omissions. Mr. Mickle thought, no doubt," says Musgrave, "that by this process he should produce a poem which in its perusal might afford a higher gratification. Nor am I prepared to say that by all readers this would be deemed a miscalculation. Let it not be supposed, however, that I wish to detract from the intrinsic merit of his translation. It is but an act of justice to admit, that it contains many passages of exquisite beauty, and that it is a performance which discovers much genius, a cultivated taste, and a brilliant imagination. Many parts of the original are rendered with great facility, elegance, and fidelity. In poetical elegance I presume not to enter into competition with him."

For his own performance Musgrave claims the merit of greater fidelity to the original; but in respect of harmony, in true poetic grace, and sublimity of diction, his translation will bear no comparison with Mickle's version; for even Southey, in the article before quoted, though very hard upon his interpolations, admits that, "Mickle was a man of genius ... a man whom we admire and respect; whose memory is without a spot, and whose name will live among the English poets." (Quarterly Review, liii. p. 29.)

It only remains for me to say, that in order to place the reader in a position to judge of the merits of this sublime effort of genius, I have distinguished Mickle's longer interpolations by printing them in Bk. i. p. 24, in Italics, and in the first 300 lines of Bk. ix. by calling the attention of the reader to the interpolation by means of a foot-note. The notes are, in general, left as written by the translator, except in some cases where it seemed advisable to curtail them. Original notes are indicated by the abbreviation "Ed."

THE EDITOR.
LONDON, 1877.

THE LIFE OF CAMOËNS BY WILLIAM JULIUS MICKLE

When the glory of the arms of Portugal had reached its meridian splendour, Nature, as if in pity of the literary rudeness of that nation, produced a great poet to record the numberless actions of high spirit performed by his countrymen. Except Osorius, the historians of Portugal are little better than dry journalists. But it is not their inelegance which rendered the poet necessary. It is the peculiar nature of poetry to give a colouring to heroic actions, and to express indignation against breaches of honour, in a spirit which at once seizes the heart of the man of feeling, and carries with it instantaneous conviction. The brilliant actions of the Portuguese form the great hinge which opened the door to the most important alterations in the civil history of mankind. And to place these actions in the light and enthusiasm of poetry—that enthusiasm which particularly assimilates the youthful breast to its own fires—was Luis de Camoëns the poet of Portugal, born.

Different cities have claimed the honour of his birth. But according to N. Antonio, and Manuel Correa, his intimate friend, this event happened at Lisbon in 1517.[6] His family was of considerable note, and originally Spanish. In 1370 Vasco Perez de Caamans, disgusted at the court of Castile, fled to that of Lisbon, where King Ferdinand immediately admitted him into his council, and gave him the lordships of Sardoal, Punnete, Marano, Amendo, and other considerable lands; a certain proof of the eminence of his rank and abilities. In the war for the succession, which broke out on the death of Ferdinand, Caamans sided with the King of Castile, and was killed in the battle of Aljabarota. But though John I., the victor, seized a great part of his estate, his widow, the daughter of Gonsalo Tereyro, grand master of the Order of Christ, and general of the Portuguese army, was not reduced beneath her rank. She had three sons, who took the name of Camoëns. The family of the eldest intermarried with the first nobility of Portugal, and even, according to Castera, with the blood royal. But the family of the second brother, whose fortune was slender, had the superior honour to produce the author of the Lusiad.

Early in life the misfortunes of the poet began. In his infancy, Simon Vaz de Camoëns, his father, commander of a vessel, was shipwrecked at Goa, where, with his life, the greatest part of his fortune was lost. His mother, however, Anne de Macedo of Santarem, provided for the education of her son Luis, at the University of Coimbra. What he acquired there his works discover; an intimacy with the classics, equal to that of a Scaliger, but directed by the taste of a Milton or a Pope.

When he left the university he appeared at court. He was a polished scholar and very handsome,[7] possessing a most engaging mien and address, with the finest complexion, which, added to the natural ardour and gay vivacity of his deposition, rendered him an accomplished gentleman. Courts are the scenes of intrigue, and intrigue was fashionable at Lisbon. But the particulars of the amours of Camoëns rest unknown. This only appears: he had aspired above his rank, for he was banished from the court; and in several of his sonnets he ascribes this misfortune to love.

He now retired to his mother's friends at Santarem. Here he renewed his studies, and began his poem on the discovery of India. John III. at this time prepared an armament against Africa. Camoëns, tired of his inactive, obscure life, went to Ceuta in this expedition, and greatly distinguished his valour in several rencontres. In a naval engagement with the Moors in the Straits of Gibraltar, Camoëns, in the conflict of boarding, where he was among the foremost, lost his right eye. Yet neither the hurry of actual service, nor the dissipation of the camp, could stifle his genius. He continued his Lusiadas; and several of his most beautiful sonnets were written in Africa, while, as he expresses it,

"One hand the pen, and ant the sword employ'd."

The fame of his valour had now reached the Court, and he obtained permission to return to Lisbon. But while he solicited an establishment which he had merited in the ranks of battle, the malignity of evil tongues (as he calls it in one of his letters) was injuriously poured upon him. Though the bloom of his early youth was effaced by several years residence under the scorching sky of Africa, and though altered by the loss of an eye, his presence gave uneasiness to the gentlemen of some families of the first rank where he had formerly visited. Jealousy is the characteristic of the Spanish and Portuguese; its resentment knows no bounds, and Camoëns now found it prudent to banish himself from his native country. Accordingly, in 1553 he hailed for India, with a resolution never to return. As the ship left the Tagus he exclaimed, in the words of the sepulchral monument of Scipio Africanus, "Ingrata patria, non possidebis ossa mea!" (Ungrateful country, thou shalt not possess my bones!) But he knew not what evils in the East would awaken the remembrance of his native fields.

When Camoëns arrived in India, an expedition was ready to sail to revenge the King of Cochin on the King of Pimenta. Without any rest on shore after his long voyage, he joined this armament, and, in the conquest of the Alagada Islands, displayed his usual bravery. But his modesty, perhaps, is his greatest praise. In a sonnet he mentions this expedition: "We went to punish the King of Pimenta," says he, "e succedeones bem" (and we succeeded well). When it is considered that the poet bore no inconsiderable share in the victory, no ode can conclude more elegantly, more happily than this.

In the year following, he attended Manuel de Vasconcello in an expedition to the Red Sea. Here, says Faria, as Camoëns had no use for his sword, he employed his pen. Nor was his activity confined to the fleet or camp. He visited Mount Felix, and the adjacent inhospitable regions of Africa, which he so strongly pictures in the Lusiad, and in one of his little pieces, where he laments the absence of his mistress.

When he returned to Goa, he enjoyed a tranquility which enabled him to bestow his attention on his epic poem. But this serenity was interrupted, perhaps by his own imprudence. He wrote some satires which gave offence, and by order of the viceroy, Francisco Barreto, he was banished to China.

Men of poor abilities are more conscious of their embarrassment and errors than is commonly believed. When men of this kind are in power, they affect great solemnity; and every expression of the most distant tendency to lessen their dignity is held as the greatest of crimes. Conscious, also, how severely the man of genius can hurt their interest, they bear an instinctive antipathy against him, are uneasy even in his company, and, on the slightest pretence, are happy to drive him from them. Camoëns was thus situated at Goa; and never was there a fairer field for satire than the rulers of India at that time afforded. Yet, whatever esteem the prudence of Camoëns may lose in our idea, the nobleness of his disposition will doubly gain. And, so conscious was he of his real integrity and innocence, that in one of his sonnets he wishes no other revenge on Barreto than that the cruelty of his exile should ever be remembered.[8]

The accomplishments and manners of Camoëns soon found him friends, though under the disgrace of banishment. He was appointed Commissary of the estates of deceased persons, in the island of Macao, a Portuguese settlement on the coast of China. Here he continued his Lusiad; and here, also, after five years residence, he acquired a fortune, though small, yet equal to his wishes. Don Constantine de Braganza was now Viceroy of India; and Camoëns, desirous to return to Goa, resigned his charge. In a ship, freighted by himself, he set sail, but was shipwrecked in the gulf near the mouth of the river Meekhaun, in Cochin China. All he had acquired was lost in the waves: his poems, which he held in one hand, while he swam with the other, were all he found himself possessed of when he stood friendless on the unknown shore. But the natives gave him a most humane reception; this he has immortalized in the prophetic song in the tenth Lusiad;[9] and in the seventh he tells us that here he lost the wealth which satisfied his wishes.

Agora da esperança ja adquirida, etc.

"Now blest with all the wealth fond hope could crave, Soon I beheld that wealth beneath the wave For ever lost;—My life like Judah's Heaven-doom'd king of yore By miracle prolong'd."

On the banks of the Meekhaun, he wrote his beautiful paraphrase of the 137th Psalm, where the Jews, in the finest strain of poetry, are represented as hanging their harps on the willows by the rivers of Babylon, and weeping their exile from their native country. Here Camoëns continued some time, till an opportunity offered to carry him to Goa. When he arrived at that city, Don Constantine de Braganza, the viceroy, whose characteristic was politeness, admitted him into intimate friendship, and Camoëns was happy till Count Redondo assumed the government. Those who had formerly procured the banishment of the satirist were silent while Constantine was in power. But now they exerted all their arts against him. Redondo, when he entered on office, pretended to be the friend of Camoëns; yet, with the most unfeeling indifference, he suffered the innocent man to be thrown into the common prison. After all the delay of bringing witnesses, Camoëns, in a public trial, fully refuted every accusation against his conduct while commissary at Macao, and his enemies were loaded with ignominy and reproach. But Camoëns had some creditors; and these detained him in prison a considerable time, till the gentlemen of Goa began to be ashamed that a man of his singular merit should experience such treatment among them. He was set at liberty; and again he assumed the profession of arms, and received the allowance of a gentleman-volunteer, a character at that time common in Portuguese India. Soon after, Pedro Barreto (appointed governor of the fort of Sofála), by high promises, allured the poet to attend him thither. The governor of a distant fort, in a barbarous country, shares in some measure the fate of an exile. Yet, though the only motive of Barreto was, in this unpleasant situation, to retain the conversation of Camoëns at his table, it was his least care to render the life of his guest agreeable. Chagrined with his treatment, and a considerable time having elapsed in vain dependence upon Barreto, Camoëns resolved to return to his native country. A ship, on the homeward voyage, at this time touched at Sofála, and several gentlemen[10] who were on board were desirous that Camoëns should accompany them. But this the governor ungenerously endeavoured to prevent, and charged him with a debt for board. Anthony de Cabral, however, and Hector de Sylveyra, paid the demand, and Camoëns, says Faria, and the honour of Barreto were sold together.

After an absence of sixteen years, Camoëns, in 1569, returned to Lisbon, unhappy even in his arrival, for the pestilence then raged in that city, and prevented his publishing for three years. At last, in 1572, he printed his Lusiad, which, in the opening of the first book, in a most elegant turn of compliment, he addressed to his prince, King Sebastian, then in his eighteenth year. The king, says the French translator, was so pleased with his merit, that he gave the author a pension of 4000 reals, on condition that he should reside at court. But this salary, says the same writer, was withdrawn by Cardinal Henry, who succeeded to the crown of Portugal, lost by Sebastian at the battle of Alcazar.

But this story of the pension is very doubtful. Correa and other contemporary authors do not mention it, though some late writers have given credit to it. If Camoëns, however, had a pension, it is highly probable that Henry deprived him of it. While Sebastian was devoted to the chase, his grand-uncle, the cardinal, presided at the council board, and Camoëns, in his address to the king, which closes the Lusiad, advises him to exclude the clergy from State affairs. It was easy to see that the cardinal was here intended. And Henry, besides, was one of those statesmen who can perceive no benefit resulting to the public from elegant literature. But it ought also to be added in completion of his character, that under the narrow views and weak hands of this Henry, the kingdom of Portugal fell into utter ruin; and on his death, which closed a short inglorious reign, the crown of Lisbon, after a faint struggle, was annexed to that of Spain. Such was the degeneracy of the Portuguese, a degeneracy lamented in vain by Camoëns, whose observation of it was imputed to him as a crime.

Though the great[11] patron of theological literature—a species the reverse of that of Camoëns—certain it is, that the author of the Lusiad was utterly neglected by Henry, under whose inglorious reign he died in all the misery of poverty. By some, it is said, he died in an almshouse. It appears, however, that he had not even the certainty of subsistence which these houses provide. He had a black servant, who had grown old with him, and who had long experienced his master's humanity. This grateful dependant, a native of Java, who, according to some writers, saved his master's life in the unhappy shipwreck where he lost his effects, begged in the streets of Lisbon for the only man in Portugal on whom God had bestowed those talents which have a tendency to erect the spirit of a downward age. To the eye of a careful observer, the fate of Camoëns throws great light on that of his country, and will appear strictly connected with it. The same ignorance, the same degenerate spirit, which suffered Camoëns to depend on his share of the alms begged in the streets by his old hoary servant—the same spirit which caused this, sank the kingdom of Portugal into the most abject vassalage ever experienced by a conquered nation. While the grandees of Portugal were blind to the ruin which impended over them, Camoëns beheld it with a pungency of grief which hastened his end. In one of his letters he has these remarkable words, "Em fim accaberey à vida, e verràm todos que fuy afeiçoada a minho patria," etc.—"I am ending the course of my life, the world will witness how I have loved my country. I have returned, not only to die in her bosom, but to die with her." In another letter, written a little before his death, he thus, yet with dignity, complains, "Who has seen on so small a theatre as my poor bed, such a representation of the disappointments of Fortune. And I, as if she could not herself subdue me, I have yielded and become of her party; for it were wild audacity to hope to surmount such accumulated evils."

In this unhappy situation, in 1579, in his sixty-second year, the year after the fatal defeat of Don Sebastian, died Luis de Camoëns, the greatest literary genius ever produced by Portugal; in martial courage and spirit of honour nothing inferior to her greatest heroes. And in a manner suitable to the poverty in which he died was he buried. Soon after, however, many epitaphs honoured his memory; the greatness of his merit was universally confessed, and his Lusiad was translated into various languages.[12] Nor ought it to be omitted, that the man so miserably neglected by the weak king Henry, was earnestly enquired after by Philip of Spain when he assumed the crown of Lisbon. When Philip heard that Camoëns was dead, both his words and his countenance expressed his disappointment and grief.

From the whole tenor of his life, and from that spirit which glows throughout the Lusiad, it evidently appears that the courage and manners of Camoëns flowed from true greatness and dignity of soul. Though his polished conversation was often courted by the great, he appears so distant from servility that his imprudence in this respect is by some highly blamed. Yet the instances of it by no means deserve that severity of censure with which some writers have condemned him. Unconscious of the feelings of a Camoëns, they knew not that a carelessness in securing the smiles of fortune, and an open honesty of indignation, are almost inseparable from the enthusiasm of fine imagination. The truth is, the man possessed of true genius feels his greatest happiness in the pursuits and excursions of the mind, and therefore makes an estimate of things very different from that of him whose unremitting attention is devoted to his external interest. The profusion of Camoëns is also censured. Had he dissipated the wealth he acquired at Macao, his profusion indeed had been criminal; but it does not appear that he ever enjoyed any other opportunity of acquiring independence. But Camoëns was unfortunate, and the unfortunate man is viewed—

"Through the dim shade his fate casts o'er him: A shade that spreads its evening darkness o'er His brightest virtues, while it shows his foibles Crowding and obvious as the midnight stars, Which, in the sunshine of prosperity Never had been descried."

Yet, after the strictest discussion, when all the causes are weighed together, the misfortunes of Camoëns will appear the fault and disgrace of his age and country, and not of the man. His talents would have secured him an apartment in the palace of Augustus, but such talents are a curse to their possessor in an illiterate nation. In a beautiful, digressive exclamation at the end of the Lusiad, he affords us a striking view of the neglect which he experienced. Having mentioned how the greatest heroes of antiquity revered and cherished the muse, he thus characterizes the nobility of his own age and country.

"Alas! on Tago's hapless shore alone The muse is slighted, and her charms unknown; For this, no Virgil here attunes the lyre, No Homer here awakes the hero's fire; Unheard, in vain their native poet sings, And cold neglect weighs dawn the muse's wings."

In such an age, and among such a barbarous nobility, what but wretched neglect could be the fate of a Camoëns! After all, however, if he was imprudent on his first appearance at the court of John III.; if the honesty of his indignation led him into great imprudence, as certainly it did, when at Goa he satirised the viceroy and the first persons in power; yet let it also be remembered, that "The gifts of imagination bring the heaviest task upon the vigilance of reason; and to bear those faculties with unerring rectitude, or invariable propriety, requires a degree of firmness and of cool attention, which doth not always attend the higher gifts of the mind. Yet, difficult as nature herself seems to have rendered the task of regularity to genius, it is the supreme consolation of dullness and of folly to point with Gothic triumph to those excesses which are the overflowings of faculties they never enjoyed. Perfectly unconscious that they are indebted to their stupidity for the consistency of their conduct, they plume themselves on an imaginary virtue which has its origin in what is really their disgrace.—Let such, if such dare approach the shrine of Camoëns, withdraw to a respectful distance; and should they behold the ruins of genius, or the weakness of an exalted mind, let them be taught to lament that nature has left the noblest of her works imperfect."[13]

DISSERTATION ON THE LUSIAD, AND ON EPIC POETRY BY THE TRANSLATOR.

When Voltaire was in England, previous to his publication of his Henriade, he published in English an essay on the epic poetry of the European nations. In this he both highly praised, and severely attacked, the Lusiad. In his French editions of this essay, he has made various alterations, at different times, in the article on Camoëns. It is not, however, improper to premise, that some most amazing falsities will be here detected; the gross misrepresentation of every objection refuted; and demonstration brought, that when Voltaire wrote his English essay, his knowledge of the Lusiad was entirely borrowed from the bold, harsh, unpoetical version of Fanshaw.

"While Trissino," says Voltaire, "was clearing away the rubbish in Italy, which barbarity and ignorance had heaped up for ten centuries in the way of the arts and sciences, Camoëns, in Portugal, steered a new course, and acquired a reputation which lasts still among his countrymen who pay as much respect to his memory as the English to Milton."

Among other passages of the Lusiad which he criticises is that where "Adamastor, the giant of the Cape of Storms, appears to them, walking in the depth of the sea; his head reaches to the clouds; the storms, the winds, the thunders, and the lightnings hang about him; his arms are extended over the waves. It is the guardian of that foreign ocean, unploughed before by any ship. He complains of being obliged to submit to fate, and to the audacious undertaking of the Portuguese, and foretells them all the misfortunes they must undergo in the Indies. I believe that such a fiction would be thought noble and proper in all ages, and in all nations.

"There is another, which perhaps would have pleased the Italians as well as the Portuguese, but no other nation besides: it is the enchanted island, called the Island of Bliss, which the fleet finds in its way home, just rising from the sea, for their comfort, and for their reward. Camoëns describes that place, as Tasso some years after depicted his island of Armida. There a supernatural power brings in all the beauties, and presents all the pleasures which nature can afford, and the heart may wish for; a goddess, enamoured with Vasco de Gama, carries him to the top of a high mountain, from whence she shows him all the kingdoms of the earth, and foretells the fate of Portugal.

"After Camoëns hath given loose to his fancy, in the description of the pleasures which Gama and his crew enjoyed in the island, he takes care to inform the reader that he ought to understand by this fiction nothing but the satisfaction which the virtuous man feels, and the glory which accrues to him, by the practice of virtue; but the best excuse for such an invention is the charming style in which it is delivered (if we may believe the Portuguese), for the beauty of the elocution sometimes makes amends for the faults of the poet, as the colouring of Rubens makes some defects in his figures pass unregarded.

"There is another kind of machinery continued throughout all the poem, which nothing can excuse; that is, an injudicious mixture of the heathen gods with our religion. Gama in a storm addresses his prayers to Christ, but it is Venus who comes to his relief; the heroes are Christians, and the poet heathen. The main design which the Portuguese are supposed to have (next to promoting their trade) is to propagate Christianity; yet Jupiter, Bacchus, and Venus, have in their hands all the management of the voyage. So incongruous a machinery casts a blemish upon the whole poem; yet it shows at the same time how prevailing are its beauties since the Portuguese like it with all its faults."

The Lusiad, says Voltaire, contains "a sort of epic poetry unheard of before. No heroes are wounded a thousand different ways; no woman enticed away, and the world overturned for her cause." But the very want of these, in place of supporting the objection intended by Voltaire, points out the happy judgment and peculiar excellence of Camoëns. If Homer has given us all the fire and hurry of battles, he has also given us all the uninteresting, tiresome detail. What reader but must be tired with the deaths of a thousand heroes, who are never mentioned before, nor afterwards, in the poem. Yet, in every battle we are wearied out with such Gazette-returns of the slain and wounded as—

"Hector Priamides when Zeus him glory gave, Assæus first, Autonoüs, he slew; Ophites, Dolops, Klytis' son beside; Opheltius also, Agelaüs too, Æsymnus, and the battle-bide Hippónoüs, chiefs on Danaian side, And then, the multitude."

HOMER'S Iliad, bk. xi. 299, et seq., (W. G. T. BARTER'S translation.)

And corresponding to it is Virgil's Æneid, bk. x. line 747, et seq.:—

"By Cædicus Alcathoüs was slain; Sacrator laid Hydaspes on the plain; Orsès the strong to greater strength must yield, He, with Parthenius, were by Rapo killed. Then brave Messapus Ericetès slew, Who from Lycaón's blood his lineage drew."

DRYDEN'S version.

With, such catalogues is every battle extended; and what can be more tiresome than such uninteresting descriptions, and their imitations! If the idea of the battle be raised by such enumeration, still the copy and original are so near each other that they can never please in two separate poems. Nor are the greater part of the battles of the Æneid much more distant than those of the Iliad. Though Virgil with great art has introduced a Camilla, a Pallas, and a Lausus, still, in many particulars, and in the action upon the whole, there is such a sameness with the Iliad, that the learned reader of the Æneid is deprived of the pleasure inspired by originality. If the man of taste, however, will be pleased to mark how the genius of a Virgil has managed a war after Homer, he will certainly be tired with a dozen epic poems in the same style. Where the siege of a town and battles are the subject of an epic, there will, of necessity, in the characters and circumstances, be a resemblance to Homer; and such poem must therefore want originality. Happily for Tasso, the variation of manners, and his masterly superiority over Homer in describing his duels, has given to his Jerusalem an air of novelty. Yet, with all the difference between Christian and pagan heroes, we have a Priam, an Agamemnon, an Achilles, etc., armies slaughtered, and a city besieged. In a word, we have a handsome copy of the Iliad in the Jerusalem Delivered. If some imitations, however, have been successful, how many other epics of ancient and modern times have hurried down the stream of oblivion! Some of their authors had poetical merit, but the fault was in the choice of their subjects. So fully is the strife of war exhausted by Homer, that Virgil and Tasso could add to it but little novelty; no wonder, therefore, that so many epics on battles and sieges have been suffered to sink into utter neglect. Camoëns, perhaps, did not weigh these circumstances, but the strength of his poetical genius directed him. He could not but feel what it was to read Virgil after Homer; and the original turn and force of his mind led him from the beaten track of Helen's and Lavinia's, Achilles's and Hector's sieges and slaughters, where the hero hews down, and drives to flight, whole armies with his own sword. Camoëns was the first who wooed the modern Epic Muse, and she gave him the wreath of a first lover; a sort of epic poetry unheard of before; or, as Voltaire calls it, une nouvelle espèce d'epopée; and the grandest subject it is (of profane history) which the world has ever beheld.[14] A voyage esteemed too great for man to dare; the adventures of this voyage through unknown oceans deemed unnavigable; the eastern world happily discovered, and for ever indissolubly joined and given to the western; the grand Portuguese empire in the East founded; the humanization of mankind, and universal commerce the consequence! What are the adventures of an old, fabulous hero's arrival in Britain, what are Greece and Latium in arms for a woman compared to this! Troy is in ashes, and even the Roman empire is no more. But the effects of the voyage, adventures, and bravery of the hero of the Lusiad will be felt and beheld, and perhaps increase in importance, while the world shall remain.

Happy in his choice, happy also was the genius of Camoëns in the method of pursuing his subject. He has not, like Tasso, given it a total appearance of fiction; nor has he, like Lucan, excluded allegory and poetical machinery. Whether he intended it or not (for his genius was sufficient to suggest its propriety), the judicious precept of Petronius[15] is the model of the Lusiad. That elegant writer proposes a poem on the civil war, and no poem, ancient or modern, merits the character there sketched out in any degree comparative to the Lusiad. A truth of history is preserved; yet, what is improper for the historian, the ministry of Heaven is employed, and the free spirit of poetry throws itself into fictions which makes the whole appear as an effusion of prophetic fury, and not like a rigid detail of facts, given under the sanction of witnesses. Contrary to Lucan, who, in the above rules, drawn from the nature of poetry, is severely condemned by Petronius, Camoëns conducts his poem per ambages Deorumque ministeria. The apparition, which in the night hovers athwart the fleet near the Cape of Good Hope, is the grandest fiction in human composition; the invention his own! In the Island of Venus, the use of which fiction in an epic poem is also his own, he has given the completest assemblage of all the flowers which have ever adorned the bowers of love. And, never was the furentis animi vaticinatio more conspicuously displayed than in the prophetic song, the view of the spheres, and the globe of the earth. Tasso's imitation of the Island of Venus is not equal to the original; and, though "Virgil's myrtles[16] dropping blood are nothing to Tasso's enchanted forest," what are all Ismeno's enchantments to the grandeur and horror of the appearance, prophecy, and vanishment of the spectre of Camoëns![17] It has long been agreed among critics, that the solemnity of religious observances gives great dignity to the historical narrative of epic poetry. Camoëns, in the embarkation of the fleet, and in several other places, is peculiarly happy in the dignity of religious allusions. Manners and character are also required in the epic poem. But all the epics which have appeared are, except two, mere copies of the Iliad in these respects. Every one has its Agamemnon, Achilles, Ajax, and Ulysses; its calm, furious, gross, and intelligent hero. Camoëns and Milton happily left this beaten track, this exhausted field, and have given us pictures of manners unknown in the Iliad, the Æneid, and all those poems which may be classed with the Thebaid. The Lusiad abounds with pictures of manners, from those of the highest chivalry to those of the rudest, fiercest, and most innocent barbarism. In the fifth, sixth, and ninth books, Leonardo and Veloso are painted in stronger colours than any of the inferior characters in Virgil. But character, indeed, is not the excellence of the Æneid. That of Monzaida, the friend of Gama, is much superior to that of Achates. The base, selfish, perfidious and cruel character of the Zamorim and the Moors, are painted in the strongest colours; and the character of Gama himself is that of the finished hero. His cool command of his passions, his deep sagacity, his fixed intrepidity, his tenderness of heart, his manly piety, and his high enthusiasm in the love of his country are all displayed in the superlative degree. Let him who objects the want of character to the Lusiad, beware lest he stumble upon its praise; lest he only say, it wants an Achilles, a Hector, and a Priam. And, to the novelty of the manners of the Lusiad let the novelty of fire-arms also be added. It has been said that the buckler, the bow, and the spear, must continue the arms of poetry. Yet, however unsuccessful others may have been, Camoëns has proved that fire-arms may be introduced with the greatest dignity, and the finest effect in the epic poem.

As the grand interest of commerce and of mankind forms the subject of the Lusiad, so, with great propriety, as necessary accompaniments to the voyage of his hero, the author has given poetical pictures of the four parts of the world—in the third book a view of Europe; in the fifth, a view of Africa; and in the tenth, a picture of Asia and America. Homer and Virgil have been highly praised for their judgment in the choice of subjects which interested their countrymen, and Statius has been as severely condemned for his uninteresting choice. But, though the subject of Camoëns be particularly interesting to his own countrymen, it has also the peculiar happiness to be the poem of every trading nation. It is the epic poem of the birth of commerce, and, in a particular manner, the epic poem of whatever country has the control and possession of the commerce of India.[18]

An unexhausted fertility and variety of poetical description, an unexhausted elevation of sentiment, and a constant tenor of the grand simplicity of diction, complete the character of the Lusiad of Camoëns: a poem which, though it has hitherto received from the public most unmerited neglect, and from the critics most flagrant injustice, was yet better understood by the greatest poet of Italy. Tasso never did his judgment more credit than when he confessed that he dreaded Camoëns as a rival; or his generosity more honour than when he addressed the elegant sonnet to the hero of the Lusiad, commencing—

"Vasco, le cui felici, ardite antenne In contro al sol, che ne riporta il giorno."

It only remains to give some account of the version of the Lusiad which is now offered to the public. Beside the translations mentioned in the life of Camoëns, M. Duperron De Castera, in 1735, gave, in French prose, a loose unpoetical paraphrase[19] of the Lusiad. Nor does Sir Richard Fanshaw's English version, published during the usurpation of Cromwell, merit a better character. Though stanza be rendered for stanza, though at first view it has the appearance of being exceedingly literal, this version is nevertheless exceedingly unfaithful. Uncountenanced by his original, Fanshaw—

"Teems with many a dead-born just."[20]

Nor had he the least idea of the dignity of the epic style,[21] or of the true spirit of poetical translation. For this, indeed, no definite rule can be given. The translator's feelings alone must direct him, for the spirit of poetry is sure to evaporate in literal translation.

Indeed, literal translation of poetry is a solecism. You may construe your author, indeed, but, if with some translators you boast that you have left your author to speak for himself, that you have neither added nor diminished, you have in reality grossly abused him, and deceived yourself. Your literal translation can have no claim to the original felicities of expression; the energy, elegance, and fire of the original poetry. It may bear, indeed, a resemblance; but such a one as a corpse in the sepulchre bears to the former man when he moved in the bloom and vigour of life.

Nec verbum verbo curabis reddere, fidus Interpres,

was the taste of the Augustan age. None but a poet can translate a poet. The freedom which this precept gives, will, therefore, in a poet's hands, not only infuse the energy, elegance, and fire of his author's poetry into his own version, but will give it also the spirit of an original.

He who can construe may perform all that is claimed by the literal translator. He who attempts the manner of translation prescribed by Horace, ventures upon a task of genius. Yet, however daring the undertaking, and however he may have failed in it, the translator acknowledges, that in this spirit he has endeavoured to give the Lusiad in English. Even farther liberties, in one or two instances, seemed to him advantageous—But a minuteness[22] in the mention of these will not appear with a good grace in this edition of his work; and besides, the original is in the hands of the world.

If a concatenation of events centred in one great action—events which gave birth to the present commercial system of the world—if these be of the first importance in the civil history of mankind, then the Lusiad, of all other poems, challenges the attention of the philosopher, the politician, and the gentleman.

In contradistinction to the Iliad and the Æneid, the Paradise Lost has been called the Epic Poem of Religion. In the same manner may the Lusiad be named the Epic Poem of Commerce. The happy completion of the most important designs of Henry, Duke of Viseo, prince of Portugal, to whom Europe owes both Gama and Columbus, both the eastern and the western worlds, constitutes the subject of this celebrated epic poem. But before we proceed to the historical introduction necessary to elucidate a poem founded on such an important period of history, some attention is due to the opinion of those theorists in political philosophy who lament that India was ever discovered, and who assert that increase of trade is only the parent of degeneracy, and the nurse of every vice.

Much, indeed, may be urged on this side of the question; but much, also, may be urged against every institution relative to man. Imperfection, if not necessary to humanity, is at least the certain attendant on everything human. Though some part of the traffic with many countries resemble Solomon's importation of apes and peacocks; though the superfluities of life, the baubles of the opulent, and even the luxuries which enervate the irresolute and administer disease, are introduced by the intercourse of navigation, yet the extent of the benefits which attend it are also to be considered before the man of cool reason will venture to pronounce that the world is injured, and rendered less virtuous and happy by the increase of commerce.

If a view of the state of mankind, where commerce opens no intercourse between nation and nation be neglected, unjust conclusions will certainly follow. Where the state of barbarians, and of countries under different degrees of civilization are candidly weighed, we may reasonably expect a just decision. As evidently as the appointment of nature gives pasture to the herds, so evidently is man born for society. As every other animal is in its natural state when in the situation which its instinct requires, so man, when his reason is cultivated, is then, and only then, in the state proper to his nature. The life of the naked savage, who feeds on acorns and sleeps like a beast in his den, is commonly called the natural state of man; but, if there be any propriety in this assertion, his rational faculties compose no part of his nature, and were given not to be used. If the savage, therefore, live in a state contrary to the appointment of nature, it must follow that he is not so happy as nature intended him to be. And a view of his true character will confirm this conclusion. The reveries, the fairy dreams of a Rousseau, may figure the paradisaical life of a Hottentot, but it is only in such dreams that the superior happiness of the barbarian exists. The savage, it is true, is reluctant to leave his manner of life; but, unless we allow that he is a proper judge of the modes of living, his attachment to his own by no means proves that he is happier than he might otherwise have been. His attachment only exemplifies the amazing power of habit in reconciling the human breast to the most uncomfortable situations. If the intercourse of mankind in some instances be introductive of vice, the want of it as certainly excludes the exertion of the noblest virtues; and, if the seeds of virtue are indeed in the heart, they often lie dormant, and even unknown to the savage possessor. The most beautiful description of a tribe of savages (which we may be assured is from real life) occurs in these words:[23] And the five spies of Dan "came to Laish, and saw the people that were there, how they dwelt careless, after the manner of the Zidonians, quiet and secure; and there was no magistrate in the land, that might put them to shame in anything...." And the spies said to their brethren, "Arise, that we may go up against them; for we have seen the land, and, behold, it is very good.... And they came unto Laish, unto a people that were at quiet and secure: and they smote them with the edge of the sword, and burnt the city with fire. And there was no deliverer, because it was far from Zidon, and they had no business with any man." However the happy simplicity of this society may please the man of fine imagination, the true philosopher will view the men of Laish with other eyes. However virtuous he may suppose one generation, it requires an alteration of human nature to preserve the children of the next in the same generous estrangement from the selfish passions—from those passions which are the parents of the acts of injustice. When his wants are easily supplied, the manners of the savage will be simple, and often humane, for the human heart is not vicious without objects of temptation. But these will soon occur; he that gathers the greatest quantity of fruit will be envied by the less industrious. The uninformed mind seems insensible of the idea of the right of possession which the labour of acquirement gives. When want is pressing, and the supply at hand, the only consideration with such minds is the danger of seizing it; and where there is no magistrate to put to shame in anything, depredation will soon display all its horrors. Let it even be admitted that the innocence of the men of Laish could secure them from the consequences of their own unrestrained desires, could even this impossibility be surmounted, still are they a wretched prey to the first invaders, and because they have no business with any man, they will find no deliverer. While human nature is the same, the fate of Laish will always be the fate of the weak and defenceless; and thus the most amiable description of savage life raises in our minds the strongest imagery of the misery and impossible continuance of such a state. But if the view of these innocent people terminate in horror, with what contemplation shall we behold the wilds of Africa and America? The tribes of America, it is true, have degrees of policy greatly superior to anything understood by the men of Laish. Great masters of martial oratory, their popular assemblies are schools open to all their youth. In these they not only learn the history of their nation, and what they have to fear from the strength and designs of their enemies, but they also imbibe the most ardent spirit of war. The arts of stratagem are their study, and the most athletic exercises of the field their employment and delight; and, what is their greatest praise, they have magistrates "to put them to shame." They inflict no corporeal punishment on their countrymen, it is true; but a reprimand from an elder, delivered in the assembly, is esteemed by them a deeper degradation and severer punishment than any of those too often most impolitically adopted by civilized nations. Yet, though possessed of this advantage—an advantage impossible to exist in a large commercial empire—and though masters of great martial policy, their condition, upon the whole, is big with the most striking demonstration of the misery and unnatural state of such very imperfect civilization. "Multiply and replenish the earth" is an injunction of the best political philosophy ever given to man. Nature has appointed man to cultivate the earth, to increase in number by the food which its culture gives, and by this increase of brethren to remove some, and to mitigate all, the natural miseries of human life. But in direct opposition to this is the political state of the wild aborigines of America. Their lands, luxuriant in climate, are often desolate wastes, where thousands of miles hardly support a few hundreds of savage hunters. Attachment to their own tribe constitutes their highest idea of virtue; but this virtue includes the most brutal depravity, makes them esteem the man of every other tribe as an enemy, as one with whom nature had placed them in a state of war, and had commanded to destroy.[24] And to this principle their customs and ideas of honour serve as rituals and ministers. The cruelties practised by the American savages on their prisoners of war (and war is their chief employment) convey every idea expressed by the word diabolical, and give a most shocking view of the degradation of human nature. But what peculiarly completes the character of the savage is his horrible superstition. In the most distant nations the savage is, in this respect, the same. The terror of evil spirits continually haunts him; his God is beheld as a relentless tyrant, and is worshipped often with cruel rites, always with a heart full of horror and fear. In all the numerous accounts of savage worship, one trace of filial dependence is not to be found. The very reverse of that happy idea is the hell of the ignorant mind. Nor is this barbarism confined alone to those ignorant tribes whom we call savages. The vulgar of every country possess it in certain degrees, proportionated to their opportunities of conversation with the more enlightened. Sordid disposition and base ferocity, together with the most unhappy superstition, are everywhere the proportionate attendants of ignorance and severe want. And ignorance and want are only removed by intercourse and the offices of society. So self-evident are these positions, that it requires an apology for insisting upon them; but the apology is at hand. He who has read knows how many eminent writers,[25] and he who has conversed knows how many respectable names, connect the idea of innocence and happiness with the life of the savage and the unimproved rustic. To fix the character of the savage is therefore necessary, ere we examine the assertion, that "it had been happy for both the old and the new worlds if the East and West Indies had never been discovered." The bloodshed and the attendant miseries which the unparalleled rapine and cruelties of the Spaniards spread over the new world, indeed disgrace human nature. The great and flourishing empires of Mexico and Peru, steeped in the blood of forty millions of their sons, present a melancholy prospect, which must excite the indignation of every good heart. Yet such desolation is not the certain consequence of discovery. And, even should we allow that the depravity of human nature is so great that the avarice of the merchant and rapacity of the soldier will overwhelm with misery every new-discovered country, still, are there other, more comprehensive views, to be taken, ere we decide against the intercourse introduced by navigation. When we weigh the happiness of Europe in the scale of political philosophy, we are not to confine our eye to the dreadful ravages of Attila the Hun, or of Alaric the Goth. If the waters of a stagnated lake are disturbed by the spade when led into new channels, we ought not to inveigh against the alteration because the waters are fouled at the first; we are to wait to see the streamlets refine and spread beauty and utility through a thousand vales which they never visited before. Such were the conquests of Alexander, temporary evils, but civilization and happiness followed in the bloody track. And, though disgraced with every barbarity, happiness has also followed the conquests of the Spaniards in the other hemisphere. Though the villainy of the Jesuits defeated their schemes of civilization in many countries, the labours of that society have been crowned with a success in Paraguay and in Canada, which reflects upon their industry the greatest honour. The customs and cruelties of many American tribes still disgrace human nature, but in Paraguay and Canada the natives have been brought to relish the blessings of society, and the arts of virtuous and civil life. If Mexico is not so populous as it once was, neither is it so barbarous;[26] the shrieks of the human victim do not now resound from temple to temple, nor does the human heart, held up reeking to the sun, imprecate the vengeance of Heaven on the guilty empire. And, however impolitically despotic the Spanish governments may be, still do these colonies enjoy the opportunities of improvement, which in every age arise from the knowledge of commerce and of letters—opportunities which were never enjoyed in South America under the reigns of Montezuma and Atabalipa. But if from Spanish, we turn our eyes to British America, what a glorious prospect! Here, formerly, on the wild lawn, perhaps twice in the year, a few savage hunters kindled their evening fire, kindled it more to protect them from evil spirits and beasts of prey, than from the cold, and with their feet pointed to it, slept on the ground. Here, now, population spreads her thousands, and society appears in all its blessings of mutual help, and the mutual lights of intellectual improvement. "What work of art, or power, or public utility, has ever equalled the glory of having peopled a continent, without guilt or bloodshed, with a multitude of free and happy commonwealths; to have given them the best arts of life and government!" To have given a savage continent an image of the British Constitution is, indeed, the greatest glory of the British crown, "a greater than any other nation ever acquired;" and from the consequences of the genius of Henry, Duke of Viseo, did the British American empire arise, an empire which, unless retarded by the illiberal and inhuman spirit of religious fanaticism, will in a few centuries, perhaps, be the glory of the world.

Stubborn indeed must be the theorist who will deny the improvement, virtue, and happiness which, in the result, the voyage of Columbus has spread over the western world. The happiness which Europe and Asia have received from the intercourse with each other, cannot hitherto, it must be owned, be compared either with the possession of it, or the source of its increase established in America. Yet, let the man of the most melancholy views estimate all the wars and depredations which are charged upon the Portuguese and other European nations, still will the eastern world appear considerably advantaged by the voyage of Gama. If seas of blood have been shed by the Portuguese, nothing new was introduced into India. War and depredation were no unheard-of strangers on the banks of the Ganges, nor could the nature of the civil establishments of the eastern nations secure a lasting peace. The ambition of their native princes was only diverted into new channels, into channels which, in the natural course of human affairs, will certainly lead to permanent governments, established on improved laws and just dominion. Yet, even ere such governments are formed, is Asia no loser by the arrival of Europeans. The horrid massacres and unbounded rapine which, according to their own annals, followed the victories of their Asian conquerors were never equalled by the worst of their European vanquishers. Nor is the establishment of improved governments in the East the dream of theory. The superiority of the civil and military arts of the British, notwithstanding the hateful character of some individuals, is at this day beheld in India with all the astonishment of admiration; and admiration is always followed, though often with retarded steps, by the strong desire of similar improvement. Long after the fall of the Roman empire the Roman laws were adopted by nations which ancient Rome esteemed as barbarous. And thus, in the course of ages, the British laws, according to every test of probability, will have a most important effect, will fulfil the prophecy of Camoëns, and transfer to the British the high compliment he pays to his countrymen—

"Beneath their sway majestic, wise, and mild,
Proud of her victor's laws thrice happier India smiled."

In former ages, and within these few years, the fertile empire of India has exhibited every scene of human misery, under the undistinguishing ravages of their Mohammedan and native princes; ravages only equalled in European history by those committed under Atilla, surnamed "the scourge of God," and "the destroyer of nations." The ideas of patriotism and of honour were seldom known in the cabinets of the eastern princes till the arrival of the Europeans. Every species of assassination was the policy of their courts, and every act of unrestrained rapine and massacre followed the path of victory. But some of the Portuguese governors, and many of the English officers, have taught them that humanity to the conquered is the best, the truest policy. The brutal ferocity of their own conquerors is now the object of their greatest dread; and the superiority of the British in war has convinced their princes,[27] that an alliance with the British is the surest guarantee of their national peace and prosperity. While the English East India Company are possessed of their present greatness, it is in their power to diffuse over the East every blessing which flows from the wisest and most humane policy. Long ere the Europeans arrived, a failure of the crop of rice, the principal food of India, had spread the devastations of famine over the populous plains of Bengal. And never, from the seven years' famine of ancient Egypt to the present day, was there a natural scarcity in any country which did not enrich the proprietors of the granaries. The Mohammedan princes, and Moorish traders have often added all the horrors of an artificial, to a natural, famine. But, however some Portuguese or other governors may stand accused, much was left for the humanity of the more exalted policy of an Albuquerque, or a Castro. And under such European governors as these, the distresses of the East have often been alleviated by a generosity of conduct, and a train of resources formerly unknown in Asia. Absurd and impracticable were that scheme which would introduce the British laws into India without the deepest regard to the manners and circumstances peculiar to the people. But that spirit of liberty upon which they are founded, and that security of property which is their leading principle, must in time have a wide and stupendous effect. The abject spirit of Asiatic submission will be taught to see, and to claim, those rights of nature, of which the dispirited and passive Hindus could, till lately, hardly form an idea. From this, as naturally as the noon succeeds the dawn, must the other blessings of civilization arise. For, though the four great castes of

India are almost inaccessible to the introduction of other manners, and of other literature than their own, happily there is in human nature a propensity to change. Nor may the political philosopher be deemed an enthusiast who would boldly prophesy, that unless the British be driven from India the general superiority which they bear will, ere many generations shall have passed, induce the most intelligent of India to break the shackles of their absurd superstitions,[28] and lead them to partake of those advantages which arise from the free scope and due cultivation of the rational powers. In almost every instance the Indian institutions are contrary to the feelings and wishes of nature. And ignorance and bigotry, their two chief pillars, can never secure unalterable duration. We have certain proof that the horrid custom of burning the wives along with the body of the deceased husband has continued for upwards of fifteen hundred years; we are also certain that within these twenty years it has begun to fall into disuse. Together with the alteration of this most striking feature of Indian manners, other assimilations to European sentiments have already taken place. Nor can the obstinacy even of the conceited Chinese always resist the desire of imitating the Europeans, a people who in arts and arms are so greatly superior to themselves. The use of the twenty-four letters, by which we can express every language, appeared at first as miraculous to the Chinese. Prejudice cannot always deprive that people, who are not deficient in selfish cunning, of the ease and expedition of an alphabet; and it is easy to foresee that, in the course of a few centuries, some alphabet will certainly take the place of the 60,000 arbitrary marks which now render the cultivation of the Chinese literature not only a labour of the utmost difficulty, but even the attainment impossible beyond a very limited degree. And from the introduction of an alphabet, what improvements may not be expected from the laborious industry of the Chinese! Though most obstinately attached to their old customs, yet there is a tide in the manners of nations which is sudden and rapid, and which acts with a kind of instinctive fury against ancient prejudice and absurdity. It was that nation of merchants, the Phœnicians, which diffused the use of letters through the ancient, and commerce will undoubtedly diffuse the same blessings through the modern, world.

To this view of the political happiness which is sure to be introduced in proportion to civilization, let the divine add what may be reasonably expected from such opportunity of the increase of religion. A factory of merchants, indeed, has seldom been found to be a school of piety; yet, when the general manners of a people become assimilated to those of a more rational worship, something more than ever was produced by an infant mission, or the neighbourhood of an infant colony, may then be reasonably expected, and even foretold.

In estimating the political happiness of a people, nothing is of greater importance than their capacity of, and tendency to, improvement. As a dead lake, to continue our former illustration, will remain in the same state for ages and ages, so would the bigotry and superstitions of the East continue the same. But if the lake is begun to be opened into a thousand rivulets, who knows over what unnumbered fields, barren before, they may diffuse the blessings of fertility, and turn a dreary wilderness into a land of society and joy.

In contrast to this, let the Gold Coast and other immense regions of Africa be contemplated—

"Afric behold; alas, what altered view! Her lands uncultured, and her sons untrue; Ungraced with all that sweetens human life, Savage and fierce they roam in brutal strife; Eager they grasp the gifts which culture yields, Yet naked roam their own neglected fields.... Unnumber'd tribes as bestial grazers stray, By laws unform'd, unform'd by Reason's sway. Far inward stretch the mournful sterile dales, Where on the parch'd hill-side pale famine wails."

LUSIAD X.

Let us consider how many millions of these unhappy savages are dragged from their native fields, and cut off for ever from all the hopes and all the rights to which human birth entitled them. And who would hesitate to pronounce that negro the greatest of patriots, who, by teaching his countrymen the arts of society, should teach them to defend themselves in the possession of their fields, their families, and their own personal liberties?

Evident, however, as it is, that the voyages of Gama and Columbus have already carried a superior degree of happiness, and the promise of infinitely more, to the eastern and western worlds; yet the advantages to Europe from the discovery of these regions may perhaps be denied. But let us view what Europe was, ere the genius of Don Henry gave birth to the spirit of modern discovery.

Several ages before this period the feudal system had degenerated into the most absolute tyranny. The barons exercised the most despotic authority over their vassals, and every scheme of public utility was rendered impracticable by their continual petty wars with each other; to which they led their dependents as dogs to the chase. Unable to read, or to write his own name, the chieftain was entirely possessed by the most romantic opinion of military glory, and the song of his domestic minstrel constituted his highest idea of fame. The classic authors slept on the shelves of the monasteries, their dark but happy asylum, while the life of the monks resembled that of the fattened beeves which loaded their tables. Real abilities were indeed possessed by a Duns Scotus and a few others; but these were lost in the most trifling subtleties of a sophistry which they dignified with the name of casuistical divinity. Whether Adam and Eve were created with navels? and How many thousand angels might at the same instant dance upon the point of the finest needle without one jostling another? were two of the several topics of like importance which excited the acumen and engaged the controversies of the learned. While every branch of philosophical, of rational investigation, was thus unpursued and unknown, commerce, which is incompatible with the feudal system, was equally neglected and unimproved. Where the mind is enlarged and enlightened by learning, plans of commerce will rise into action, and these, in return, will from every part of the world bring new acquirements to philosophy and science. The birth of learning and commerce may be different, but their growth is mutual and dependent upon each other. They not only assist each other, but the same enlargement of mind which is necessary for perfection in the one is also necessary for perfection in the other; and the same causes impede, and are alike destructive of, both. The INTERCOURSE of mankind is the parent of each. According to the confinement or extent of intercourse, barbarity or civilization proportionately prevail. In the dark, monkish ages, the intercourse of the learned was as much impeded and confined as that of the merchant. A few unwieldy vessels coasted the shores of Europe, and mendicant friars and ignorant pilgrims carried a miserable account of what was passing in the world from monastery to monastery. What doctor had last disputed on the peripatetic philosophy at some university, or what new heresy had last appeared, not only comprised the whole of their literary intelligence, but was delivered with little accuracy, and received with as little attention. While this thick cloud of mental darkness overspread the western world, was Don Henry, prince of Portugal, born; born to set mankind free from the feudal system, and to give to the whole world every advantage, every light that may possibly be diffused by the intercourse of unlimited commerce:—

"For then from ancient gloom emerg'd The rising world of trade: the genius, then, Of navigation, that in hopeless sloth Had slumber'd on the vast Atlantic deep For idle ages, starting heard at last The Lusitanian prince, who, Heaven-inspir'd, To love of useful glory rous'd mankind, And in unbounded commerce mix'd the world."

THOMSON.

In contrast to this melancholy view of human nature, sunk in barbarism and benighted with ignorance, let the present state of Europe be impartially estimated. Yet, though the great increase of opulence and learning cannot be denied, there are some who assert that virtue and happiness have as greatly declined. And the immense overflow of riches, from the East in particular, has been pronounced big with destruction to the British empire. Everything human, it is true, has its dark as well as its bright side; but let these popular complaints be examined, and it will be found that modern Europe, and the British empire in a very particular manner, have received the greatest and most solid advantages from the modern, enlarged system of commerce. The magic of the old romances, which could make the most withered, deformed hag, appear as the most beautiful virgin, is every day verified in popular declamation. Ancient days are there painted in the most amiable simplicity, and the modern in the most odious colours. Yet, what man of fortune in England lives in that stupendous gross luxury which every day was exhibited in the Gothic castles of the old chieftains! Four or five hundred knights and squires in the domestic retinue of a warlike earl was not uncommon, nor was the pomp of embroidery inferior to the profuse waste of their tables; in both instances unequalled by all the mad excesses of the present age.

While the baron thus lived in all the wild glare of Gothic luxury, agriculture was almost totally neglected, and his meaner vassals fared harder, infinitely less comfortably, than the meanest industrious labourers of England do now; where the lands are uncultivated, the peasants, ill-clothed, ill-lodged, and poorly fed, pass their miserable days in sloth and filth, totally ignorant of every advantage, of every comfort which nature lays at their feet. He who passes from the trading towns and cultured fields of England to those remote villages of Scotland or Ireland which claim this description, is astonished at the comparative wretchedness of their destitute inhabitants; but few consider that these villages only exhibit a view of what Europe was ere the spirit of commerce diffused the blessings which naturally flow from her improvements. In the Hebrides the failure of a harvest almost depopulates an island. Having little or no traffic to purchase grain, numbers of the young and hale betake themselves to the continent in quest of employment and food, leaving a few, less adventurous, behind, to beget a new race, the heir of the same fortune. Yet from the same cause, from the want of traffic, the kingdom of England has often felt more dreadful effects than these. Even in the days when her Henries and Edwards plumed themselves with the trophies of France, how often has famine spread all her horrors over city and village? Our modern histories neglect this characteristic feature of ancient days; but the rude chronicles of these ages inform us, that three or four times in almost every reign was England thus visited. The failure of the crop was then severely felt, and two bad harvests in succession were almost insupportable. But commerce has now opened another scene, has armed government with the happiest power that can be exerted by the rulers of a nation—the power to prevent every extremity[29] which may possibly arise from bad harvests; extremities, which, in former ages, were esteemed more dreadful visitations of the wrath of Heaven than the pestilence itself. Yet modern London is not so certainly defended against the latter, its ancient visitor, than the commonwealth by the means of commerce, under a just and humane government, is secured against the ravages of the former. If, from these great outlines of the happiness enjoyed by a commercial over an uncommercial nation, we turn our eyes to the manners, the advantages will be found no less in favour of the civilized.

Whoever is inclined to declaim at the vices of the present age, let him read, and be convinced, that the Gothic ages were less virtuous. If the spirit of chivalry prevented effeminacy, it was the foster-father of a ferocity of manners now happily unknown. Rapacity, avarice, and effeminacy are the vices ascribed to the increase of commerce; and in some degree, it must be confessed, they follow her steps. Yet infinitely more dreadful, as every palatinate in Europe often felt, were the effects of the two first under the feudal lords than can possibly be experienced under any system of trade. The virtues and vices of human nature are the same in every age: they only receive different modifications, and are dormant, or awakened into action, under different circumstances. The feudal lord had it infinitely more in his power to be rapacious than the merchant. And whatever avarice may attend the trader, his intercourse with the rest of mankind lifts him greatly above that brutish ferocity which actuates the savage, often the rustic, and in general characterizes the ignorant part of mankind. The abolition of the feudal system, a system of absolute slavery, and that equality of mankind which affords the protection of property, and every other incitement to industry, are the glorious gifts which the spirit of commerce, awakened by Prince Henry of Portugal, has bestowed upon Europe in general; and, as if directed by the manes of his mother, a daughter of England, upon the British empire in particular. In the vice of effeminacy alone, perhaps, do we exceed our ancestors; yet, even here we have infinitely the advantage over them. The brutal ferocity of former ages is now lost, and the general mind is humanized. The savage breast is the native soil of revenge; a vice, of all others, peculiarly stamped with the character of hell. But the mention of this was reserved for the character of the savages of Europe. The savage of every country is implacable when injured; but among some, revenge has its measure. When an American Indian is murdered his kindred pursue the murderer; and, as soon as blood has atoned for blood, the wilds of America hear the hostile parties join in their mutual lamentations over the dead, whom, as an oblivion of malice, they bury together. But the measure of revenge, never to be full, was left for the demi-savages of Europe. The vassals of the feudal lord entered into his quarrels with the most inexorable rage. Just or unjust was no consideration of theirs. It was a family feud; no farther inquiry was made; and from age to age, the parties, who never injured each other, breathed nothing but mutual rancour and revenge. And actions, suitable to this horrid spirit, everywhere confessed its virulent influence. Such were the late days of Europe, admired by the ignorant for the innocence of manners. Resentment of injury, indeed, is natural; and there is a degree which is honest, and though warm, far from inhuman. But if it is the hard task of humanized virtue to preserve the feeling of an injury unmixed with the slightest criminal wish of revenge, how impossible is it for the savage to attain the dignity of forgiveness, the greatest ornament of human nature. As in individuals, a virtue will rise into a vice, generosity into blind profusion, and even mercy into criminal lenity, so civilized manners will lead the opulent into effeminacy. But let it be considered, this consequence is by no means the certain result of civilization. Civilization, on the contrary, provides the most effectual preventive of this evil. Where classical literature prevails the manly spirit which it breathes must be diffused; whenever frivolousness predominates, when refinement degenerates into whatever enervates the mind, literary ignorance is sure to complete the effeminate character. A mediocrity of virtues and of talents is the lot of the great majority of mankind; and even this mediocrity, if cultivated by a liberal education, will infallibly secure its possessor against those excesses of effeminacy which are really culpable. To be of plain manners it is not necessary to be a clown, or to wear coarse clothes; nor is it necessary to lie on the ground and feed like the savage to be truly manly. The beggar who, behind the hedge, divides his offals with his dog has often more of the real sensualist than he who dines at an elegant table. Nor need we hesitate to assert, that he who, unable to preserve a manly elegance of manners, degenerates into the petit maître, would have been, in any age or condition, equally insignificant and worthless. Some, when they talk of the debauchery of the present age, seem to think that the former ages were all innocence. But this is ignorance of human nature. The debauchery of a barbarous age is gross and brutal; that of a gloomy, superstitious one, secret, excessive, and murderous; that of a more polished one, much happier for the fair sex,[30] and certainly in no sense so big with political unhappiness. If one disease has been imported from America,[31] the most valuable medicines have likewise been brought from those regions; and distempers, which were thought invincible by our forefathers, are now cured. If the luxuries of the

Indies usher disease to our tables the consequence is not unknown; the wise and the temperate receive no injury, and intemperance has been the destroyer of mankind in every age. The opulence of ancient Rome produced a luxury of manners which proved fatal to that mighty empire. But the effeminate sensualists of those ages were not men of intellectual cultivation. The enlarged ideas, the generous and manly feelings inspired by a liberal education, were utterly unknown to them. Unformed by that wisdom which arises from science and true philosophy, they were gross barbarians, dressed in the mere outward tinsel of civilization.[32] Where the enthusiasm of military honour characterizes the rank of gentlemen that nation will rise into empire. But no sooner does conquest give a continued security than the mere soldier degenerates; and the old veterans are soon succeeded by a new generation, illiterate as their fathers, but destitute of their virtues and experience. Polite literature not only humanizes the heart, but also wonderfully strengthens and enlarges the mind. Moral and political philosophy are its peculiar provinces, and are never happily cultivated without its assistance. But, where ignorance characterizes the body of the nobility, the most insipid dissipation and the very idleness and effeminacy of luxury are sure to follow. Titles and family are then the only merit, and the few men of business who surround the throne have it then in their power to aggrandize themselves by riveting the chains of slavery. A stately grandeur is preserved, but it is only outward; all is decayed within, and on the first storm the weak fabric falls to the dust. Thus rose and thus fell the empire of Rome, and the much wider one of Portugal. Though the increase of wealth did, indeed, contribute to that corruption of manners which unnerved the Portuguese, certain it is the wisdom of legislature might certainly have prevented every evil which Spain and Portugal have experienced from their acquisitions in the two Indies.[33] Every evil which they have suffered from their acquirements arose, as shall be hereafter demonstrated, from their general ignorance, which rendered them unable to investigate or apprehend even the first principles of civil and commercial philosophy. And what other than the total eclipse of their glory could be expected from a nobility, rude and unlettered as those of Portugal are described by the author of the Lusiad—a court and nobility who sealed the truth of all his complaints against them by suffering that great man, the light of their age, to die in an almshouse! What but the fall of their state could be expected from barbarians like these! Nor can the annals of mankind produce one instance of the fall of empire where the character of the nobles was other than that ascribed to his countrymen by Camoëns.

MICKLE'S SKETCH OF THE HISTORY OF THE DISCOVERY OF INDIA

No lesson can be of greater national importance than the history of the rise and the fall of a commercial empire. The view of what advantages were acquired, and of what might have been still added; the means by which such empire might have been continued, and the errors by which it was lost, are as particularly conspicuous in the naval and commercial history of Portugal as if Providence had intended to give a lasting example to mankind; a chart, where the course of the safe voyage is pointed out, and where the shelves and rocks, and the seasons of tempest are discovered and foretold.

The history of Portugal, as a naval and commercial power, begins with the designs of Prince Henry. But as the enterprises of this great man, and the completion of his designs are intimately connected with the state of Portugal, a short view of the progress of the power, and of the character of that kingdom, will be necessary to elucidate the history of the revival of commerce, and the subject of the Lusiad.

During the centuries when the effeminated Roman provinces of Europe were desolated by the irruptions of the northern barbarians, the Saracens spread the same horrors of brutal conquest over the finest countries of the eastern world. The northern conquerors of the finer provinces of Europe embraced the Christian religion as professed by the monks, and, contented with the luxuries of their new settlements, their military spirit soon declined. The Saracens, on the other hand, having embraced the religion of Mohammed, their rage for war received every addition which can possibly be inspired by religious enthusiasm. Not only the spoils of the vanquished, but Paradise itself was to be obtained by their sabres. Strengthened and inspired by a commission which they esteemed divine, the rapidity of their conquests far exceeded those of the Goths and Vandals. The majority of the inhabitants of every country they subdued embraced their religion and imbibed their principles; thus, the professors of Mohammedanism became the most formidable combination ever leagued together against the rest of mankind. Morocco and the adjacent countries had now received the doctrines of the Koran, and the arms of the Saracens spread slaughter and desolation from the south of Spain to Italy, and the islands of the Mediterranean. All the rapine and carnage committed by the Gothic conquerors were now amply returned on their less warlike posterity. In Spain, and the province now called Portugal, the Mohammedans erected powerful kingdoms, and their lust of conquest threatened destruction to every Christian power. But a romantic military spirit revived in Europe under the auspices of Charlemagne. The Mohammedans, during the reign of this sovereign, made a most formidable irruption into Europe; France in particular felt the weight of their fury. By the invention of new military honours that monarch drew the adventurous youth of every Christian power to his standards, which eventually resulted in the crusades, the beginning of which, in propriety, should be dated from his reign. Few indeed are the historians of this period, but enough remains to prove, that though the writers of the old romance seized upon it, and added the inexhaustible machinery of magic to the adventures of their heroes, yet the origin of their fictions was founded on historical facts.[34] Yet, however this period may thus resemble the fabulous ages of Greece, certain it is, that an Orlando, a Rinaldo, a Rugero, and other celebrated names in romance, acquired great honour in the wars which were waged against the Saracens, the invaders of Europe. In these romantic wars, by which the power of the Mohammedans was checked, several centuries elapsed, when Alonzo, King of Castile, apprehensive that the whole force of the Mohammedans of Spain and Morocco was ready to fall upon him, prudently imitated the conduct of Charlemagne. He availed himself of the spirit of chivalry, and demanded leave of Philip I. of France, and other princes, that volunteers from their dominions might be allowed to distinguish themselves, under his banners, against the Saracens. His desire was no sooner known than a brave army of volunteers thronged to his standard, and Alonzo was victorious. Honours and endowments were liberally distributed among the champions; and to Henry, a younger son of the Duke of Burgundy, he gave his daughter, Teresa, in marriage, with the sovereignty of the countries south of Galicia as a dowry, commissioning him to extend his dominions by the expulsion of the Moors. Henry, who reigned by the title of Count, improved every advantage which offered. The two rich provinces of Entro Minho e Douro, and Tras os Montes, yielded to his arms; great part of Beira also was subdued, and the Moorish King of Lamego became his tributary. Many thousands of Christians, who had lived in miserable subjection to the Moors, took shelter under the generous protection of Count Henry. Great numbers of the Moors also changed their religion, and chose rather to continue in the land where they were born than be exposed to the severities and injustice of their native governors. And thus, one of the most beautiful[35] and fertile spots of the world, with the finest climate, in consequence of a crusade[36] against the Mohammedans, became in the end the kingdom of Portugal, a sovereignty which in course of time spread its influence far over the world.

Count Henry, after a successful reign, was succeeded by his infant son, Don Alonzo-Henry, who, having surmounted the dangers which threatened his youth, became the founder of the Portuguese monarchy. In 1139 the Moors of Spain and Barbary united their forces to recover the dominions from which they had been driven by the Christians. According to the accounts of the Portuguese writers, the Moorish army amounted to near 400,000 men; nor is this number incredible when we consider what armies they at other times have brought into the field, and that at this time they came to take possession of lands from which they had been expelled. Don Alonzo, however, with a very small army, gave them battle on the plains of Ourique, and after a struggle of six hours, obtained a most glorious and complete victory, and one which was crowned with an event of the utmost importance. On the field of battle Don Alonzo was proclaimed King of Portugal by his victorious soldiers, and he in return conferred the rank of nobility on the whole army. The constitution of the monarchy, however, was not settled, nor was Alonzo invested with the regalia till six years after this memorable victory. The kind of government the Portuguese had submitted to under the Spaniards and Moors, and the advantages which they saw were derived from their own valour, had taught them the love of liberty, while Alonzo himself understood the spirit of his subjects too well to make the least attempt to set himself up as a despotic monarch. After six years spent in further victories, he called an assembly of the prelates, nobility, and commons, to meet at Lamego. When the assembly opened, Alonzo appeared seated on the throne, but without any other mark of regal dignity. Before he was crowned, the constitution of the state was settled, and eighteen statutes were solemnly confirmed by oath[37] as the charter of king and people; statutes diametrically opposite to the divine right and arbitrary power of kings, principles which inculcate and demand the unlimited passive obedience of the subject.

The founders of the Portuguese monarchy transmitted to their heirs those generous principles of liberty which complete and adorn the martial character. The ardour of the volunteer, an ardour unknown to the slave and the mercenary, added to the most romantic ideas of military glory, characterized the Portuguese under the reigns of their first monarchs. Engaged in almost continual war with the Moors, this spirit rose higher and higher; and the desire to extirpate Mohammedanism—the principle which animated the wish of victory in every battle—seemed to take deeper root in every age. Such were the manners, and such the principles of the people who were governed by the successors of Alonzo I.—a succession of great men who proved themselves worthy to reign over so military and enterprising a nation.

By a continued train of victories the Portuguese had the honour to drive the Moors from Europe. The invasions of European soil by these people were now requited by successful expeditions into Africa. Such was the manly spirit of these ages, that the statutes of Lamego received additional articles in favour of liberty, a convincing proof that the general heroism of a people depends upon the principles of freedom. Alonzo IV.,[38] though not an amiable character, was perhaps the greatest warrior, politician, and monarch of his age. After a reign of military splendour, he left his throne to his son Pedro, surnamed the Just. Ideas of equity and literature were now diffused by this great prince,[39] who was himself a polite scholar, and a most accomplished gentleman. Portugal began to perceive the advantages of cultivated talents, and to feel its superiority over the barbarous politics of the ignorant Moors. The great Pedro, however, was succeeded by a weak prince, and the heroic spirit of the Portuguese seemed to exist no more under his son Fernando, surnamed the Careless.

Under John I.[40] all the virtues of the Portuguese again shone forth with redoubled lustre. Happily for Portugal, his father had bestowed an excellent education upon this prince, which, added to his great natural talents, rendered him one of the greatest of monarchs. Conscious of the superiority which his own liberal education gave him, he was assiduous to bestow the same advantages upon his children, and he himself often became their preceptor in science and useful knowledge. Fortunate in all his affairs, he was most of all fortunate in his family. He had many sons, and he lived to see them become men of parts and of action, whose only emulation was to show affection to his person and to support his administration by their great abilities.

All the sons of John excelled in military exercises, and in the literature of their age; Don Edward and Don Pedro[41] were particularly educated for the cabinet, and the mathematical genius of Don Henry received every encouragement which a king and a father could give to ripen it into perfection and public utility.

History was well known to Prince Henry, and his turn of mind peculiarly enabled him to make political observations upon it. The history of ancient Tyre and Carthage showed him what a maritime nation might hope to become; and the flourishing colonies of the Greeks were the frequent topic of his conversation. Where Grecian commerce extended its influence the deserts became cultivated fields, cities rose, and men were drawn from the woods and caverns to unite in society. The Romans, on the other hand, when they destroyed Carthage, buried in her ruins the fountain of civilization, improvement and opulence. They extinguished the spirit of commerce, and the agriculture of the conquered nations. And thus, while the luxury of Rome consumed the wealth of her provinces, her uncommercial policy dried up the sources of its continuance. Nor were the inestimable advantages of commerce the sole motives of Henry. All the ardour that the love of his country could awaken conspired to stimulate the natural turn of his genius for the improvement of navigation.

As the kingdom of Portugal had been wrested from the Moors, and established by conquest, so its existence still depended on the superiority of force of arms; and even before the birth of Henry, the superiority of the Portuguese navies had been of the utmost consequence to the protection of the state. Whatever, therefore, might curb the power of the Moors, was of the utmost importance to the existence of Portugal. Such were the views and circumstances which united to inspire the designs of Henry, designs which were powerfully enforced by the religion of that prince. Desire to extirpate Mohammedanism was synonymous with patriotism in Portugal. It was the principle which gave birth to, and supported their monarchy. Their kings avowed it; and Prince Henry always professed, that to propagate the Gospel and extirpate Mohammedanism, was the great purpose of all his enterprises. The same principles, it is certain, inspired King Emmanuel, under whom the eastern world was discovered by Gama.[42]

The crusades, which had rendered the greatest political service to Spain and Portugal, had begun now to have some effect upon the commerce of Europe. The Hanse Towns had received charters of liberty, and had united together for the protection of their trade against the pirates of the Baltic. The Lombards had opened a lucrative traffic with the ports of Egypt, from whence they imported into Europe the riches of India; and Bruges, the mart between them and the Hanse Towns, was, in consequence, surrounded with the best agriculture of these ages,[43] a certain proof of the dependence of agriculture upon the extent of commerce. The Hanse Towns were liable, however, to be buried in the victories of a tyrant, and the trade with Egypt was exceedingly insecure and precarious. Europe was still enveloped in the dark mists of ignorance; commerce still crept, in an infant state, along the coasts, nor were the ships adapted for long voyages. A successful tyrant might have overwhelmed the system of commerce entirely, for it stood on a much narrower basis than in the days of Phœnician and Greek colonization. A broader and more permanent foundation of commerce than the world had yet seen was wanting to bless mankind, and Henry, Duke of Viseo, was born to give it.

In order to promote his designs, Prince Henry was appointed Commander-in-chief of the Portuguese forces in Africa. He had already, in 1412, three years before the reduction of Ceuta,[44] sent a ship to make discoveries on the Barbary coast. Cape Nam[45] (as its name implies) was then the ne plus ultra of European navigation; the ship sent by Henry, however, passed it sixty leagues, and reached Cape Bojador. About a league and a half from Cape St. Vincent (supposed to be the Promontorium Sacrum of the Romans), Prince Henry built his town of Sagrez, the best planned and fortified town in Portugal. Here, where the view of the ocean inspired his hopes, he erected his arsenals, and built and harboured his ships. And here, leaving the temporary bustle and cares of the State to his father and brothers, he retired like a philosopher from the world in order to promote its happiness. Having received all the information he could obtain in Africa, he continued unwearied in his mathematical and geographical studies; the art of ship-building received amazing improvement under his direction, and the correctness of his ideas of the structure of the globe is now confirmed. He it was who first suggested the use of the mariner's compass, and of longitude and latitude in navigation, and demonstrated how these might be ascertained by astronomical observations. Naval adventurers were now invited from all parts to the town of Sagrez, and in 1418 Juan Gonsalez Zarco and Tristran Vaz set sail on an expedition of discovery, the circumstances of which give us a striking picture of the state of navigation ere it was remodelled by the genius of Henry.

Cape Bojador, so named from its extent,[46] runs about forty leagues to the westward, and for about six leagues off land there is a most violent current, which, dashing upon the shallows, makes a tempestuous sea. This was deemed impassable, for it had not occurred to any one that by standing out to sea the current might be avoided. To pass this formidable Cape was the commission of Zarco and Vaz, who were also ordered to survey the African coast, which, according to the information given to Henry by the Moors, extended to the Equator. Zarco and Vaz, however, lost their course in a storm, and were driven to a small island, which, in the joy of their deliverance, they named Puerto Santo, or the Holy Haven. Nor was Prince Henry less joyful of their discovery than they had been of their escape: sufficient proof of the miserable state of navigation in those days; for this island is only a few days' voyage from Sagrez.

The discoverers of Puerto Santo, accompanied by Bartholomew Perestrello, were, with three ships, sent out on farther trial. Perestrello, having sown some seeds and left some cattle at Puerto Santo, returned to Portugal.[47] Zarco and Vaz directing their course southward, in 1419, perceived something like a cloud on the water, and sailing towards it, discovered an island covered with woods, which from this circumstance they named Madeira.[48] And this rich and beautiful island was the first reward of the enterprises of Prince Henry.

Nature calls upon Portugal to be a maritime power, and her naval superiority over the Moors, was, in the time of Henry, the surest defence of her existence as a kingdom. Yet, though all his labours tended to establish that naval superiority on the surest basis, though even the religion of the age added its authority to the clearest political principles in favour of Henry, yet were his enterprises and his expected discoveries derided with all the insolence of ignorance, and the bitterness of popular clamour. Barren deserts like Lybia, it was said, were all that could be found, and a thousand disadvantages, drawn from these data, were foreseen and foretold. The great mind and better knowledge of Henry, however, were not thus to be shaken. Twelve years had elapsed since the discovery of Madeira in unsuccessful endeavours to carry navigation farther. At length, one of his captains, named Galianez, in 1434 passed the Cape of Bojador, till then invincible; an action, says Faria, not inferior to the labours of Hercules.

Galianez, the next year, accompanied by Gonsalez Baldaya, carried his discoveries many leagues farther. Having put two horsemen on shore to discover the face of the country, the adventurers, after riding several hours, saw nineteen men armed with javelins. The natives fled, and the two horsemen pursued, till one of the Portuguese, being wounded, lost the first blood that was sacrificed to the new system of commerce. A small beginning, it soon swelled into oceans, and deluged the eastern and western worlds. The cruelties of Hernando Cortez, and that more horrid barbarian, Pizarro,[49] are no more to be charged upon Don Henry and Columbus, than the villainies of the Jesuits and the horrors of the

Inquisition are to be ascribed to Him who commands us to do to our neighbour as we would wish our neighbour to do to us. But, if it be maintained that he who plans a discovery ought to foresee the miseries which the vicious will engraft upon his enterprise, let the objector be told that the miseries are uncertain, while the advantages are real and sure.

In 1440 Anthony Gonsalez brought some Moors prisoners to Lisbon. These he took two and forty leagues beyond Cape Bojador, and in 1442 he returned with his captives. One Moor escaped, but ten blacks of Guinea and a considerable quantity of gold dust were given in ransom for two others. A rivulet at the place of landing was named by Gonsalez, Rio del Oro, or the River of Gold. And the islands of Adeget, Arguim, and De las Garças were now discovered.

The negroes of Guinea, the first ever seen in Portugal, and the gold dust, excited other passions beside admiration. A company was formed at Lagos, under the auspices of Prince Henry, to carry on a traffic with the newly discovered countries; and, as the Portuguese considered themselves in a state of continual hostility with the Moors, about two hundred of these people, inhabitants of the Islands of Nar and Tider, in 1444, were brought prisoners to Portugal. Next year Gonzalo de Cintra was attacked by the Moors, fourteen leagues beyond Rio del Oro, where, with seven of his men, he was killed.

This hostile proceeding displeased Prince Henry, and in 1446 Anthony Gonsalez and two other captains were sent to enter into a treaty of peace and traffic with the natives of Rio del Oro, and also to attempt their conversion. But these proposals were rejected by the barbarians, one of whom, however, came voluntarily to Portugal, and Juan Fernandez remained with the natives, to observe their manners and the products of the country.

In 1447 upwards of thirty ships followed the route of traffic which was now opened; and John de Castilla obtained the infamy to stand the first on the list of those names whose villainies have disgraced the spirit of commerce, and afforded the loudest complaints against the progress of navigation. Dissatisfied with the value of his cargo, he seized twenty of the natives of Gomera (one of the Canaries), who had assisted him, and with whom he was in friendly alliance, and brought them as slaves to Portugal. But Prince Henry resented this outrage, and having given them some valuable presents of clothes, restored the captives to freedom and their native country.

The reduction of the Canaries was also this year attempted; but Spain having challenged the discovery of these islands, the expedition was discontinued. In the Canary Islands a singular feudal custom existed; giving to the chief man, or governor, a temporary right to the person of every bride in his district.

In 1448 Fernando Alonzo was sent ambassador to the king of Cape Verde with a treaty of trade and conversion, which was defeated at that time by the treachery of the natives. In 1449 the Azores were discovered by Gonsalo Vello; and the coast sixty leagues beyond Cape Verde was visited by the fleets of Henry. It is also certain that some of his commanders passed the equinoctial line.

Prince Henry had now, with inflexible perseverance, prosecuted his discoveries for upwards of forty years. His father, John I., concurred with him in his views, and gave him every assistance; his brother, King Edward, during his short reign, took the same interest in his expeditions as his father had done; nor was the eleven years' regency of his brother Don Pedro less auspicious to him.[50] But the misunderstanding between Pedro and his nephew Alonzo V., who took upon him the reins of government in his seventeenth year, retarded the designs of Henry, and gave him much unhappiness.[51] At his town of Sagrez, from whence he had not moved for many years, Don Henry, now in his sixty-seventh year, yielded to the stroke of fate, in the year of our Lord 1463, gratified with the certain prospect that the route to the eastern world would one day crown the enterprises to which he had given birth. He saw with pleasure the naval superiority of his country over the Moors established on the must solid basis, its trade greatly upon the increase, and flattered himself that he had given a mortal wound to Mohammedanism. To him, as to their primary author, are due all the inestimable advantages which ever have flowed, or ever will flow from the discovery of the greatest part of Africa, and of the East and West Indies. Every improvement in the state and manners of these countries, or whatever country may be yet discovered, is strictly due to him. What is an Alexander, crowned with trophies at the head of his army, compared with a Henry contemplating the ocean from his window on the rock of Sagrez! The one suggests the idea of a destroying demon, the other of a benevolent Deity.

From 1448, when Alonzo V. assumed the power of government, till the end of his reign in 1471, little progress was made in maritime affairs. Cape Catherine alone was added to the former discoveries. But under his son, John II., the designs of Prince Henry were prosecuted with renewed vigour. In 1481 the Portuguese built a fort on the Gold Coast, and the King of Portugal took the title of Lord of Guinea. Bartholomew Diaz, in 1486, reached the river which he named dell'Infante on the eastern side of Africa, but deterred by the storms of that coast from proceeding farther, on his return he had the happiness to be the discoverer of the promontory, unknown for many ages, which bounds the south of Africa. From the storms he there encountered he named it Cape of Storms; but John, elated with the promise of India, which this discovery, as he justly deemed, included, gave it the name of the Cape of Good Hope. The arts and valour of the Portuguese had now made a great impression on the minds of the Africans. The King of Congo sent the sons of some of his principal officers to Lisbon, to be instructed in arts and religion; and ambassadors from the King of Benin requested teachers to be sent to his kingdom. On the return of his subjects, the King and Queen of Congo, with 100,000 of their people, were baptized. An ambassador also arrived from the Christian Emperor of Abyssinia, and Pedro de Covillam and Alonzo de Payva were sent by land to penetrate into the East, that they might acquire whatever intelligence might facilitate the desired navigation to India. Covillam and Payva parted at Toro in Arabia, and took different routes. The former having visited Conanor, Calicut, and Goa in India, returned to Cairo, where he heard of the death of his companion. Here also he met the Rabbi Abraham of Beja, who was employed for the same purpose by King John. Covillam sent the Rabbi home with an account of what countries he had seen, and he himself proceeded to Ormuz and Ethiopia, but, as Camoëns expresses it—

"To his native shore, Enrich'd with knowledge, he return'd no more."

Men, whose genius led them to maritime affairs began now to be possessed by an ardent ambition to distinguish themselves; and the famous Columbus offered his service to King John, and was rejected. Every one knows the discoveries of this great adventurer, but his history is generally misunderstood.[52] The simple truth is, Columbus, who acquired his skill in navigation among the Portuguese, could be no stranger to the design, long meditated in that kingdom, of discovering a naval route to India, which, according to ancient geographers and the opinion of that age, was supposed to be the next land to the west of Spain. And that India and the adjacent islands were the regions sought by Columbus is also certain. John, who esteemed the route to India as almost discovered, and in the power of his own subjects, rejected the proposals of the foreigner. But Columbus met a more favourable reception from Ferdinand and Isabella, the king and queen of Castile. Columbus, therefore, proposed, as Magalhaens afterwards did, for the same reason, to steer a westward course, and having in 1492 discovered some western islands, in 1493, on his return to Spain, he put into the Tagus with great tokens of the riches of his discovery. Some of the Portuguese courtiers (the same ungenerous minds, perhaps, who advised the rejection of Columbus because he was a foreigner) proposed the assassination of that great man, thereby to conceal from Spain the advantages of his navigation. But John, though Columbus rather roughly upbraided him, looked upon him now with a generous regret, and dismissed him with honour. The King of Portugal, however, alarmed lest the discoveries of Columbus should interfere with those of his crown, gave orders to equip a war-fleet to protect his rights. But matters were adjusted by embassies, and that celebrated treaty was drawn up by which Spain and Portugal divided the western and eastern worlds between them. The eastern half of the world was allotted for the Portuguese, and the western for the Spanish navigation. A Papal Bull also, which, for obvious reasons, prohibited the propagation of the gospel in these bounds by the subjects of any other state, confirmed this amicable and extraordinary treaty.

Soon after this, however, while the thoughts of King John were intent on the discovery of India, his preparations were interrupted by his death. But his earnest desires and great designs were inherited, together with his crown, by his cousin Emmanuel; and in 1497 (the year before Columbus made the voyage in which he discovered the mouth of the river Oronoko), Vasco de Gama sailed from the Tagus for the discovery of India.

Of this voyage, the subject of the Lusiad, many particulars are necessarily mentioned in the notes; we shall therefore only allude to these, but be more explicit on the others, which are omitted by Camoëns in obedience to the rules of epic poetry.

Notwithstanding the popular clamour against the undertaking, Emmanuel was determined to prosecute the views of Prince Henry and John II. Three sloops of war and a store ship, manned with only 160 men, were fitted out; for hostility was not the purpose of this expedition. Vasco de Gama, a gentleman of good family, who, in a war with the French, had given signal proofs of his naval skill, was commissioned admiral and general, and his brother Paul, with his friend Nicholas Coello, were appointed to command under him. It is the greatest honour of kings to distinguish the characters of their officers, and to employ them accordingly. Emmanuel in many instances was happy in this talent, particularly in the choice of his admiral for the discovery of India. All the enthusiasm of desire to accomplish his end, joined with the greatest heroism, the quickest penetration, and coolest prudence, united to form the character of Gama. On his appointment he confessed to the king that his mind had long aspired to this expedition. The king expressed great confidence in his prudence and honour, and gave him, with his own hand, the colours which he was to carry. On this banner, which bore the cross of the military Order of Christ, Gama, with great enthusiasm, took the oath of fidelity.

About four miles from Lisbon is a chapel on the sea side. To this, the day before their departure, Gama conducted the companions of his expedition. He was to encounter an ocean untried, and dreaded as unnavigable, and he knew the power of religion on minds which are not inclined to dispute its authority. The whole night was spent in the chapel in prayers for success, and in the rites of their devotion. The next day, when the adventurers marched to the fleet, the shore of Belem[53] presented one of the most solemn and affecting scenes perhaps recorded in history. The beach was covered with the inhabitants of Lisbon. A procession of priests, in their robes, sang anthems and offered up invocations to heaven. Every one looked on the adventurers as brave men going to a dreadful execution; as rushing upon certain death; and the vast multitude caught the fire of devotion, and joined aloud in prayers for their success. The relations, friends, and acquaintances of the voyagers wept; all were affected; the sight was general; Gama himself shed manly tears on parting with his friends, but he hurried over the tender scene, and hastened on board with all the alacrity of hope. He set sail immediately, and so much affected were the thousands who beheld his departure, that they remained immovable on the shore, till the fleet, under full sail, vanished from their sight.

It was on the 8th of July when Gama left the Tagus. The flag ship was commanded by himself, the second by his brother, the third by Coello, and the store ship by Gonsalo Nunio. Several interpreters, skilled in Arabic, and other oriental languages, went along with them. Ten malefactors (men of abilities, whose sentences of death were reversed, on condition of their obedience to Gama in whatever embassies or dangers among the barbarians he might think proper to employ them), were also on board. The fleet, favoured by the weather, passed the Canary and Cape de Verde islands, but had now to encounter other fortune. Sometimes stopped by dead calms, but for the most part tossed by tempests, which increased in violence as they proceeded to the south. Thus driven far to sea they laboured through that wide ocean which surrounds St. Helena, in seas, says Faria, unknown to the Portuguese discoverers, none of whom had sailed so far to the west. From the 28th of July, the day they passed the isle of St. James, they had seen no shore, and now on November the 4th they were happily relieved by the sight of land. The fleet anchored in the large bay,[54] and Coello was sent in search of a river where they might take in wood and fresh water. Having found one, the fleet made towards it, and Gama, whose orders were to acquaint himself with the manners of the people wherever he touched, ordered a party of his men to bring him some of the natives by force, or stratagem. One they caught as he was gathering honey on the side of a mountain, and brought him to the fleet. He expressed the greatest indifference about the gold and fine clothes which they showed him, but was greatly delighted with some glasses and little brass bells. These with great joy he accepted, and was set on shore; and soon after many of the blacks came for, and were gratified with, the like trifles; in return for which they gave plenty of their best provisions. None of Gama's interpreters, however, could understand a word of their language, or obtain any information of India. The friendly intercourse between the fleet and the natives was, however, soon interrupted by the imprudence of Veloso, a young Portuguese, which occasioned a skirmish wherein Gama's life was endangered. Gama and some others were on shore taking the altitude of the sun, when in consequence of Veloso's rashness they were attacked by the blacks with great fury. Gama defended himself with an oar, and received a dart in his foot. Several others were likewise wounded, and they found safety in retreat. A discharge of cannon from the ships facilitated their escape, and Gama, esteeming it imprudent to waste his strength in attempts entirely foreign to the design of his voyage, weighed anchor, and steered in search of the extremity of Africa.

In this part of the voyage, says Osorius, "The heroism of Gama was greatly displayed." The waves swelled up like mountains, the ships seemed at one time heaved up to the clouds, and at another precipitated to the bed of the ocean. The winds were piercing cold, and so boisterous that the pilot's voice could seldom be heard, and a dismal darkness, which at that tempestuous season involves these seas, added all its horrors. Sometimes the storm drove them southward, at other times they were obliged to stand on the tack and yield to its fury, preserving what they had gained with the greatest difficulty.

"With such mad seas the daring Gama fought For many a day, and many a dreadful night, Incessant labouring round the stormy Cape, By bold ambition led."

THOMSON.

During any interval of the storm, the sailors, wearied out with fatigue, and abandoned to despair, surrounded Gama, and implored him not to suffer himself, and those committed to his care, to perish by so dreadful a death. The impossibility that men so weakened could endure much longer, and the opinion that this ocean was torn by eternal tempest, and therefore had hitherto been, and was impassable, were urged. But Gama's resolution to proceed was unalterable.[55] A conspiracy was then formed against his life. But his brother discovered it, and the courage and prudence of Gama defeated its design. He put the chief conspirators and all the pilots in irons, and he himself, his brother, Coello, and some others, stood night and day at the helm and directed the course. At last, after having many days, with unconquered mind, withstood the tempest and mutiny (molem perfidiæ) the storm suddenly ceased, and they beheld the Cape of Good Hope.

On November the 20th all the fleet doubled that promontory, and steering northward, coasted along a rich and beautiful shore, adorned with large forests and numberless herds of cattle. All was now alacrity; the hope that they had surmounted every danger revived their spirits, and the admiral was beloved and admired. Here, and at the bay, which they named St. Blas, they took in provisions, and beheld these beautiful rural scenes, described by Camoëns. And here the store sloop was burnt by order of the admiral. On December the 8th a violent tempest drove the fleet out of sight of land, and carried them to that dreadful current which made the Moors deem it impossible to double the Cape. Gama, however, though unlucky in the time of navigating these seas, was safely carried over the current by the violence of a tempest; and having recovered the sight of land, as his safest course he steered northward along the coast. On the 10th of January they discovered, about 230 miles from their last watering place, some beautiful islands, with herds of cattle frisking in the meadows. It was a profound calm, and Gama stood near to land. The natives were better dressed and more civilized than those they had hitherto seen. An exchange of presents was made, and the black king was so pleased with the politeness of Gama, that he came aboard his ship to see him. At this place, which he named Terra de Natal, Gama left two of the malefactors before mentioned to procure what information they could against his return. On the 15th of January, in the dusk of the evening, they came to the mouth of a large river, whose banks were shaded with trees laden with fruit. On the return of day they saw several little boats with palm-tree leaves making towards them, and the natives came aboard without hesitation or fear. Gama received them kindly, gave them an entertainment, and some silken garments, which they received with visible joy. Only one of them, however, could speak a little broken Arabic. From him Fernan Martinho learned that not far distant was a country where ships, in shape and size like Gama's, frequently resorted. This gave the fleet great encouragement, and the admiral named this place "The River of Good Signs."

Here, while Gama refitted his ships, the crews were attacked with a violent scurvy, which carried off several of his men. Having taken in fresh provisions, on the 24th of February he set sail, and on the 1st of March they descried four islands on the coast of Mozambique. From one of these they perceived seven vessels in full sail bearing to the fleet. The Râis, or captain, knew Gama's ship by the admiral's ensign, and made up to her, saluting her with loud huzzas and instruments of music. Gama received them aboard, and entertained them with great kindness. The interpreters talked with them in Arabic. The island, in which was the principal harbour and trading town, they said, was governed by a deputy of the King of Quiloa; and many Arab merchants, they added, were settled here, who traded with Arabia, India, and other parts of the world. Gama was overjoyed, and the crew, with uplifted hands, returned thanks to Heaven.

Pleased with the presents which Gama sent him, and imagining that the Portuguese were Mohammedans from Morocco, the governor, dressed in rich embroidery, came to congratulate the admiral on his arrival in the east. As he approached the fleet in great pomp, Gama removed the sick out of sight, and ordered all those in health to attend above deck, armed in the Portuguese manner; for he foresaw what would happen when the Mohammedans should discover it was a Christian fleet. During the entertainment provided for him Zacocia seemed highly pleased, and asked several questions about the arms and religion of the strangers. Gama showed him his arms, and explained the force of his cannon, but he did not affect to know much about religion; however he frankly promised to show him his books of devotion whenever a few days refreshment should give him a more convenient time. In the meanwhile he entreated Zacocia to send him some pilots who might conduct him to India. Two pilots were next day brought by the governor, a treaty of peace was solemnly concluded, and every office of mutual friendship seemed to promise a lasting harmony. But it was soon interrupted. Zacocia, as soon as he found the Portuguese were Christians, used every endeavour to destroy the fleet. The life of Gama was attempted. One of the Moorish pilots deserted, and some of the Portuguese who were on shore to get fresh water were attacked by the natives, but were rescued by a timely assistance from the ships.

Besides the hatred of the Christian name, inspired by their religion, the Arabs had other reasons to wish the destruction of Gama. Before this period, they were almost the only merchants of the East; they had colonies in every place convenient for trade, and were the sole masters of the Ethiopian, Arabian, and Indian seas. They clearly foresaw the consequences of the arrival of Europeans, and every art was soon exerted to prevent such formidable rivals from effecting any footing in the East. To these Mohammedan traders the Portuguese gave the name of Moors.

Immediately after the skirmish at the watering-place, Gama, having one Moorish pilot, set sail, but was soon driven back by tempestuous weather. He now resolved to take in fresh water by force. The Moors perceiving his intention, about two thousand of them rising from ambush, attacked the Portuguese detachment. But the prudence of Gama had not been asleep. His ships were stationed with art, and his artillery not only dispersed the hostile Moors, but reduced their town, which was built of wood, into a heap of ashes. Among some prisoners taken by Paulus de Gama was a pilot, and Zacocia begging forgiveness for his treachery, sent another, whose skill in navigation he greatly commended.

A war with the Moors was now begun. Gama perceived that their jealousy of European rivals gave him nothing to expect but open hostility and secret treachery; and he knew what numerous colonies they had on every trading coast of the East. To impress them, therefore, with the terror of his arms on their first act of treachery, was worthy of a great commander. Nor was he remiss in his attention to the chief pilot who had been last sent. He perceived in him a kind of anxious endeavour to bear near some little islands, and suspecting there were unseen rocks in that course, he confidently charged the pilot with guilt, and ordered him to be severely whipped. The punishment produced a confession and promises of fidelity. And he now advised Gama to stand for Quiloa, which he assured him was inhabited by Christians. Three Ethiopian Christians had come aboard the fleet while at Zacocia's island, and the opinions then current about Prester John's country inclined Gama to try if he could find a port where he might obtain the assistance of a people of his own religion. A violent storm, however, drove the fleet from Quiloa, and being now near Mombas, the pilot advised him to enter that harbour, where, he said, there were also many Christians.

The city of Mombas is agreeably situated on an island, formed by a river which empties itself into the sea by two mouths. The buildings are lofty and of solid stone, and the country abounds with fruit-trees and cattle. Gama, happy to find a harbour where everything wore the appearance of civilization, ordered the fleet to cast anchor, which was scarcely done, when a galley, in which were 100 men in oriental costume, armed with bucklers and sabres, rowed up to the flag ship. All of these seemed desirous to come on board, but only four, who by their dress seemed officers, were admitted; nor were these allowed, till stripped of their arms. When on board they extolled the prudence of Gama in refusing admittance to armed strangers; and by their behaviour, seemed desirous to gain the good opinion of the fleet. Their country, they boasted, contained all the riches of India; and their king, they professed, was ambitious of entering into a friendly treaty with the Portuguese, with whose renown he was well acquainted. And, that a conference with his majesty and the offices of friendship might be rendered more convenient, Gama was requested to enter the harbour. As no place could be more commodious for the recovery of the sick, Gama resolved to enter the port; and in the meanwhile sent two of the pardoned criminals as an embassy to the king. These the king treated with the greatest kindness, ordered his officers to show them the strength and opulence of his city; and, on their return to the navy, he sent a present to Gama of the most valuable spices, of which he boasted such abundance, that the Portuguese, he said, if they regarded their own interest, would seek for no other India.

To make treaties of commerce was the business of Gama; and one so advantageous was not to be refused. Fully satisfied by the report of his spies, he ordered to weigh anchor and enter the harbour. His own ship led the way, when a sudden violence of the tide made Gama apprehensive of running aground. He therefore ordered the sails to be furled, and the anchors to be dropped, and gave a signal for the rest of the fleet to follow his example. This manœuvre, and the cries of the sailors in executing it, alarmed the Mozambique pilots. Conscious of their treachery, they thought their design was discovered, and leaped into the sea. Some boats of Mombas took them up, and refusing to put them on board, set them safely on shore, though the admiral repeatedly demanded the restoration of the pilots. These proofs of treachery were farther confirmed by the behaviour of the King of Mombas. In the middle of the night Gama thought he heard some noise, and on examination, found his fleet surrounded by a great number of Moors, who, with the utmost secrecy, endeavoured to cut his cables. But their scheme was defeated; and some Arabs, who remained on board, confessed that no Christians were resident either at Quiloa or Mombas. The storm which drove them from the one place, and their late escape at the other, were now beheld as manifestations of the Divine favour, and Gama, holding up his hands to heaven, ascribed his safety to the care of Providence.[56] Two days, however, elapsed before they could get clear of the rocky bay of Mombas. Having now ventured to hoist their sails, they steered for Melinda, a port, they had been told, where many merchants from India resorted. In their way thither they took a Moorish vessel, out of which Gama selected fourteen prisoners, one of whom he perceived by his mien to be a person of distinction. By this Saracen, Gama was informed that he was near Melinda, that the king was hospitable, and celebrated for his faith, and that four ships from India, commanded by Christian masters, were in that harbour. The Saracen also offered to go as Gama's messenger to the king, and promised to procure him an able pilot to conduct him to Calicut, the chief port of India.

As the coast of Melinda appeared to be dangerous, Gama anchored at some distance from the city, and, unwilling to risk the safety of any of his men, he landed the Saracen on an island opposite to Melinda. This was observed, and the stranger was brought before the king, to whom he gave so favourable an account of the politeness and humanity of Gama, that a present of several sheep, and fruits of all sorts, was sent by his majesty to the admiral, who had the happiness to find the truth of what his prisoner had told him confirmed by the masters of the four ships from India. These were Christians from Cambaya. They were transported with joy on the arrival of the Portuguese, and gave several useful instructions to the admiral.

The city of Melinda was situated in a fertile plain, surrounded with gardens and groves of orange-trees, whose flowers diffused a most grateful odour. The pastures were covered with herds; and the houses, built of square stones, were both elegant and magnificent. Desirous to make an alliance with such a state, Gama requited the civility of the king with great generosity. He drew nearer the shore, and urged his instructions as apology for not landing to wait upon his majesty in person. The apology was accepted, and the king, whose age and infirmity prevented him going on board, sent his son to congratulate Gama, and enter into a treaty of friendship. The prince, who had some time governed under the direction of his father, came in great pomp. His dress was royally magnificent, the nobles who attended him displayed all the riches of silk and embroidery, and the music of Melinda resounded all over the bay. Gama, to express his regard, met him in the admiral's barge. The prince, as soon as he came up, leaped into it, and distinguishing the admiral by his habit, embraced him with all the intimacy of old friendship. In their conversation, which was long and sprightly, he discovered nothing of the barbarian, says Osorius, but in everything showed an intelligence and politeness worthy of his high rank. He accepted the fourteen Moors, whom Gama gave to him, with great pleasure. He seemed to view Gama with enthusiasm, and confessed that the build of the Portuguese ships, so much superior to what he had seen, convinced him of the greatness of that people. He gave Gama an able pilot, named Melemo Cana, to conduct him to Calicut; and requested, that on his return to Europe, he would carry an ambassador with him to the court of Lisbon. During the few days the fleet stayed at Melinda, the mutual friendship increased, and a treaty of alliance was concluded. And now, on April 22, resigning the helm to his skilful and honest pilot, Gama hoisted sail and steered to the north. In a few days they passed the line, and the Portuguese with ecstasy beheld the appearance of their native sky. Orion, Ursa Major and Minor, and the other stars about the north pole, were now a more joyful discovery than the south pole had formerly been to them.[57] The pilot now stood out to the east, through the Indian ocean; and after sailing about three weeks, he had the happiness to congratulate Gama on the view of the mountains of Calicut, who, transported with ecstasy, returned thanks to Heaven, and ordered all his prisoners to be set at liberty.

About two leagues from Calicut, Gama ordered the fleet to anchor, and was soon surrounded by a number of boats. By one of these he sent one of the pardoned criminals to the city. The appearance of an unknown fleet on their coast brought immense crowds around the stranger, who no sooner entered Calicut, than he was lifted from his feet and carried hither and thither by the concourse. Though the populace and the stranger were alike earnest to be understood, their language was unintelligible to each other, till, happily for Gama, a Moorish merchant accosted his messenger in the Spanish tongue. The next day this Moor, who was named Monzaida, waited upon Gama on board his ship. He was a native of Tunis, and the chief person, he said, with whom John II. had at that port contracted for military stores. He was a man of abilities and great intelligence of the world, and an admirer of the Portuguese valour and honour. The engaging behaviour of Gama heightened his esteem into the sincerest attachment. Monzaida offered to be interpreter for the admiral, and to serve him in whatever besides he might possibly befriend him. And thus, by one of those unforeseen circumstances which often decide the greatest events, Gama obtained a friend who soon rendered him the most important services.

At the first interview, Monzaida gave Gama the fullest information of the climate, extent, customs, religion, and riches of India, the commerce of the Arabs, and the character of the sovereign. Calicut was not only the imperial city, but the greatest port. The king, or zamorim,[58] who resided here, was acknowledged as emperor by the neighbouring princes; and, as his revenue consisted chiefly of duties on merchandise, he had always encouraged the resort of foreigners to his ports.

Pleased with this promising prospect, Gama sent two of his officers with Monzaida to wait upon the zamorim at his palace, at Pandarene, a few miles from the city. They were admitted to the royal apartment, and delivered their embassy; to which the zamorim replied, that the arrival of the admiral of so great a prince as Emmanuel, gave him inexpressible pleasure, and that he would willingly embrace the offered alliance. In the meanwhile, as their present station was extremely dangerous, he advised them to bring the ships nearer to Pandarene, and for this purpose he sent a pilot to the fleet.

A few days after this, the zamorim sent his first minister, or catual,[59] attended by several of the nayres, or nobility, to conduct Gama to the royal palace. As an interview with the zamorim was absolutely necessary to complete the purpose of his voyage, Gama immediately agreed to it, though the treachery he had already experienced since his arrival in the eastern seas showed him the personal danger which he thus hazarded. He gave his brother, Paulus, and Coello the command of the fleet in his absence.

The revenue of the zamorim arose chiefly from the traffic of the Moors; the various colonies of these people were combined in one interest, and the jealousy and consternation which his arrival in the eastern seas had spread among them, were circumstances well known to Gama: and he knew, also, what he had to expect, both from their force and their fraud. But duty and honour required him to complete the purpose of his voyage. He left peremptory command, that if he was detained a prisoner, or any attempt made upon his life, they should take no step to save him or to reverse his fate; to give ear to no message which might come in his name for such purpose, and to enter into no negotiation on his behalf. They were to keep some boats near the shore, to favour his escape if he perceived treachery before being detained by force; yet the moment that force rendered his escape impracticable they were to set sail, and carry the tidings to the king. As this was his only concern, he would suffer no risk that might lose a man, or endanger the homeward voyage. Having left these orders, he went ashore with the catual, attended only by twelve of his own men, for he would not weaken his fleet, though he knew the pomp of attendance would in one respect have been greatly in his favour at the first court of India.

As soon as landed, he and the catual were carried in great pomp, in palanquins, upon men's shoulders, to the chief temple, and thence, amid immense crowds, to the royal palace. The apartment and dress of the zamorim were such as might be expected from the luxury and wealth of India. The emperor reclined on a magnificent couch, surrounded with his nobility and officers of state. Gama was introduced to him by a venerable old man, the chief brahmin. His majesty, by a gentle nod, appointed the admiral to sit on one of the steps of his sofa, and then demanded his embassy. It was against the custom of his country, Gama replied, to deliver his instructions in a public assembly; he therefore desired that the king and a few of his ministers would grant him a private audience. This was complied with, and Gama, in a manly speech, set forth the greatness of his sovereign Emmanuel, the fame he had heard of the zamorim, and the desire he had to enter into an alliance with so great a prince; nor were the mutual advantages of such a treaty omitted by the admiral. The zamorim, in reply, professed great esteem for the friendship of the King of Portugal, and declared his readiness to enter into a friendly alliance. He then ordered the catual to provide proper apartments for Gama in his own house; and having promised another conference, he dismissed the admiral with all the appearance of sincerity.

The character of this monarch is strongly marked in the history of Portuguese Asia. Avarice was his ruling passion; he was haughty or mean, bold or timorous, as his interest rose or fell in the balance of his judgment; wavering and irresolute whenever the scales seemed doubtful which to preponderate. He was pleased with the prospect of bringing the commerce of Europe to his harbours, but he was also influenced by the threats of the Moors.

Three days elapsed ere Gama was again permitted to see the zamorim. At this second audience he presented the letter and presents of Emmanuel. The letter was received with politeness, but the presents were viewed with an eye of contempt. Gama noticed it, and said he only came to discover the route to India, and therefore was not charged with valuable gifts, before the friendship of the state, where they might choose to traffic, was known. Yet, indeed, he brought the most valuable of all gifts, the offer of the friendship of his sovereign, and the commerce of his country. He then entreated the king not to reveal the contents of Emmanuel's letter to the Moors; and the king, with great apparent friendship, desired Gama to guard against the perfidy of that people. At this time, it is highly probable, the zamorim was sincere.

Every hour since the arrival of the fleet the Moors had held secret conferences. That one man of it might not return was their purpose; and every method to accomplish this was meditated. To influence the king against the Portuguese, to assassinate Gama, to raise a general insurrection to destroy the foreign navy, and to bribe the catual, were determined. And the catual (the master of the house where Gama was lodged) accepted the bribe, and entered into their interest. Of all these circumstances, however, Gama was apprised by his faithful interpreter, Monzaida, whose affection to the foreign admiral the Moors hitherto had not suspected. Thus informed, and having obtained the faith of an alliance from the sovereign of the first port of India, Gama resolved to elude the plots of the Moors; and accordingly, before the dawn, he set out for Pandarene, in hope to get aboard his fleet by some of the boats which he had ordered to hover about the shore.

But the Moors were vigilant. His escape was immediately known, and the catual, by the king's order, pursued and brought him back by force. The catual, however (for it was necessary for their schemes to have the ships in their power), behaved with politeness to the admiral, and promised to use all his interest in his behalf.

The eagerness of the Moors now contributed to the safety of Gama. Their principal merchants were admitted to a formal audience, when one of their orators accused the Portuguese as a nation of faithless plunderers: Gama, he said, was an exiled pirate, who had marked his course with blood and depredation. If he were not a pirate, still there was no excuse for giving such warlike foreigners any footing in a country already supplied with all that nature and commerce could give. He expatiated on the great services which the Moorish traders had rendered to Calicut; and ended with a threat, that all the Moors would leave the zamorim's ports and find some other settlement, if he permitted these foreigners any share in the commerce of his dominions.

However staggered with these arguments and threats, the zamorim was not blind to the self-interest and malice of the Moors. He therefore ordered, that the admiral should once more be brought before him. In the meanwhile the catual tried many stratagems to get the fleet into the harbour; and at last, in the name of his master, made an absolute demand that the sails and rudders should be delivered up, as the pledge of Gama's honesty. But these demands were as absolutely refused by Gama, who sent a letter to his brother by Monzaida, enforcing his former orders in the strongest manner, declaring that his fate gave him no concern, that he was only unhappy lest the fruits of all their fatigue and dangers should be lost. After two days spent in vain altercation with the catual, Gama was brought as a prisoner before the king. The king repeated his accusation; upbraided him with non-compliance to the requests of his minister; urged him, if he were an exile or a pirate, to confess freely, in which case he promised to take him into his service, and highly promote him on account of his abilities. But Gama, who with great spirit had baffled all the stratagems of the catual, behaved with the same undaunted bravery before the king. He asserted his innocence, pointed out the malice of the Moors, and the improbability of his piracy; boasted of the safety of his fleet, offered his life rather than his sails and rudders, and concluded with threats in the name of his sovereign. The zamorim, during the whole conference, eyed Gama with the keenest attention, and clearly perceived in his unfaltering mien the dignity of truth, and the consciousness that he was the admiral of a great monarch. In their late address, the Moors had treated the zamorim as somewhat dependent upon them, and he saw that a commerce with other nations would certainly lessen their dangerous importance. His avarice strongly desired the commerce of Portugal; and his pride was flattered in humbling the Moors. After many proposals, it was at last agreed, that of his twelve attendants he should leave seven as hostages; that what goods were aboard his fleet should be landed; and that Gama should be safely conducted to his ship, after which the treaty of commerce and alliance was to be finally settled. And thus, when the assassination of Gama seemed inevitable, the zamorim suddenly dropped his demand for the sails and rudders, rescued him from his determined enemies, and restored him to liberty and the command of his navy.

As soon as he was aboard[60] the goods were landed, accompanied by a letter from Gama to the zamorim, wherein he boldly complained of the treachery of the catual. The zamorim, in answer, promised to make inquiry, and punish him, if guilty; but did nothing in the affair. Gama, who had now anchored nearer to the city, every day sent two or three different persons on some business to Calicut, that as many of his men as possible might be able to give some account of India. The Moors, meanwhile, every day assaulted the ears of the king, who now began to waver; when Gama, who had given every proof of his desire of peace and friendship, sent another letter, in which he requested the zamorim to permit him to leave a consul at Calicut to manage the affairs of King Emmanuel. But to this request—the most reasonable result of a commercial treaty—the zamorim returned a refusal full of rage and indignation. Gama, now fully master of the character of the zamorim, resolved to treat a man of such an inconstant, dishonourable disposition with a contemptuous silence. This contempt was felt by the king, who, yielding to the advice of the catual and the entreaties of the Moors, seized the Portuguese goods, and ordered two of the seven hostages—the two who had the charge of the cargo—to be put in irons. The admiral remonstrated by means of Monzaida, but the king still persisted in his treacherous breach of faith. Repeated solicitations made him more haughty, and it was now the duty and interest of Gama to use force. He took a vessel, in which were six nayres, or noblemen, and nineteen of their servants. The servants he set ashore to relate the tidings, the noblemen he detained. As soon as the news had time to spread through the city, he hoisted his sails, and, though with a slow motion, seemed to proceed on his homeward voyage. The city was now in an uproar; the friends of the captive noblemen surrounded the palace, and loudly accused the policy of the Moors. The king, in all the perplexed distress of a haughty, avaricious, weak prince, sent after Gama, delivered up all the hostages, and submitted to his proposals; nay, even solicited that an agent should be left, and even descended to the meanness of a palpable lie. The two factors, he said, he had put in irons, only to detain them till he might write letters to his brother Emmanuel, and the goods he had kept on shore that an agent might be sent to dispose of them. Gama, however, perceived a mysterious trifling, and, previous to any treaty, insisted upon the restoration of the goods.

The day after this altercation Monzaida came aboard the fleet in great perturbation. The Moors, he said, had raised great commotions, and had enraged the king against the Portuguese. The king's ships were getting ready, and a numerous Moorish fleet from Mecca was daily expected. To delay Gama till this force arrived was the purpose of the Court and of the Moors, who were now confident of success. To this information Monzaida added, that the Moors, suspecting his attachment to Gama, had determined to assassinate him; that he had narrowly escaped from them; that it was impossible for him to recover his effects, and that his only hope was in the protection of Gama. Gama rewarded him with the friendship he merited, took him with him, as he desired, to Lisbon, and procured him a recompense for his services.

Almost immediately seven boats arrived loaded with the goods, and demanded the restoration of the captive noblemen. Gama took the goods on board, but refused to examine if they were entire, and also refused to deliver the prisoners. He had been promised an ambassador to his sovereign, he said, but had been so often deluded he could trust such a faithless people no longer, and would therefore carry away the captives to convince the King of Portugal what insults and injustice his ambassador and admiral had suffered from the Zamorim of Calicut. Having thus dismissed the Indians, he fired his cannon and hoisted his sails. A calm, however, detained him on the coast some days; and the zamorim, seizing the opportunity, sent what vessels he could fit out (sixty in all), full of armed men, to attack him. Though Gama's cannon were well handled, confident of their numbers, they pressed on to board him, when a sudden tempest arose, which Gama's ships rode out in safety, miserably dispersed the Indian fleet, and completed their ruin.

After this victory the admiral made a halt at a little island near the shore, where he erected a cross,[61] bearing the name and arms of his Portuguese majesty. From this place, by the hand of Monzaida, he wrote a letter to the zamorim, wherein he gave a full and circumstantial account of all the plots of the catual and the Moors. Still, however, he professed his desire of a commercial treaty, and promised to represent the zamorim in the best light to Emmanuel. The prisoners, he said, should be kindly used, were only kept as ambassadors to his sovereign, and should be returned to India when they were enabled from experience to give an account of Portugal. The letter he sent by one of the captives, who by this means obtained his liberty.

The fame of Gama had now spread over the Indian seas, and the Moors were everywhere intent on his destruction. As he was near the shore of Anchediva, he beheld the appearance of a floating isle, covered with trees, advance towards him. But his prudence was not to be thus deceived. A bold pirate, named Timoja, by linking together eight vessels full of men and covered with green boughs, thought to board him by surprise. But Gama's cannon made seven of them fly; the eighth, loaded with fruits and provision, he took. The beautiful island of Anchediva now offered a convenient place to careen his ships and refresh his men. While he stayed here, the first minister of Zabajo, king of Goa, one of the most powerful princes of India, came on board, and, in the name of his master, congratulated the admiral in the Italian tongue. Provisions, arms, and money were offered to Gama, and he was entreated to accept the friendship of Zabajo. The admiral was struck with admiration; the address and abilities of the minister appeared so conspicuous. He said he was an Italian by birth, but in sailing to Greece, had been taken by pirates, and after various misfortunes, had been necessitated to enter into the service of a Mohammedan prince, the nobleness of whose disposition he commended in the highest terms. Yet, with all his abilities, Gama perceived an artful inquisitiveness—that nameless something which does not accompany simple honesty. After a long conference, Gama abruptly upbraided him as a spy, and ordered him to be put to the torture. And this soon brought a confession, that he was a Polish Jew by birth, and was sent to examine the strength of the fleet by Zabajo, who was mustering all his power to attack the Portuguese. Gama, on this, immediately set sail, and took the spy along with him, who soon after was baptized, and named Jasper de Gama, the admiral being his godfather. He afterwards became of great service to Emmanuel.

Gama now stood westward through the Indian Ocean, and after being long delayed by calms, arrived off Magadoxa, on the coast of Africa. This place was a principal port of the Moors; he therefore levelled the walls of the city with his cannon, and burned and destroyed all the ships in the harbour. Soon after this he descried eight Moorish vessels bearing down upon him; his artillery, however, soon made them use their oars in flight, nor could Gama overtake any of them for want of wind. The hospitable harbour of Melinda was the next place he reached. His men, almost worn out with fatigue and sickness, here received a second time every assistance which an accomplished and generous prince could bestow. And having taken an ambassador on board, he again set sail, in hope that he might pass the Cape of Good Hope while the favourable weather continued; for his acquaintance with the eastern seas now suggested to him that the tempestuous season was periodical. Soon after he set sail his brother's ship struck on a sand bank, and was burnt by order of the admiral. His brother and part of the crew he took into his own ship, the rest he sent on board of Coello's; nor were more hands now alive than were necessary to man the two vessels which remained. Having taken in provisions at the island of Zanzibar (where they were kindly entertained by a Mohammedan prince of the same sect with the King of Melinda), they safely doubled the Cape of Good Hope on April 26, 1499, and continued till they reached the island of St. Iago, in favourable weather. But a tempest here separated the two ships, and gave Gama and Coello an opportunity to show the goodness of their hearts in a manner which does honour to human nature.

The admiral was now near the Azores, when Paulus de Gama, long worn with fatigue and sickness, was unable to endure the motion of the ship. Vasco, therefore, put into the island of Tercera, in hope of his brother's recovery. And such was his affection, that rather than leave him he gave the command of his ship to one of his officers. But the hope of recovery was vain. John de Sa proceeded to Lisbon with the flag ship, while the admiral remained behind to soothe the deathbed of his brother, and perform his funeral rites. Coello, meanwhile, landed at Lisbon, and hearing that Gama had not arrived, imagined he might either be shipwrecked or beating about in distress. Without seeing one of his family he immediately set sail again, on purpose to bring relief to his friend and admiral. But this generous design was prevented by an order from the king, ere he got out of the Tagus.

The particulars of the voyage were now diffused by Coello, and the joy of the king was only equalled by the admiration of the people. Yet, while all the nation was fired with zeal to express their esteem of the happy admiral, he himself, the man who was such an enthusiast to the success of his voyage that he would willingly have sacrificed his life in India to secure that success, was now in the completion of it a dejected mourner. The compliments of the Court, and the shouts of the street, were irksome to him; for his brother, the companion of his toils and dangers, was not there to share the joy. As soon as he had waited on the king, he shut himself up in a lonely house near the seaside at Belem, from whence it was some time ere he was drawn to mingle in public life.

During this important expedition, two years and almost two months elapsed. Of 160 men who went out, only 55 returned. These were all rewarded by the king. Coello was pensioned with 100 ducats a year, and made a fidalgo, or gentleman of the king's household, a degree of nobility in Portugal. The title of Don was annexed to the family of Vasco de Gama. He was appointed admiral of the eastern seas, with an annual salary of 3000 ducats, and a part of the king's arms was added to his. Public thanksgivings to Heaven were celebrated throughout the churches of the kingdom; while feasts, dramatic performances, and chivalrous entertainments (or tournaments), according to the taste of that age, demonstrated the joy of Portugal.

Pedro Alvarez Cabral was the second Portuguese admiral who sailed for India. He entered into alliance with Trimumpara, king of Cochin, and high priest of Malabar. (See Bk. x. p. 302.)

Gama, having left six ships for the protection of Cochin and Cananor, had sailed for Portugal with twelve ships, laden with the riches of the East. As soon as his departure was made known, the zamorim made great preparations to attack Cochin—a city situated on an island, divided by an arm of the sea from the main-land. At one part, however, this creek was fordable at low water. The zamorim having renewed the war, at length, by force of numbers and bribery, took the city; and the King of Cochin, stripped of his dominions, but still faithful to the Portuguese, fled to the island of Viopia. Francisco Albuquerque, with other commanders, having heard of the fate of Cochin, set sail for its relief; the garrison of the zamorim fled, and Trimumpara was restored to his throne. Every precaution by which the passage to the island of Cochin might be secured was now taken by Pacheco. The Portuguese took the sacrament, and devoted themselves to death. The King of Cochin's troops amounted only to 5000 men, while the army of the zamorim numbered 57,000, provided with brass cannon, and assisted by two Italian engineers. Yet this immense army, laying siege to Cochin, was defeated. Seven times the zamorim raised new armies; yet they were all vanquished at the fords of Cochin, by the intrepidity and stratagems of Pacheco. In the later battles the zamorim exposed himself to the greatest danger, and was sometimes sprinkled with the blood of his slain attendants—a circumstance mentioned in the Lusiad, bk. x. p. 304. He then had recourse to fraud and poison; but all his attempts were baffled. At last, in despair, he resigned his throne, and shut himself up for the rest of his days in one of the temples.

Soon after the kingdom of Cochin was restored to prosperity Pacheco was recalled. The King of Portugal paid the highest compliments to his valour, and gave him the government of a possession of the crown in Africa. But merit always has enemies: Pacheco was accused and brought to Lisbon in irons, where he remained for a considerable time chained in a dungeon. He was at length tried, and after a full investigation of the charges made against him, was honourably acquitted. His services to his country were soon forgotten, his merits were no longer thought of, and the unfortunate Pacheco ended his days in an alms-house—a circumstance referred to in the Lusiad, bk. x. p. 305.

BOOK VI

THE ARGUMENT

Gama's long recital being concluded, the poet resumes the thread of his story in his own person. The Portuguese admiral enters into an alliance with the King of Melinda, assures him that the vessels of his nation will always in future anchor on his shores. Gama receives from the monarch a faithful pilot to conduct him to India. Bacchus now has recourse to Neptune, at whose palace the divinities of the sea assemble. The gods of the sea consent to let loose the winds and waves against the daring navigators. During the night the sailors on the watch relate to each other amusing stories. Veloso urges them to relate some proud feats of war. The history of the contest of the twelve knights of England with the twelve of Portugal is then told. A violent tempest assails the fleet. Vivid picture of a storm at sea. Gama addresses his prayer to God; and Venus, with her nymphs so captivates the storm-gods that a calm ensues. The boy at the mast-head raises a joyful cry of Land! re-echoed by the whole crew. The pilot informs the Portuguese that they are now approaching the kingdom of Calicut. The poet's reflections.

With heart sincere the royal pagan joy'd,
And hospitable rites each hour employ'd,
For much the king the Lusian band admir'd,
And, much their friendship and their aid desir'd;
Each hour the gay festivity prolongs,
Melindian dances, and Arabian songs;
Each hour in mirthful transport steals away,
By night the banquet, and the chase by day;
And now, the bosom of the deep invites,
And all the pride of Neptune's festive rites;
Their silken banners waving o'er the tide,
A jovial band, the painted galleys ride;
The net and angle various hands employ,
And Moorish timbrels sound the notes of joy.
Such was the pomp, when Egypt's beauteous[400] queen

Bade all the pride of naval show convene,
In pleasure's downy bosom, to beguile
Her love-sick warrior:[401] o'er the breast of Nile,
Dazzling with gold, the purple ensigns flow'd,
And to the lute the gilded barges row'd;
While from the wave, of many a shining hue,
The anglers' lines the panting fishes drew.

Now, from the West the sounding breezes blow,
And far the hoary flood was yet to plough:
The fountain and the field bestow'd their store,
And friendly pilots from the friendly shore,
Train'd in the Indian deep, were now aboard,
When GAMA, parting from Melinda's lord,
The holy vows of lasting peace renew'd,
For, still the king for lasting friendship sued;
That Lusus' heroes in his port supplied,
And tasted rest, he own'd his dearest pride,
And vow'd, that ever while the seas they roam,
The Lusian fleets should find a bounteous home,
And, ever from the gen'rous shore receive
Whate'er his port, whate'er his land could give.[402]
Nor less his joy the grateful chief declar'd;
And now, to seize the valued hours prepar'd.
Full to the wind the swelling sails he gave,
And, his red prows divide the foamy wave:
Full to the rising sun the pilot steers,
And, far from shore through middle ocean bears.
The vaulted sky now widens o'er their heads,
Where first the infant morn his radiance sheds.
And now, with transport sparkling in his eyes,
Keen to behold the Indian mountains rise,
High on the decks each Lusian hero smiles,
And, proudly in his thoughts reviews his toils.
When the stern demon, burning with disdain,
Beheld the fleet triumphant plough the main:
The powers of heav'n, and heav'n's dread lord he knew,
Resolv'd in Lisbon glorious to renew
The Roman honours—raging with despair
From high Olympus' brow he cleaves the air,
On earth new hopes of vengeance to devise,
And sue that aid denied him in the skies;
Blaspheming Heav'n, he pierc'd the dread abode
Of ocean's lord, and sought the ocean's god.
Deep, where the bases of the hills extend,
And earth's huge ribs of rock enormous bend,
Where, roaring through the caverns, roll the waves
Responsive as the aërial tempest raves,

The ocean's monarch, by the Nereid train,
And wat'ry gods encircled, holds his reign.
Wide o'er the deep, which line could ne'er explore,
Shining with hoary sand of silver ore,
Extends the level, where the palace rears
Its crystal towers, and emulates the spheres;
So, starry bright, the lofty turrets blaze,
And, vie in lustre with the diamond's rays.
Adorn'd with pillars, and with roofs of gold,
The golden gates their massy leaves unfold:
Inwrought with pearl the lordly pillars shine,
The sculptur'd walls confess a hand divine.
Here, various colours in confusion lost,
Old Chaos' face and troubled image boast.
Here, rising from the mass, distinct and clear,
Apart, the four fair elements appear.
High o'er the rest ascends the blaze of fire,
Nor, fed by matter did the rays aspire,
But, glow'd ætherial, as the living flame,
Which, stol'n from heav'n, inspir'd the vital frame.
Next, all-embracing air was spread around,
Thin as the light, incapable of wound;
The subtle power the burning south pervades,
And penetrates the depth of polar shades.
Here, mother Earth, with mountains crown'd, is seen,
Her trees in blossom, and her lawns in green;
The lowing beeves adorn the clover vales,
The fleecy dams bespread the sloping dales;
Here, land from land the silver streams divide;
The sportive fishes through the crystal tide,
Bedropt with gold their shining sides display:
And here, old Ocean rolls his billows gray:
Beneath the moon's pale orb his current flows,
And, round the earth, his giant arms he throws.
Another scene display'd the dread alarms
Of war in heav'n, and mighty Jove in arms;
Here, Titan's race their swelling nerves distend
Like knotted oaks, and from their bases rend
And tower the mountains to the thund'ring sky,
While round their heads the forky lightnings fly;
Beneath huge Etna vanquish'd Typhon lies,[403]
And vomits smoke and fire against the darken'd skies.
Here, seems the pictur'd wall possess'd of life:
Two gods contending[404] in the noble strife,
The choicest boon to humankind to give,
Their toils to lighten, or their wants relieve:
While Pallas here appears to wave her hand,[405]
The peaceful olive's silver boughs expand:

Here, while the ocean's god indignant frown'd,
And rais'd his trident from the wounded ground,
As yet entangled in the earth, appears
The warrior horse; his ample chest he rears,
His wide red nostrils smoke, his eye-balls glare,
And his fore-hoofs, high pawing, smite the air.

Though wide, and various, o'er the sculptur'd stone[406]
The feats of gods, and godlike heroes shone;
On speed the vengeful demon views no more:
Forward he rushes through the golden door,
Where ocean's king, enclos'd with nymphs divine,
In regal state receives the king of wine:[407]
"O Neptune!" instant as he came, he cries,
"Here let my presence wake no cold surprise.
A friend I come, your friendship to implore
Against the Fates unjust, and Fortune's power;
Beneath whose shafts the great Celestials bow,
Yet ere I more, if more you wish to know,
The wat'ry gods in awful senate call,
For all should hear the wrong that touches all."
Neptune alarm'd, with instant speed commands
From ev'ry shore to call the wat'ry bands:
Triton, who boasts his high Neptunian race,
Sprung from the god by Salacé's[408] embrace,
Attendant on his sire the trumpet sounds,
Or, through the yielding waves, his herald, bounds:
Huge is his bulk, deform'd, and dark his hue;
His bushy beard, and hairs that never knew
The smoothing comb, of seaweed rank and long,   }
Around his breast and shoulders dangling hung,   }
And, on the matted locks black mussels clung;   }
A shell of purple on his head he bore,[409]
Around his loins no tangling garb he wore,
But all was cover'd with the slimy brood,
The snaily offspring of the unctuous flood;
And now, obedient to his dreadful sire,
High o'er the wave his brawny arms aspire;
To his black mouth his crooked shell applied,
The blast rebellows o'er the ocean wide:
Wide o'er their shores, where'er their waters flow,
The wat'ry powers the awful summons know;
And instant, darting to the palace hall,
Attend the founder of the Dardan wall;[410]
Old Father Ocean, with his num'rous race
Of daughters and of sons, was first in place.
Nereus and Doris, from whose nuptials sprung
The lovely Nereid train, for ever young,

Who people ev'ry sea on ev'ry strand,
Appear'd, attended with their filial band;
And changeful Proteus, whose prophetic mind[411]
The secret cause of Bacchus' rage divin'd,
Attending, left the flocks, his scaly charge,
To graze the bitter, weedy foam at large.
In charms of power the raging waves to tame,
The lovely spouse of ocean's sov'reign came.[412]
From Heaven and Vesta sprung the birth divine,
Her snowy limbs bright through the vestments shine.
Here, with the dolphin, who persuasive led
Her modest steps to Neptune's spousal bed,
Fair Amphitrité mov'd, more sweet, more gay
Than vernal fragrance, and the flowers of May;
Together with her sister-spouse she came,
The same their wedded lord, their love the same;
The same the brightness of their sparkling eyes,
Bright as the sun, and azure as the skies.
She, who, the rage of Athamas to shun,[414]
Plung'd in the billows with her infant son;
A goddess now, a god the smiling boy,
Together sped; and Glaucus lost to joy,[415]
Curs'd in his love by vengeful Circé's hate,
Attending, wept his Scylla's hapless fate.

And now, assembled in the hall divine,
The ocean gods in solemn council join;
The goddesses on pearl embroid'ry sat,
The gods, on sparkling crystal chairs of state,
And, proudly honour'd, on the regal throne,
Beside the ocean's lord, Thyoneus[416] shone.
High from the roof the living amber glows,[417]
High from the roof the stream of glory flows,
And, richer fragrance far around exhales
Than that which breathes on fair Arabia's gales.

Attention now, in list'ning silence waits:
The power, whose bosom rag'd against the Fates,
Rising, casts round his vengeful eyes, while rage
Spread o'er his brows the wrinkled seams of age.
"O thou," he cries, "whose birthright sov'reign sway,
From pole to pole, the raging waves obey;
Of human race 'tis thine to fix the bounds,
And fence the nations with thy wat'ry mounds:
And thou, dread power, O Father Ocean, hear,
Thou, whose wide arms embrace the world's wide sphere,
'Tis thine the haughtiest victor to restrain,
And bind each nation in its own domain:

And you, ye gods, to whom the seas are giv'n,
Your just partition with the gods of heav'n;
You who, of old unpunish'd never bore
The daring trespass of a foreign oar;
You who beheld, when Earth's dread offspring strove[418]
To scale the vaulted sky, the seat of Jove:
Indignant Jove deep to the nether world
The rebel band in blazing thunders hurl'd.
Alas! the great monition lost on you,
Supine you slumber, while a roving crew,
With impious search, explore the wat'ry way,
And, unresisted, through your empire stray:
To seize the sacred treasures of the main,
Their fearless prows your ancient laws disdain:
Where, far from mortal sight his hoary head
Old Ocean hides, their daring sails they spread,
And their glad shouts are echo'd where the roar
Of mounting billows only howl'd before.
In wonder, silent, ready Boreas[419] sees
Your passive languor, and neglectful ease;
Ready, with force auxiliar, to restrain
The bold intruders on your awful reign;
Prepar'd to burst his tempests, as of old,
When his black whirlwinds o'er the ocean roll'd,
And rent the Mynian[420] sails, whose impious pride
First brav'd their fury, and your power defied.
Nor deem that, fraudful, I my hope deny;
My darken'd glory sped me from the sky.
How high my honours on the Indian shore!
How soon these honours must avail no more!
Unless these rovers, who with doubled shame
To stain my conquests, bear my vassal's[421] name,
Unless they perish on the billowy way.
Then rouse, ye gods, and vindicate your sway.
The powers of heaven, in vengeful anguish, see
The tyrant of the skies, and Fate's decree;
The dread decree, that to the Lusian train
Consigns, betrays your empire of the main:
Say, shall your wrong alarm the high abodes?
Are men exalted to the rank of gods?
O'er you exalted, while in careless ease
You yield the wrested trident of the seas,
Usurp'd your monarchy, your honours stain'd,
Your birthright ravish'd, and your waves profan'd!
Alike the daring wrong to me, to you,
And, shall my lips in vain your vengeance sue!
This, this to sue from high Olympus bore—"
More he attempts, but rage permits no more.

Fierce, bursting wrath the wat'ry gods inspires,
And, their red eye-balls burn with livid fires:
Heaving and panting struggles evr'y breast,
With the fierce billows of hot ire oppress'd.
Twice from his seat divining Proteus rose,
And twice he shook, enrag'd, his sedgy brows:
In vain; the mandate was already giv'n,
From Neptune sent, to loose the winds of heav'n:
In vain; though prophecy his lips inspir'd,
The ocean's queen his silent lips requir'd.
Nor less the storm of headlong rage denies,
Or counsel to debate, or thought to rise.
And now, the God of Tempests swift unbinds
From their dark caves the various rushing winds:
High o'er the storm the power impetuous rides,
His howling voice the roaring tempest guides;
Right to the dauntless fleet their rage he pours,
And, first their headlong outrage tears the shores:
A deeper night involves the darken'd air,
And livid flashes through the mountains glare:
Uprooted oaks, with all their leafy pride,
Roll thund'ring down the groaning mountain's side;
And men and herds in clam'rous uproar run,
The rocking towers and crashing woods to shun.

While, thus, the council of the wat'ry state
Enrag'd, decreed the Lusian heroes' fate,
The weary fleet before the gentle gale
With joyful hope display'd the steady sail;
Thro' the smooth deep they plough'd the length'ning way;
Beneath the wave the purple car of day
To sable night the eastern sky resign'd,
And, o'er the decks cold breath'd the midnight wind.
All but the watch in warm pavilions slept,
The second watch the wonted vigils kept:
Supine their limbs, the mast supports the head,
And the broad yard-sail o'er their shoulders spread
A grateful cover from the chilly gale,
And sleep's soft dews their heavy eyes assail.
Languid against the languid power they strive,
And, sweet discourse preserves their thoughts alive.
When Leonardo, whose enamour'd thought
In every dream the plighted fair one sought—
"The dews of sleep what better to remove
Than the soft, woful, pleasing tales of love?"
"Ill-timed, alas!" the brave VELOSO cries,
"The tales of love, that melt the heart and eyes.
The dear enchantments of the fair I know,

The fearful transport, and the rapturous woe:
But, with our state ill suits the grief or joy;
Let war, let gallant war our thoughts employ:
With dangers threaten'd, let the tale inspire
The scorn of danger, and the hero's fire."
His mates with joy the brave VELOSO hear,
And, on the youth the speaker's toil confer.
The brave VELOSO takes the word with joy,
"And truth," he cries, "shall these slow hours decoy.
The warlike tale adorns our nation's fame,
The twelve of England give the noble theme.

"When Pedro's gallant heir, the valiant John,
Gave war's full splendour to the Lusian throne,
In haughty England, where the winter spreads
His snowy mantle o'er the shining meads,[422]
The seeds of strife the fierce Erynnis sows;[423]
The baleful strife from court dissension rose.
With ev'ry charm adorn'd, and ev'ry grace,
That spreads its magic o'er the female face,
Twelve ladies shin'd the courtly train among,
The first, the fairest of the courtly throng;
But, Envy's breath revil'd their injur'd name,
And stain'd the honour of their virgin fame.
Twelve youthful barons own'd the foul report,
The charge at first, perhaps, a tale of sport.
Ah, base the sport that lightly dares defame
The sacred honour of a lady's name!
What knighthood asks the proud accusers yield,
And, dare the damsels' champions to the field.[424]
'There let the cause, as honour wills, be tried,
And, let the lance and ruthless sword decide.'
The lovely dames implore the courtly train,
With tears implore them, but implore in vain.
So fam'd, so dreaded tower'd each boastful knight,
The damsels' lovers shunn'd the proffer'd fight.
Of arm unable to repel the strong,
The heart's each feeling conscious of the wrong,
When, robb'd of all the female breast holds dear,
Ah Heaven, how bitter flows the female tear!
To Lancaster's bold duke the damsels sue;
Adown their cheeks, now paler than the hue
Of snowdrops trembling to the chilly gale,
The slow-pac'd crystal tears their wrongs bewail.
When down the beauteous face the dew-drop flows,
What manly bosom can its force oppose!
His hoary curls th' indignant hero shakes,
And, all his youthful rage restor'd, awakes:

'Though loth,' he cries, 'to plunge my bold compeers
In civil discord, yet, appease your tears:
From Lusitania'—for, on Lusian ground
Brave Lancaster had strode with laurel crown'd;
Had mark'd how bold the Lusian heroes shone,
What time he claim'd the proud Castilian throne,[425]
How matchless pour'd the tempest of their might,
When, thund'ring at his side, they rul'd the fight:
Nor less their ardent passion for the fair,
Gen'rous and brave, he view'd with wond'ring care,
When, crown'd with roses, to the nuptial bed
The warlike John his lovely daughter led—
'From Lusitania's clime,' the hero cries,
'The gallant champions of your fame shall rise.
Their hearts will burn (for well their hearts I know)
To pour your vengeance on the guilty foe.
Let courtly phrase the heroes' worth admire,
And, for your injur'd names, that worth require:
Let all the soft endearments of the fair,
And words that weep your wrongs, your wrongs declare.
Myself the heralds to the chiefs will send,
And to the king, my valiant son, commend.'
He spoke; and twelve of Lusian race he names
All noble youths, the champions of the dames.
The dames, by lot, their gallant champions choose,[426]
And each her hero's name, exulting, views.
Each in a various letter hails her chief,
And, earnest for his aid, relates her grief:
Each to the king her courtly homage sends,
And valiant Lancaster their cause commends.
Soon as to Tagus' shores the heralds came,
Swift through the palace pours the sprightly flame
Of high-soul'd chivalry; the monarch glows
First on the listed field to dare the foes;
But regal state withheld. Alike their fires,
Each courtly noble to the toil aspires:
High on his helm, the envy of his peers,
Each chosen knight the plume of combat wears.
In that proud port, half circled by the wave,
Which Portugallia to the nation gave,
A deathless name,[427] a speedy sloop receives
The sculptur'd bucklers, and the clasping greaves,
The swords of Ebro, spears of lofty size,
And breast-plates, flaming with a thousand dyes,
Helmets high plum'd, and, pawing for the fight,
Bold steeds, whose harness shone with silv'ry light
Dazzling the day. And now, the rising gale
Invites the heroes, and demands the sail,

When brave Magricio thus his peers address'd,
'Oh, friends in arms, of equal powers confess'd,
Long have I hop'd through foreign climes to stray,
Where other streams than Douro wind their way;
To note what various shares of bliss and woe
From various laws and various customs flow;
Nor deem that, artful, I the fight decline;
England shall know the combat shall be mine.
By land I speed, and, should dark fate prevent,
(For death alone shall blight my firm intent),
Small may the sorrow for my absence be,
For yours were conquest, though unshar'd by me.
Yet, something more than human warms my breast,
And sudden whispers,[428] In our fortunes blest,
Nor envious chance, nor rocks, nor whelmy tide,
Shall our glad meeting at the list divide.'

"He said; and now, the rites of parting friends
Sufficed, through Leon and Castile he bends.
On many a field, enrapt, the hero stood,
And the proud scenes of Lusian conquest view'd.
Navarre he pass'd, and pass'd the dreary wild,
Where rocks on rocks o'er yawning glens are pil'd;
The wolf's dread range, where, to the ev'ning skies
In clouds involv'd, the cold Pyrenians rise.
Through Gallia's flow'ry vales, and wheaten plains
He strays, and Belgia now his steps detains.
There, as forgetful of his vow'd intent,
In various cares the fleeting days he spent:
His peers, the while, direct to England's strand,
Plough the chill northern wave; and now, at land,
Adorn'd in armour, and embroid'ry gay,
To lordly London hold the crowded way:
Bold Lancaster receives the knights with joy;
The feast, and warlike song each hour employ.
The beauteous dames, attending, wake their fire,
With tears enrage them, and with smiles inspire.
And now, with doubtful blushes rose the day,
Decreed the rites of wounded fame to pay.
The English monarch gives the listed bounds,
And, fix'd in rank, with shining spears surrounds.
Before their dames the gallant knights advance,
(Each like a Mars), and shake the beamy lance:
The dames, adorn'd in silk and gold, display
A thousand colours glitt'ring to the day:
Alone in tears, and doleful mourning, came,
Unhonour'd by her knight, Magricio's dame.
'Fear not our prowess,' cry the bold eleven,

'In numbers, not in might, we stand uneven.
More could we spare, secure of dauntless might,
When for the injur'd female name we fight.'

"Beneath a canopy of regal state,
High on a throne, the English monarch sat,
All round, the ladies and the barons bold,
Shining in proud array, their stations hold.
Now, o'er the theatre the champions pour,
And facing three to three, and four to four,
Flourish their arms in prelude. From the bay
Where flows the Tagus to the Indian sea,
The sun beholds not, in his annual race,
A twelve more sightly, more of manly grace
Than tower'd the English knights. With frothing jaws,
Furious, each steed the bit restrictive gnaws,
And, rearing to approach the rearing foe,
Their wavy manes are dash'd with foamy snow:
Cross-darting to the sun a thousand rays,
The champions' helmets as the crystal blaze.
Ah now, the trembling ladies' cheeks how wan!
Cold crept their blood; when, through the tumult ran
A shout, loud gath'ring; turn'd was ev'ry eye
Where rose the shout, the sudden cause to spy.
And lo, in shining arms a warrior rode,
With conscious pride his snorting courser trod;
Low to the monarch, and the dames he bends,
And now, the great Magricio joins his friends.
With looks that glow'd, exulting rose the fair,
Whose wounded honour claim'd the hero's care.
Aside the doleful weeds of mourning thrown,
In dazzling purple, and in gold she shone.
Now, loud the signal of the fight rebounds,
Quiv'ring the air, the meeting shock resounds
Hoarse, crashing uproar; griding splinters spring
Far round, and bucklers dash'd on bucklers ring.
Their swords flash lightning; darkly reeking o'er
The shining mail-plates flows the purple gore.
Torn by the spur, the loosen'd reins at large,
Furious, the steeds in thund'ring plunges charge;
Trembles beneath their hoofs the solid ground,
And, thick the fiery sparkles flash around,
A dreadful blaze! With pleasing horror thrill'd,
The crowd behold the terrors of the field.
Here, stunn'd and stagg'ring with the forceful blow,
A bending champion grasps the saddle-bow;
Here, backward bent, a falling knight reclines,
His plumes, dishonour'd, lash the courser's loins.

So, tir'd and stagger'd toil'd the doubtful fight,
When great Magricio, kindling all his might,
Gave all his rage to burn: with headlong force,
Conscious of victory, his bounding horse
Wheels round and round the foe; the hero's spear
Now on the front, now flaming on the rear,
Mows down their firmest battle; groans the ground   }
Beneath his courser's smiting hoofs: far round   }
The cloven helms and splinter'd shields resound.   }
Here, torn and trail'd in dust the harness gay,
From the fall'n master springs the steed away;
Obscene with dust and gore, slow from the ground
Rising, the master rolls his eyes around,
Pale as a spectre on the Stygian coast,
In all the rage of shame confus'd, and lost:
Here, low on earth, and o'er the riders thrown,
The wallowing coursers and the riders groan:
Before their glimm'ring vision dies the light,
And, deep descends the gloom of death's eternal night.
They now who boasted, 'Let the sword decide,'
Alone in flight's ignoble aid confide:
Loud to the skies the shout of joy proclaims
The spotless honour of the ladies' names.

"In painted halls of state, and rosy bowers,
The twelve brave Lusians crown the festive hours.
Bold Lancaster the princely feast bestows,
The goblet circles, and the music flows;
And ev'ry care, the transport of their joy,
To tend the knights the lovely dames employ;
The green-bough'd forests by the lawns of Thames
Behold the victor-champions, and the dames
Rouse the tall roe-buck o'er the dews of morn,
While, through the dales of Kent resounds the bugle-horn.
The sultry noon the princely banquet owns,
The minstrel's song of war the banquet crowns:
And, when the shades of gentle ev'ning fall,
Loud with the dance resounds the lordly hall:
The golden roofs, while Vesper shines, prolong
The trembling echoes of the harp and song.
Thus pass'd the days on England's happy strand,
Till the dear mem'ry of their natal land
Sigh'd for the banks of Tagus. Yet, the breast
Of brave Magricio spurns the thoughts of rest.
In Gaul's proud court he sought the listed plain,
In arms, an injur'd lady's knight again.
As Rome's Corvinus[429] o'er the field he strode,
And, on the foe's huge cuirass proudly trod.

No more by tyranny's proud tongue revil'd,
The Flandrian countess on her hero smil'd.[430]
The Rhine another pass'd, and prov'd his might,[431]
A fraudful German dar'd him to the fight.
Strain'd in his grasp, the fraudful boaster fell—"
Here sudden stopp'd the youth; the distant yell
Of gath'ring tempest sounded in his ears,
Unheard, unheeded by his list'ning peers.
Earnest, at full, they urge him to relate
Magricio's combat, and the German's fate.
When, shrilly whistling through the decks, resounds
The master's call, and loud his voice rebounds:
Instant from converse, and from slumber, start
Both bands, and instant to their toils they dart.
"Aloft, oh speed, down, down the topsails!" cries
The master: "sudden from my earnest eyes
Vanish'd the stars; slow rolls the hollow sigh,
The storm's dread herald." To the topsails fly
The bounding youths, and o'er the yardarms whirl
The whizzing ropes, and swift the canvas furl;
When, from their grasp the bursting tempests bore
The sheets half-gather'd, and in fragments tore.
"Strike, strike the mainsail!" loud again he rears
His echoing voice; when, roaring in their ears,
As if the starry vault, by thunders riv'n,
Rush'd downward to the deep the walls of heav'n,
With headlong weight a fiercer blast descends,
And, with sharp whirring crash, the mainsail rends;
Loud shrieks of horror through the fleet resound;
Bursts the torn cordage; rattle far around
The splinter'd yardarms; from each bending mast,
In many a shred, far streaming on the blast
The canvas floats; low sinks the leeward side,
O'er the broad vessels rolls the swelling tide:
"Oh strain each nerve!" the frantic pilot cries—
"Oh now!"—and instant every nerve applies,
Tugging what cumbrous lay, with strainful force;
Dash'd by the pond'rous loads, the surges hoarse
Roar in new whirls: the dauntless soldiers ran
To pump, yet, ere the groaning pump began
The wave to vomit, o'er the decks o'erthrown
In grovelling heaps, the stagger'd soldiers groan:
So rolls the vessel, not the boldest three,
Of arm robustest, and of firmest knee,
Can guide the starting rudder; from their hands
The helm bursts; scarce a cable's strength commands
The stagg'ring fury of its starting bounds,
While to the forceful, beating surge resounds

The hollow crazing hulk: with kindling rage
The adverse winds the adverse winds engage,
As, from its base of rock their banded power
Strove in the dust to strew some lordly tower,
Whose dented battlements in middle sky
Frown on the tempest and its rage defy;
So, roar'd the winds: high o'er the rest upborne
On the wide mountain-wave's slant ridge forlorn,
At times discover'd by the lightnings blue,
Hangs GAMA'S lofty vessel, to the view
Small as her boat; o'er Paulus' shatter'd prore
Falls the tall mainmast, prone, with crashing roar;
Their hands, yet grasping their uprooted hair,
The sailors lift to heaven in wild despair,
The Saviour-God each yelling voice implores.
Nor less from brave Coello's war-ship pours
The shriek, shrill rolling on the tempest's wings:
Dire as the bird of death at midnight sings
His dreary howlings in the sick man's ear,
The answ'ring shriek from ship to ship they hear.

Now, on the mountain-billows upward driv'n,
The navy mingles with the clouds of heav'n;
Now, rushing downward with the sinking waves,
Bare they behold old Ocean's vaulty caves.
The eastern blast against the western pours,
Against the southern storm the northern roars:
From pole to pole the flashy lightnings glare,
One pale, blue, twinkling sheet enwraps the air;
In swift succession now the volleys fly,
Darted in pointed curvings o'er the sky;
And, through the horrors of the dreadful night,
O'er the torn waves they shed a ghastly light;
The breaking surges flame with burning red,
Wider, and louder still the thunders spread,
As if the solid heav'ns together crush'd,
Expiring worlds on worlds expiring rush'd,
And dim-brow'd Chaos struggled to regain
The wild confusion of his ancient reign.
Not such the volley when the arm of Jove
From heav'n's high gates the rebel Titans drove;
Not such fierce lightnings blaz'd athwart the flood,
When, sav'd by Heaven, Deucalion's vessel rode
High o'er the delug'd hills. Along the shore
The halcyons, mindful of their fate, deplore;[432]
As beating round, on trembling wings they fly,
Shrill through the storm their woful clamours die.
So, from the tomb, when midnight veils the plains,

With shrill, faint voice, th' untimely ghost complains.[433]
The am'rous dolphins to their deepest caves
In vain retreat, to fly the furious waves;
High o'er the mountain-capes the ocean flows,
And tears the aged forests from their brows:
The pine and oak's huge, sinewy roots uptorn,
And, from their beds the dusky sands upborne
On the rude whirlings of the billowy sweep,
Imbrown the surface of the boiling deep.
High to the poop the valiant GAMA springs,
And all the rage of grief his bosom wrings,
Grief to behold, the while fond hope enjoy'd
The meed of all his toils, that hope destroy'd.
In awful horror lost, the hero stands,
And rolls his eyes to heav'n, and spreads his hands,
While to the clouds his vessel rides the swell,
And now, her black keel strikes the gates of hell;
"O Thou," he cries, "whom trembling heav'n obeys,
Whose will the tempest's furious madness sways,
Who, through the wild waves, ledd'st Thy chosen race,
While the high billows stood like walls of brass:[434]
O Thou, while ocean bursting o'er the world
Roar'd o'er the hills, and from the sky down hurl'd
Rush'd other headlong oceans; oh, as then
The second father of the race of men[435]
Safe in Thy care the dreadful billows rode,
Oh! save us now, be now the Saviour-God!
Safe in Thy care, what dangers have we pass'd!
And shalt Thou leave us, leave us now at last
To perish here—our dangers and our toils
To spread Thy laws unworthy of Thy smiles;
Our vows unheard? Heavy with all thy weight,
Oh horror, come! and come, eternal night!"

He paus'd;—then round his eyes and arms he threw
In gesture wild, and thus: "Oh happy you!
You, who in Afric fought for holy faith,
And, pierc'd with Moorish spears, in glorious death
Beheld the smiling heav'ns your toils reward,
By your brave mates beheld the conquest shar'd;
Oh happy you, on every shore renown'd!
Your vows respected, and your wishes crown'd."

He spoke; redoubled rag'd the mingled blasts;
Through the torn cordage and the shatter'd masts
The winds loud whistled, fiercer lightnings blaz'd,
And louder roars the doubled thunders rais'd,
The sky and ocean blending, each on fire,

Seem'd as all Nature struggled to expire.
When now, the silver star of Love appear'd,[436]
Bright in the east her radiant front she rear'd;
Fair, through the horrid storm, the gentle ray
Announc'd the promise of the cheerful day;
From her bright throne Celestial Love beheld
The tempest burn, and blast on blast impell'd:
"And must the furious demon still," she cries,
"Still urge his rage, nor all the past suffice!
Yet, as the past, shall all his rage be vain—"
She spoke, and darted to the roaring main;
Her lovely nymphs she calls, the nymphs obey,
Her nymphs the virtues who confess her sway;
Round ev'ry brow she bids the rose-buds twine,
And ev'ry flower adown the locks to shine,
The snow-white lily, and the laurel green,
And pink and yellow as at strife be seen.
Instant, amid their golden ringlets strove
Each flow'ret, planted by the hand of Love;
At strife, who first th' enamour'd powers to gain,
Who rule the tempests and the waves restrain:
Bright as a starry band the Nereids shone,
Instant old Eolus' sons their presence[437] own;
The winds die faintly, and, in softest sighs,
Each at his fair one's feet desponding lies:
The bright Orithia, threatening, sternly chides
The furious Boreas, and his faith derides;
The furious Boreas owns her powerful bands:
Fair Galatea, with a smile commands
The raging Notus, for his love, how true,
His fervent passion and his faith she knew.
Thus, every nymph her various lover chides;
The silent winds are fetter'd by their brides;
And, to the goddess of celestial loves,
Mild as her look, and gentle as her doves,
In flow'ry bands are brought. Their am'rous flame
The queen approves, and "ever burn the same,"
She cries, and joyful on the nymphs' fair hands,
Th' Eolian race receive the queen's commands,
And vow, that henceforth her Armada's sails
Should gently swell with fair propitious gales.[438]

Now, morn, serene, in dappled grey arose
O'er the fair lawns where murm'ring Ganges flows;
Pale shone the wave beneath the golden beam,
Blue, o'er the silver flood, Malabria's mountains gleam;
The sailors on the main-top's airy round,
"Land, land!" aloud with waving hands resound;

Aloud the pilot of Melinda cries,
"Behold, O chief, the shores of India rise!"
Elate, the joyful crew on tip-toe trod,
And every breast with swelling raptures glow'd;
GAMA's great soul confess'd the rushing swell,
Prone on his manly knees the hero fell;
"O bounteous heav'n!" he cries, and spreads his hands
To bounteous heav'n, while boundless joy commands
No further word to flow. In wonder lost,
As one in horrid dreams through whirlpools toss'd,
Now, snatch'd by demons, rides the flaming air,
And howls, and hears the howlings of despair;
Awak'd, amaz'd, confus'd with transport glows,
And, trembling still, with troubled joy o'erflows;
So, yet affected with the sickly weight
Left by the horrors of the dreadful night,
The hero wakes, in raptures to behold
The Indian shores before his prows unfold:
Bounding, he rises, and, with eyes on fire,
Surveys the limits of his proud desire.

O glorious chief, while storms and oceans rav'd,
What hopeless toils thy dauntless valour brav'd!
By toils like thine the brave ascend to heav'n,
By toils like thine immortal fame is giv'n.
Not he, who daily moves in ermine gown,
Who nightly slumbers on the couch of down;
Who proudly boasts through heroes old to trace
The lordly lineage of his titled race;
Proud of the smiles of every courtier lord,
A welcome guest at every courtier's board;
Not he, the feeble son of ease, may claim
Thy wreath, O GAMA, or may hope thy fame.
'Tis he, who nurtur'd on the tented field,
From whose brown cheek each tint of fear expell'd,
With manly face unmov'd, secure, serene,
Amidst the thunders of the deathful scene,
From horror's mouth dares snatch the warrior's crown,
His own his honours, all his fame his own:
Who, proudly just to honour's stern commands,
The dogstar's rage on Afric's burning sands,
Or the keen air of midnight polar skies,
Long watchful by the helm, alike defies:
Who, on his front, the trophies of the wars,
Bears his proud knighthood's badge, his honest scars;
Who, cloth'd in steel, by thirst, by famine worn,
Through raging seas by bold ambition borne,
Scornful of gold, by noblest ardour fir'd,

Each wish by mental dignity inspir'd,
Prepar'd each ill to suffer, or to dare,
To bless mankind, his great, his only care;
Him whom her son mature Experience owns,
Him, him alone Heroic Glory crowns.

Once more the translator is tempted to confess his opinion, that the contrary practice of Homer and Virgil affords, in reality, no reasonable objection against the exclamatory exuberances of Camoëns. Homer, though the father of the epic poem, has his exuberances, which violently trespass against the first rule of the epopea, the unity of the action. A rule which, strictly speaking, is not outraged by the digressive exclamations of Camoëns. The one now before us, as the severest critic must allow, is happily adapted to the subject of the book. The great dangers which the hero had hitherto encountered are particularly described. He is afterwards brought in safety to the Indian shore, the object of his ambition, and of all his toils. The exclamation, therefore, on the grand hinge of the poem has its propriety, and discovers the warmth of its author's genius. It must also please, as it is strongly characteristic of the temper of our military poet. The manly contempt with which he speaks of the luxurious, inactive courtier, and the delight and honour with which he talks of the toils of the soldier, present his own active life to the reader of sensibility. His campaigns in Africa, where in a gallant attack he lost an eye, his dangerous life at sea, and the military fatigues, and the battles in which he bore an honourable share in India, rise to our idea, and possess us with an esteem and admiration of our martial poet, who thus could look back with a gallant enthusiasm (though his modesty does not mention himself) on all the hardships he had endured; who thus could bravely esteem the dangers to which he had been exposed, and by which he had severely suffered, as the most desirable occurrences of his life, and the ornament of his name.

END OF THE SIXTH BOOK

BOOK VII

THE ARGUMENT

The poet, having expatiated on the glorious achievements of the Portuguese, describes the Germans, English, French, and Italians, reproaching them for their profane wars and luxury, while they ought to have been employed in opposing the enemies of the Christian faith. He then describes the western peninsula of India—the shores of Malabar—and Calicut, the capital of the Zamorim, where Gama had landed. Monsaide, a Moor of Barbary, is met with, who addresses Gama in Spanish, and offers to serve him as interpreter, Monsaide gives him a particular account of everything in India. The Zamorim invites Gama to an audience. The catual, or prime minister, with his officers, visits the ships, and embraces the opportunity of asking Gama to relate to him the history of Portugal.

Hail glorious chief![439] where never chief before
Forc'd his bold way, all hail on India's shore!
And hail, Ye Lusian heroes, fair and wide
What groves of palm, to haughty Rome denied,
For you by Ganges' length'ning banks unfold!
What laurel-forests on the shores of gold

For you their honours ever verdant rear,
Proud, with their leaves, to twine the Lusian spear!

Ah Heav'n! what fury Europe's sons controls!
What self-consuming discord fires their souls!
'Gainst her own breast her sword Germania turns,
Through all her states fraternal rancour burns;[440]
Some, blindly wand'ring, holy faith disclaim,[441]
And, fierce through all, wild rages civil flame.
High sound the titles of the English crown,
"King of Jerusalem,"[442] his old renown!
Alas, delighted with an airy name,
The thin, dim shadow of departed fame,
England's stern monarch, sunk in soft repose,
Luxurious riots mid his northern snows:
Or, if the starting burst of rage succeed,
His brethren are his foes, and Christians bleed;
While Hagar's brutal race his titles stain,   }
In weeping Salem unmolested reign,   }
And with their rites impure her holy shrines profane.   }
And thou, O Gaul,[443] with gaudy trophies plum'd.
"Most Christian" nam'd; alas, in vain assum'd!
What impious lust of empire steels thy breast[444]
From their just lords the Christian lands to wrest!
While holy faith's hereditary foes[445]
Possess the treasures where Cynifio flows;[446]
And all secure, behold their harvests smile
In waving gold along the banks of Nile.
And thou, O lost to glory, lost to fame,
Thou dark oblivion of thy ancient name,
By every vicious luxury debas'd,
Each noble passion from thy breast eras'd,
Nerveless in sloth, enfeebling arts thy boast,
O Italy, how fall'n, how low, how lost![447]
In vain, to thee, the call of glory sounds,
Thy sword alone thy own soft bosom wounds.

Ah, Europe's sons, ye brother-powers, in you
The fables old of Cadmus[448] now are true;
Fierce rose the brothers from the dragon teeth,
And each fell, crimson'd with a brother's death.
So, fall the bravest of the Christian name,[449]
While dogs unclean[450] Messiah's lore blaspheme,
And howl their curses o'er the holy tomb,
While to the sword the Christian race they doom.
From age to age, from shore to distant shore,
By various princes led, their legions pour;
United all in one determin'd aim,

From ev'ry land to blot the Christian name.
Then wake, ye brother-powers, combin'd awake,
And, from the foe the great example take.
If empire tempt ye, lo, the East expands,
Fair and immense, her summer-garden lands:
There, boastful Wealth displays her radiant store;
Pactol and Hermus' streams, o'er golden ore,
Roll their long way; but, not for you they flow,
Their treasures blaze on the stern sultan's brow:
For him Assyria plies the loom of gold,
And Afric's sons their deepest mines unfold
To build his haughty throne. Ye western powers,
To throw the mimic bolt of Jove is yours,
Yours all the art to wield the arms of fire,
Then, bid the thunders of the dreadful tire
Against the walls of dread Byzantium[451] roar,
Till, headlong driven from Europe's ravish'd shore
To their cold Scythian wilds, and dreary dens,
By Caspian mountains, and uncultur'd fens,
(Their fathers' seats beyond the Wolgian Lake,[452])
The barb'rous race of Saracen betake.
And hark, to you the woful Greek exclaims;
The Georgian fathers and th' Armenian dames,
Their fairest offspring from their bosoms torn,
(A dreadful tribute!)[453] loud imploring mourn.
Alas, in vain! their offspring captive led,
In Hagar's[454] sons' unhallow'd temples bred,
To rapine train'd, arise a brutal host,
The Christian terror, and the Turkish boast.

Yet sleep, ye powers of Europe, careless sleep,
To you in vain your eastern brethren weep;
Yet, not in vain their woe-wrung tears shall sue,
Though small the Lusian realms, her legions few,
The guardian oft by Heav'n ordain'd before,
The Lusian race shall guard Messiah's lore.
When Heav'n decreed to crush the Moorish foe
Heav'n gave the Lusian spear to strike the blow.
When Heav'n's own laws o'er Afric's shores were heard,
The sacred shrines the Lusian heroes rear'd;[455]
Nor shall their zeal in Asia's bounds expire,
Asia, subdu'd, shall fume with hallow'd fire.
When the red sun the Lusian shore forsakes,
And on the lap of deepest west[456] awakes,
O'er the wild plains, beneath unincens'd skies
The sun shall view the Lusian altars rise.
And, could new worlds by human step be trod,
Those worlds should tremble at the Lusian nod.[457]

And now, their ensigns blazing o'er the tide,
On India's shore the Lusian heroes ride.
High to the fleecy clouds resplendent far
Appear the regal towers of Malabar,
Imperial Calicut,[458] the lordly seat
Of the first monarch of the Indian state.
Right to the port the valiant GAMA bonds,
With joyful shouts, a fleet of boats attends:
Joyful, their nets they leave and finny prey,
And, crowding round the Lusians, point the way.
A herald now, by VASCO'S high command
Sent to the monarch, treads the Indian strand;
The sacred staff he bears, in gold he shines,
And tells his office by majestic signs.
As, to and fro, recumbent to the gale,
The harvest waves along the yellow dale,
So, round the herald press the wond'ring throng,
Recumbent waving as they pour along,
And much his manly port and strange attire,
And much his fair and ruddy hue admire:
When, speeding through the crowd, with eager haste,
And honest smiles, a son of Afric press'd;
Enrapt with joy the wond'ring herald hears
Castilia's manly tongue salute his ears.[459]
"What friendly angel from thy Tago's shore
Has led thee hither?" cries the joyful Moor.
Then, hand in hand (the pledge of faith) conjoin'd—
"Oh joy beyond the dream of hope to find,
To hear a kindred voice," the Lusian cried,
"Beyond unmeasur'd gulfs and seas untried;
Untried, before our daring keels explor'd
Our fearless way! O Heav'n, what tempests roar'd,
While, round the vast of Afric's southmost land,
Our eastward bowsprits sought the Indian strand!"
Amaz'd, o'erpower'd, the friendly stranger stood—
"A path now open'd through the boundless flood!
The hope of ages, and the dread despair,
Accomplish'd now, and conquer'd!"—Stiff his hair
Rose thrilling, while his lab'ring thoughts pursued
The dreadful course by GAMA'S fate subdued.
Homeward, with gen'rous warmth o'erflow'd, he leads
The Lusian guest, and swift the feast succeeds;
The purple grape, and golden fruitage smile;
And each choice viand of the Indian soil
Heap'd o'er the board, the master's zeal declare;
The social feast the guest and master share:
The sacred pledge of eastern faith[460] approv'd,

By wrath unalter'd, and by wrong unmov'd.
Now, to the fleet the joyful herald bends,
With earnest pace the Heav'n-sent friend attends:
Now, down the river's sweepy stream they glide,
And now, their pinnace cuts the briny tide:
The Moor, with transport sparkling in his eyes,
The well-known make of GAMA'S navy spies,
The bending bowsprit, and the mast so tall,
The sides black, frowning as a castle wall,
The high-tower'd stern, the lordly nodding prore,
And the broad standard slowly waving o'er
The anchor's moony[461] fangs. The skiff he leaves,
Brave GAMA'S deck his bounding step receives;
And, "Hail!" he cries: in transport GAMA sprung,
And round his neck with friendly welcome hung;
Enrapt, so distant o'er the dreadful main,
To hear the music of the tongue of Spain.
And now, beneath a painted shade of state,
Beside the admiral, the stranger sat.
Of India's clime, the natives, and the laws,
What monarch sways them, what religion awes?
Why from the tombs devoted to his sires
The son so far? the valiant chief inquires.
In act to speak the stranger waves his hand,
The joyful crew in silent wonder stand,
Each gently pressing on, with greedy ear,
As erst the bending forests stoop'd to hear
In Rhodope,[462] when Orpheus' heavenly strain,
Deplor'd his lost Eurydice in vain;
While, with a mien that gen'rous friendship won
From ev'ry heart, the stranger thus began:—

"Your glorious deeds, ye Lusians, well I know,
To neighb'ring earth the vital air I owe;
Yet—though my faith the Koran's lore revere;
So taught my sires; my birth at proud Tangier,
A hostile clime to Lisbon's awful name—
I glow, enraptur'd, o'er the Lusian fame;
Proud though your nation's warlike glories shine,
These proudest honours yield, O chief, to thine;
Beneath thy dread achievements low they fall,
And India's shore, discover'd, crowns them all.
Won by your fame, by fond affection sway'd,
A friend I come, and offer friendship's aid.
As, on my lips Castilia's language glows,
So, from my tongue the speech of India flows:
Mozaide my name, in India's court belov'd,
For honest deeds (but time shall speak) approv'd.

When India's monarch greets his court again,
(For now the banquet on the tented plain:
And sylvan chase his careless hours employ),[463]
When India's mighty lord, with wond'ring joy,
Shall hail you welcome on his spacious shore
Through oceans never plough'd by keel before,
Myself shall glad interpreter attend,
Mine ev'ry office of the faithful friend.
Ah! but a stream, the labour of the oar,
Divides my birthplace from your native shore;
On shores unknown, in distant worlds, how sweet
The kindred tongue, the kindred face, to greet!
Such now my joy; and such, O Heav'n, be yours!
Yes, bounteous Heav'n your glad success secures.
Till now impervious, Heav'n alone subdued
The various horrors of the trackless flood:
Heav'n sent you here for some great work divine,
And Heav'n inspires my breast your sacred toils to join.

"Vast are the shores of India's wealthful soil;
Southward sea-girt she forms a demi-isle:
His cavern'd cliffs with dark-brow'd forests crown'd,
Hemodian Taurus[464] frowns her northern bound:
From Caspia's lake th' enormous mountain[464] spreads,
And, bending eastward, rears a thousand heads:
Far to extremest sea the ridges thrown,
By various names, through various tribes are known:
Here down the waste of Taurus' rocky side
Two infant rivers pour the crystal tide,
Indus the one, and one the Ganges nam'd,
Darkly of old through distant nations fam'd:
One eastward curving holds his crooked way,
One to the west gives his swoll'n tide to stray:
Declining southward many a land they lave,
And, widely swelling, roll the sea-like wave,
Till the twin offspring of the mountain sire
Both in the Indian deep engulf'd expire:
Between these streams, fair smiling to the day,
The Indian lands their wide domains display,
And many a league, far to the south they bend,
From the broad region where the rivers end,
Till, where the shores to Ceylon's isle oppose,
In conic form the Indian regions close.
To various laws the various tribes incline,
And various are the rites esteem'd divine:
Some, as from Heav'n, receive the Koran's lore,
Some the dread monsters of the wild adore;
Some bend to wood and stone the prostrate head,

And rear unhallow'd altars to the dead.
By Ganges' banks, as wild traditions tell,[465]
Of old the tribes liv'd healthful by the smell;
No food they knew, such fragrant vapours rose
Rich from the flow'ry lawns where Ganges flows:
Here now the Delhian, and the fierce Pathàn,
Feed their fair flocks; and here, a heathen clan,
Stern Dekhan's sons the fertile valleys till,
A clan, whose hope to shun eternal ill,
Whose trust from ev'ry stain of guilt to save,
Is fondly plac'd in Ganges' holy wave;[466]
If to the stream the breathless corpse be giv'n
They deem the spirit wings her way to heav'n.
Here by the mouths, where hallow'd Ganges ends,
Bengala's beauteous Eden wide extends,
Unrivall'd smile her fair luxurious vales:
And here Cambaya[467] spreads her palmy dales;
A warlike realm, where still the martial race
From Porus,[468] fam'd of yore, their lineage trace.
Narsinga[469] here displays her spacious line,
In native gold her sons and ruby shine:
Alas, how vain! these gaudy sons of fear,
Trembling, bow down before each hostile spear.
And now, behold!"—and while he spoke he rose,
Now, with extended arm, the prospect shows,—
"Behold these mountain tops of various size
Blend their dim ridges with the fleecy skies:
Nature's rude wall, against the fierce Canar[470]
They guard the fertile lawns of Malabar.
Here, from the mountain to the surgy main,
Fair as a garden, spreads the smiling plain:
And lo, the empress of the Indian powers,
Their lofty Calicut, resplendent towers;
Hers ev'ry fragrance of the spicy shore,
Hers ev'ry gem of India's countless store:
Great Samoreem, her lord's imperial style,
The mighty lord of India's utmost soil:
To him the kings their duteous tribute pay,
And, at his feet, confess their borrow'd sway.
Yet higher tower'd the monarchs ancients boast,
Of old one sov'reign rul'd the spacious coast.
A votive train, who brought the Koran's lore,
(What time great Perimal the sceptre bore),
From blest Arabia's groves to India came;
Life were their words, their eloquence a flame
Of holy zeal: fir'd by the powerful strain,
The lofty monarch joins the faithful train,
And vows, at fair Medina's[471] shrine, to close

His life's mild eve in prayer, and sweet repose.
Gifts he prepares to deck the prophet's tomb,
The glowing labours of the Indian loom,
Orissa's spices, and Golconda's gems;
Yet, e'er the fleet th' Arabian ocean stems,
His final care his potent regions claim,
Nor his the transport of a father's name:
His servants, now, the regal purple wear,
And, high enthron'd, the golden sceptres bear.
Proud Cochim one, and one fair Chalé sways,
The spicy isle another lord obeys;
Coulam and Cananoor's luxurious fields,
And Cranganore to various lords he yields.
While these, and others thus the monarch grac'd,
A noble youth his care unmindful pass'd:
Save Calicut, a city poor and small,
Though lordly now, no more remain'd to fall:
Griev'd to behold such merit thus repaid,
The sapient youth the 'king of kings' he made,
And, honour'd with the name, great Zamoreem,
The lordly, titled boast of power supreme.
And now, great Perimal[472] resigns his reign,
The blissful bowers of Paradise to gain:
Before the gale his gaudy navy flies,
And India sinks for ever from his eyes.
And soon to Calicut's commodious port
The fleets, deep-edging with the wave, resort:
Wide o'er the shore extend the warlike piles,
And all the landscape round luxurious smiles.
And now, her flag to ev'ry gale unfurl'd,
She towers, the empress of the eastern world:
Such are the blessings sapient kings bestow,
And from thy stream such gifts, O Commerce, flow.

"From that sage youth, who first reign'd 'king of kings,'
He now who sways the tribes of India springs.
Various the tribes, all led by fables vain,
Their rites the dotage of the dreamful brain.
All, save where Nature whispers modest care,
Naked, they blacken in the sultry air.
The haughty nobles and the vulgar race
Never must join the conjugal embrace;
Nor may the stripling, nor the blooming maid,
(Oh, lost to joy, by cruel rites betray'd!)
To spouse of other than their father's art,
At Love's connubial shrine unite the heart:
Nor may their sons (the genius and the view
Confin'd and fetter'd) other art pursue.

Vile were the stain, and deep the foul disgrace,
Should other tribe touch one of noble race;
A thousand rites, and washings o'er and o'er,
Can scarce his tainted purity restore.
Poleas[473] the lab'ring lower clans are nam'd:
By the proud Nayres the noble rank is claim'd;
The toils of culture, and of art they scorn,
The warrior's plumes their haughty brows adorn;
The shining falchion brandish'd in the right,
Their left arm wields the target in the fight;
Of danger scornful, ever arm'd they stand
Around the king, a stern barbarian band.
Whate'er in India holds the sacred name
Of piety or lore, the Brahmins claim:
In wildest rituals, vain and painful, lost,
Brahma,[474] their founder, as a god they boast.[475]
To crown their meal no meanest life expires,
Pulse, fruit, and herbs alone their board requires:
Alone, in lewdness riotous and free,
No spousal ties withhold, and no degree:
Lost to the heart-ties, to his neighbour's arms,
The willing husband yields his spouse's charms:
In unendear'd embraces free they blend;
Yet, but the husband's kindred may ascend
The nuptial couch: alas, too blest, they know   }
Nor jealousy's suspense, nor burning woe;   }
The bitter drops which oft from dear affection flow.   }
But, should my lips each wond'rous scene unfold,
Which your glad eyes will soon amaz'd behold,
Oh, long before the various tale could run,
Deep in the west would sink yon eastern sun.
In few, all wealth from China to the Nile,
All balsams, fruit, and gold on India's bosom smile."

While thus, the Moor his faithful tale reveal'd,
Wide o'er the coast the voice of Rumour swell'd;
As, first some upland vapour seems to float
Small as the smoke of lonely shepherd cote,
Soon o'er the dales the rolling darkness spreads,
And wraps in hazy clouds the mountain heads,
The leafless forest and the utmost lea;
And wide its black wings hover o'er the sea:
The tear-dropp'd bough hangs weeping in the vale,
And distant navies rear the mist-wet sail.
So, Fame increasing, loud and louder grew,
And to the sylvan camp resounding flew:
"A lordly band," she cries, "of warlike mien,
Of face and garb in India never seen,

Of tongue unknown, through gulfs undar'd before,
Unknown their aim, have reach'd the Indian shore."
To hail their chief the Indian lord prepares,
And to the fleet he sends his banner'd Nayres:
As to the bay the nobles press along,
The wond'ring city pours th' unnumber'd throng.
And now brave GAMA, and his splendid train,
Himself adorn'd in all the pride of Spain,
In gilded barges slowly bend to shore,
While to the lute the gently falling oar
Now, breaks the surges of the briny tide,
And now, the strokes the cold fresh stream divide.
Pleas'd with the splendour of the Lusian band,
On every bank the crowded thousands stand.
Begirt with, high-plum'd nobles, by the flood
The first great minister of India stood,
The Catual[476] his name in India's tongue:
To GAMA swift the lordly regent sprung;
His open arms the valiant chief enfold,
And now he lands him on the shore of gold:
With pomp unwonted India's nobles greet
The fearless heroes of the warlike fleet.
A couch on shoulders borne, in India's mode,
(With gold the canopy and purple glow'd),
Receives the Lusian captain; equal rides
The lordly catual, and onward guides,
While GAMA'S train, and thousands of the throng
Of India's sons, encircling, pour along.
To hold discourse in various tongues they try;
In vain; the accents unremember'd die,
Instant as utter'd. Thus, on Babel's plain
Each builder heard his mate, and heard in vain.
GAMA the while, and India's second lord,
Hold glad responses, as the various word
The faithful Moor unfolds. The city gate
They pass'd, and onward, tower'd in sumptuous state,
Before them now the sacred temple rose;
The portals wide the sculptur'd shrines disclose.
The chiefs advance, and, enter'd now, behold
The gods of wood, cold stone, and shining gold;
Various of figure, and of various face,
As the foul demon will'd the likeness base.
Taught to behold the rays of godhead shine
Fair imag'd in the human face divine,
With sacred horror thrill'd, the Lusians view'd
The monster forms, Chimera-like, and rude.[477]
Here, spreading horns a human visage bore,
So, frown'd stern Jove in Lybia's fane of yore.

One body here two various faces rear'd;
So, ancient Janus o'er his shrine appear'd.
A hundred arms another brandish'd wide;
So, Titan's son[478] the race of heaven defied.
And here, a dog his snarling tusks display'd;
Anubis, thus in Memphis' hallow'd shade
Grinn'd horrible. With vile prostrations low
Before these shrines the blinded Indians bow.[479]
And now, again the splendid pomp proceeds;
To India's lord the haughty regent leads.
To view the glorious leader of the fleet
Increasing thousands swell o'er every street;
High o'er the roofs the struggling youths ascend,
The hoary fathers o'er the portals bend,
The windows sparkle with the glowing blaze
Of female eyes, and mingling diamond's rays.
And now, the train with solemn state and slow,
Approach the royal gate, through many a row
Of fragrant wood-walks, and of balmy bowers,
Radiant with fruitage, ever gay with flowers.
Spacious the dome its pillar'd grandeur spread,
Nor to the burning day high tower'd the head;
The citron groves around the windows glow'd,
And branching palms their grateful shade bestow'd;
The mellow light a pleasing radiance cast;
The marble walls Dædalian sculpture grac'd
Here India's fate,[480] from darkest times of old,
The wondrous artist on the stone enroll'd;
Here, o'er the meadows, by Hydaspes' stream,
In fair array the marshall'd legions seem:
A youth of gleeful eye the squadrons led,
Smooth was his cheek, and glow'd with purest red:
Around his spear the curling vine-leaves wav'd;
And, by a streamlet of the river lav'd,
Behind her founder, Nysa's walls were rear'd;[481]
So breathing life the ruddy god appear'd,
Had Semele beheld the smiling boy,[482]
The mother's heart had proudly heav'd with joy.
Unnumber'd here, were seen th' Assyrian throng,
That drank whole rivers as they march'd along:
Each eye seem'd earnest on their warrior queen,[483]
High was her port, and furious was her mien;
Her valour only equall'd by her lust;
Fast by her side her courser paw'd the dust,
Her son's vile rival; reeking to the plain
Fell the hot sweat-drops as he champ'd the rein.
And here display'd, most glorious to behold,
The Grecian banners, op'ning many a fold,

Seem'd trembling on the gale; at distance far
The Ganges lav'd the wide-extended war.
Here, the blue marble gives the helmets' gleam;
Here, from the cuirass shoots the golden beam.
A proud-eyed youth, with palms unnumber'd gay,
Of the bold veterans led the brown array;
Scornful of mortal birth enshrin'd he rode,
Call'd Jove his father,[484] and assum'd the god.

While dauntless GAMA and his train survey'd
The sculptur'd walls, the lofty regent said:
"For nobler wars than these you wond'ring see
That ample space th' eternal fates decree:
Sacred to these th' unpictur'd wall remains,
Unconscious yet of vanquish'd India's chains.
Assur'd we know the awful day shall come,
Big with tremendous fate, and India's doom.
The sons of Brahma, by the god their sire
Taught to illume the dread divining fire,
From the drear mansions of the dark abodes
Awake the dead, or call th' infernal gods;
Then, round the flame, while glimm'ring ghastly blue,
Behold the future scene arise to view.
The sons of Brahma, in the magic hour,
Beheld the foreign foe tremendous lower;
Unknown their tongue, their face, and strange attire,
And their bold eye-balls burn'd with warlike ire:
They saw the chief o'er prostrate India rear
The glitt'ring terrors of his awful spear.
But, swift behind these wint'ry days of woe
A spring of joy arose in liveliest glow,
Such gentle manners, leagued with wisdom, reign'd
In the dread victors, and their rage restrain'd.
Beneath their sway majestic, wise, and mild,
Proud of her victors' laws, thrice happier India smil'd.
So, to the prophets of the Brahmin train
The visions rose, that never rose in vain."

The regent ceas'd; and now, with solemn pace,
The chiefs approach the regal hall of grace.
The tap'stried walls with gold were pictur'd o'er,
And flow'ry velvet spread the marble floor.[485]
In all the grandeur of the Indian state,
High on a blazing couch, the monarch sat,
With starry gems the purple curtains shin'd,
And ruby flowers and golden foliage twin'd
Around the silver pillars: high o'er head
The golden canopy its radiance shed:

Of cloth of gold the sov'reign's mantle shone,
And, his high turban flam'd with precious stone
Sublime and awful was his sapient mien,
Lordly his posture, and his brow serene.
A hoary sire, submiss on bended knee,
(Low bow'd his head), in India's luxury,
A leaf,[486] all fragrance to the glowing taste,
Before the king each little while replac'd.
The patriarch Brahmin (soft and slow he rose),
Advancing now, to lordly GAMA bows,
And leads him to the throne; in silent state
The monarch's nod assigns the captain's seat;
The Lusian train in humbler distance stand:
Silent, the monarch eyes the foreign band
With awful mien; when valiant GAMA broke
The solemn pause, and thus majestic spoke:—

"From where the crimson sun of ev'ning laves
His blazing chariot in the western waves,
I come, the herald of a mighty king,
And, holy vows of lasting friendship bring
To thee, O monarch, for resounding Fame
Far to the west has borne thy princely name;
All India's sov'reign thou! Nor deem I sue,
Great as thou art, the humble suppliant's due.
Whate'er from western Tagus to the Nile,
Inspires the monarch's wish, the merchant's toil,
From where the north-star gleams o'er seas of frost,
To Ethiopia's utmost burning coast,
Whate'er the sea, whate'er the land bestows,
In my great monarch's realm unbounded flows.
Pleas'd thy high grandeur and renown to hear,
My sov'reign offers friendship's bands sincere:
Mutual he asks them, naked of disguise,
Then, every bounty of the smiling skies
Shower'd on his shore and thine, in mutual flow,
Shall joyful Commerce on each shore bestow.
Our might in war, what vanquish'd nations fell
Beneath our spear, let trembling Afric tell;
Survey my floating towers, and let thine ear,
Dread as it roars, our battle-thunder hear.
If friendship then thy honest wish explore,
That dreadful thunder on thy foes shall roar.
Our banners o'er the crimson field shall sweep,
And our tall navies ride the foamy deep,
Till not a foe against thy land shall rear
Th' invading bowsprit, or the hostile spear:
My king, thy brother, thus thy wars shall join,

The glory his, the gainful harvest thine."

Brave GAMA spake; the pagan king replies,
"From lands which now behold the morning rise,
While eve's dim clouds the Indian sky enfold,
Glorious to us an offer'd league we hold.
Yet shall our will in silence rest unknown,
Till what your land, and who the king you own,
Our council deeply weigh. Let joy the while,
And the glad feast, the fleeting hours beguile.
Ah! to the wearied mariner, long toss'd
O'er briny waves, how sweet the long-sought coast!
The night now darkens; on the friendly shore
Let soft repose your wearied strength restore,
Assur'd an answer from our lips to bear,
Which, not displeas'd, your sov'reign lord shall hear.
More now we add not."[487] From the hall of state
Withdrawn, they now approach the regent's gate;
The sumptuous banquet glows; all India's pride
Heap'd on the board the royal feast supplied.
Now, o'er the dew-drops of the eastern lawn
Gleam'd the pale radiance of the star of dawn,
The valiant GAMA on his couch repos'd,
And balmy rest each Lusian eye-lid clos'd:
When the high catual, watchful to fulfil
The cautious mandates of his sov'reign's will,
In secret converse with the Moor retires;
And, earnest, much of Lusus' sons inquires;
What laws, what holy rites, what monarch sway'd
The warlike race? When thus the just Mozaide:—

"The land from whence these warriors well I know,
(To neighb'ring earth my hapless birth I owe)
Illustrious Spain, along whose western shores
Grey-dappled eve the dying twilight pours.—
A wondrous prophet gave their holy lore,
The godlike seer a virgin mother bore,
Th' Eternal Spirit on the human race
(So be they taught) bestow'd such awful grace.
In war unmatch'd, they rear the trophied crest:
What terrors oft have thrill'd my infant breast[488]
When their brave deeds my wond'ring fathers told;
How from the lawns, where, crystalline and cold,
The Guadiana rolls his murm'ring tide,
And those where, purple by the Tago's side,
The length'ning vineyards glisten o'er the field,
Their warlike sires my routed sires expell'd:
Nor paus'd their rage; the furious seas they brav'd,

Nor loftiest walls, nor castled mountains saved;
Round Afric's thousand bays their navies rode,
And their proud armies o'er our armies trod.
Nor less, let Spain through all her kingdoms own,
O'er other foes their dauntless valour shone:
Let Gaul confess, her mountain-ramparts wild,
Nature in vain the hoar Pyrenians pil'd.
No foreign lance could e'er their rage restrain,
Unconquer'd still the warrior race remain.
More would you hear, secure your care may trust
The answer of their lips, so nobly just,
Conscious of inward worth, of manners plain,
Their manly souls the gilded lie disdain.
Then, let thine eyes their lordly might admire,
And mark the thunder of their arms of fire:
The shore, with trembling, hears the dreadful sound,
And rampir'd walls lie smoking on the ground.
Speed to the fleet; their arts, their prudence weigh,
How wise in peace, in war how dread, survey."

With keen desire the craftful pagan burn'd
Soon as the morn in orient blaze return'd,
To view the fleet his splendid train prepares;
And now, attended by the lordly Nayres,
The shore they cover, now the oarsmen sweep
The foamy surface of the azure deep:
And now, brave Paulus gives the friendly hand,
And high on GAMA'S lofty deck they stand.
Bright to the day the purple sail-cloths glow,
Wide to the gale the silken ensigns flow;
The pictur'd flags display the warlike strife;
Bold seem the heroes, as inspir'd by life.
Here, arm to arm, the single combat strains,
Here, burns the combat on the tented plains
General and fierce; the meeting lances thrust,
And the black blood seems smoking on the dust.
With earnest eyes the wond'ring regent views
The pictur'd warriors, and their history sues.
But now the ruddy juice, by Noah found,[489]
In foaming goblets circled swiftly round,
And o'er the deck swift rose the festive board;
Yet, smiling oft, refrains the Indian lord:
His faith forbade with other tribe to join
The sacred meal, esteem'd a rite divine.[490]
In bold vibrations, thrilling on the ear,
The battle sounds the Lusian trumpets rear;
Loud burst the thunders of the arms of fire,
Slow round the sails the clouds of smoke aspire,

And rolling their dark volumes o'er the day
The Lusian war, in dreadful pomp, display.
In deepest thought the careful regent weigh'd
The pomp and power at GAMA'S nod bewray'd;
Yet, seem'd alone in wonder to behold
The glorious heroes, and the wars half told
In silent poesy.—Swift from the board
High crown'd with wine, uprose the Indian lord;
Both the bold GAMAS, and their gen'rous peer,
The brave Coello, rose, prepar'd to hear
Or, ever courteous, give the meet reply:
Fix'd and inquiring was the regent's eye:
The warlike image of a hoary sire,
Whose name shall live till earth and time expire,
His wonder fix'd, and more than human glow'd
The hero's look; his robes of Grecian mode;
A bough, his ensign, in his right he wav'd,
A leafy bough.—But I, fond man depraved!
Where would I speed, as madd'ning in a dream,
Without your aid, ye Nymphs of Tago's stream!
Or yours, ye Dryads of Mondego's bowers!
Without your aid how vain my wearied powers!
Long yet, and various lies my arduous way
Through low'ring tempests and a boundless sea.
Oh then, propitious hear your son implore,
And guide my vessel to the happy shore.
Ah! see how long what perilous days, what woes
On many a foreign coast around me rose,
As, dragg'd by Fortune's chariot-wheels along,
I sooth'd my sorrows with the warlike song:[491]
Wide ocean's horrors length'ning now around,
And, now my footsteps trod the hostile ground;
Yet, mid each danger of tumultuous war
Your Lusian heroes ever claim'd my care:
As Canace[492] of old, ere self-destroy'd,
One hand the pen, and one the sword employ'd,
Degraded now, by poverty abhorr'd,
The guest dependent at the lordling's board:
Now blest with all the wealth fond hope could crave,
Soon I beheld that wealth beneath the wave
For ever lost;[493] myself escap'd alone,
On the wild shore all friendless, hopeless, thrown;
My life, like Judah's heaven-doom'd king of yore,[494]
By miracle prolong'd; yet not the more
To end my sorrows: woes succeeding woes
Belied my earnest hopes of sweet repose:
In place of bays around my brows to shed
Their sacred honours, o'er my destin'd head

Foul Calumny proclaim'd the fraudful tale,
And left me mourning in a dreary jail.[495]
Such was the meed, alas! on me bestow'd,   }
Bestow'd by those for whom my numbers glow'd,   }
By those who to my toils their laurel honours ow'd. }

Ye gentle nymphs of Tago's rosy bowers,
Ah, see what letter'd patron-lords are yours!
Dull as the herds that graze their flow'ry dales,
To them in vain the injur'd muse bewails:
No fost'ring care their barb'rous hands bestow,
Though to the muse their fairest fame they owe.
Ah, cold may prove the future priest of fame
Taught by my fate: yet, will I not disclaim
Your smiles, ye muses of Mondego's shade;
Be still my dearest joy your happy aid!
And hear my vow: Nor king, nor loftiest peer
Shall e'er from me the song of flatt'ry hear;
Nor crafty tyrant, who in office reigns,
Smiles on his king, and binds the land in chains;
His king's worst foe: nor he whose raging ire,
And raging wants, to shape his course, conspire;
True to the clamours of the blinded crowd,
Their changeful Proteus, insolent and loud:
Nor he whose honest mien secures applause,
Grave though he seem, and father of the laws,
Who, but half-patriot, niggardly denies
Each other's merit, and withholds the prize:
Who spurns the muse,[496] nor feels the raptur'd strain,
Useless by him esteem'd, and idly vain:
For him, for these, no wreath my hand shall twine;
On other brows th' immortal rays shall shine:
He who the path of honour ever trod,
True to his king, his country, and his God,
On his blest head my hands shall fix the crown
Wove of the deathless laurels of renown.

END OF THE SEVENTH BOOK

BOOK VIII

THE ARGUMENT

Description of the pictures, given by Paulus. The heroes of Portugal, from Lusus, one of the companions
of Bacchus (who gave his name to Portugal), and Ulysses, the founder of Lisbon, down to Don Pedro and

Don Henrique (Henry), the conquerors of Ceuta, are all represented in the portraits of Gama, and are characterized by appropriate verses. Meanwhile the zamorim has recourse to the oracles of his false gods, who make him acquainted with the future dominion of the Portuguese over India, and the consequent ruin of his empire. The Mohammedan Arabs conspire against the Portuguese. The zamorim questions the truth of Gama's statement, and charges him with being captain of a band of pirates. Gama is obliged to give up to the Indians the whole of his merchandise as ransom, when he obtains permission to re-embark. He seizes several merchants of Calicut, whom he detains on board his ship as hostages for his two factors, who were on land to sell his merchandise. He afterwards liberates the natives, whom he exchanges for his two companions. In Mickle's translation this portion of the original is omitted, and the factors are released in consequence of a victory gained by Gama.

With eye unmov'd the silent CATUAL[497] view'd
The pictur'd sire[498] with seeming life endu'd;
A verdant vine-bough waving in his right,
Smooth flow'd his sweepy beard of glossy white,
When thus, as swift the Moor unfolds the word,
The valiant Paulus to the Indian lord:—

"Bold though these figures frown, yet bolder far
These godlike heroes shin'd in ancient war.
In that hoar sire, of mien serene, august,
Lusus behold, no robber-chief unjust;
His cluster'd bough—the same which Bacchus bore[499]—
He waves, the emblem of his care of yore;
The friend of savage man, to Bacchus dear,
The son of Bacchus, or the bold compeer,
What time his yellow locks with vine-leaves curl'd,
The youthful god subdued the savage world,
Bade vineyards glisten o'er the dreary waste,
And humaniz'd the nations as he pass'd.
Lusus, the lov'd companion of the god,
In Spain's fair bosom fix'd his last abode,
Our kingdom founded, and illustrious reign'd
In those fair lawns, the bless'd Elysium feign'd,[500]
Where, winding oft, the Guadiana roves,
And Douro murmurs through, the flow'ry groves.
Here, with his bones, he left his deathless fame,
And Lusitania's clime shall ever bear his name.
That other chief th' embroider'd silk displays,
Toss'd o'er the deep whole years of weary days,
On Tago's banks, at last, his vows he paid:
To wisdom's godlike power, the Jove-born maid,[501]
Who fir'd his lips with eloquence divine,
On Tago's banks he rear'd the hallow'd shrine.
Ulysses he, though fated to destroy,
On Asian ground, the heav'n-built towers of Troy,[502]
On Europe's strand, more grateful to the skies,
He bade th' eternal walls of Lisbon rise."[503]

"But who that godlike terror of the plain,
Who strews the smoking field with heaps of slain?
What num'rous legions fly in dire dismay,
Whose standards wide the eagle's wings display?"
The pagan asks: the brother chief[504] replies:—
"Unconquer'd deem'd, proud Rome's dread standard flies,
His crook thrown by, fir'd by his nation's woes,
The hero-shepherd Viriatus rose;
His country sav'd proclaim'd his warlike fame,
And Rome's wide empire trembled at his name.
That gen'rous pride which Rome to Pyrrhus bore,[505]
To him they show'd not; for they fear'd him more.
Not on the field o'ercome by manly force,
Peaceful he slept; and now, a murder'd corse,
By treason slain, he lay. How stern, behold,
That other hero, firm, erect, and bold:
The power by which he boasted he divin'd,
Beside him pictur'd stands, the milk-white hind:
Injur'd by Rome, the stern Sertorius fled
To Tago's shore, and Lusus' offspring led;
Their worth he knew; in scatter'd flight he drove
The standards painted with the birds of Jove.
And lo, the flag whose shining colours own
The glorious founder of the Lusian throne!
Some deem the warrior of Hungarian race,[506]
Some from Lorraine the godlike hero trace.
From Tagus' banks the haughty Moor expell'd,
Galicia's sons, and and Leon's warriors quell'd,
To weeping Salem's[507] ever-hallow'd meads,
His warlike bands the holy Henry leads;
By holy war to sanctify his crown,
And, to his latest race, auspicious waft it down."

"And who this awful chief?" aloud exclaims
The wond'ring regent. "O'er the field he flames
In dazzling steel; where'er he bends his course
The battle sinks beneath his headlong force:
Against his troops, though few, the num'rous foes
In vain their spears and tow'ry walls oppose.
With smoking blood his armour sprinkled o'er,
High to the knees his courser paws in gore:
O'er crowns and blood-stain'd ensigns scatter'd round
He rides; his courser's brazen hoofs resound."
"In that great chief," the second GAMA cries,
"The first Alonzo[508] strikes thy wond'ring eyes.
From Lusus' realm the pagan Moors he drove;
Heav'n, whom he lov'd, bestow'd on him such love,

Beneath him, bleeding of its mortal wound,
The Moorish strength lay prostrate on the ground.
Nor Ammon's son, nor greater Julius dar'd
With troops so few, with hosts so num'rous warr'd:
Nor less shall Fame the subject heroes own:
Behold that hoary warrior's rageful frown!
On his young pupil's flight[509] his burning eyes
He darts, and, 'Turn thy flying host,' he cries,
'Back to the field!' The vet'ran and the boy
Back to the field exult with furious joy:
Their ranks mow'd down, the boastful foe recedes,
The vanquish'd triumph, and the victor bleeds.
Again, that mirror of unshaken faith,
Egaz behold, a chief self-doom'd to death.[510]
Beneath Castilia's sword his monarch lay;
Homage he vow'd his helpless king should pay;
His haughty king reliev'd, the treaty spurns,
With conscious pride the noble Egaz burns;
His comely spouse and infant race he leads,
Himself the same, in sentenced felons' weeds,
Around their necks the knotted halters bound,
With naked feet they tread the flinty ground;
And, prostrate now before Castilia's throne,
Their offer'd lives their monarch's pride atone.
Ah Rome! no more thy gen'rous consul boast.[511]
Whose 'lorn submission sav'd his ruin'd host:
No father's woes assail'd his stedfast mind;
The dearest ties the Lusian chief resign'd.

"There, by the stream, a town besieged behold,
The Moorish tents the shatter'd walls enfold.
Fierce as the lion from the covert springs,
When hunger gives his rage the whirlwind's wings;
From ambush, lo, the valiant Fuaz pours,
And whelms in sudden rout th'astonish'd Moors.
The Moorish king[512] in captive chains he sends;
And, low at Lisbon's throne, the royal captive bends.
Fuaz again the artist's skill displays;
Far o'er the ocean shine his ensign's rays:
In crackling flames the Moorish galleys fly,
And the red blaze ascends the blushing sky:
O'er Avila's high steep the flames aspire,
And wrap the forests in a sheet of fire:
There seem the waves beneath the prows to boil;
And distant, far around for many a mile,
The glassy deep reflects the ruddy blaze;
Far on the edge the yellow light decays,
And blends with hov'ring blackness. Great and dread

Thus shone the day when first the combat bled,
The first our heroes battled on the main,
The glorious prelude of our naval reign,
Which, now the waves beyond the burning zone,
And northern Greenland's frost-bound billows own.
Again behold brave Fuaz dares the fight!
O'erpower'd he sinks beneath the Moorish might;
Smiling in death the martyr-hero lies,
And lo, his soul triumphant mounts the skies.
Here now, behold, in warlike pomp portray'd,
A foreign navy brings the pious aid.[513]
Lo, marching from the decks the squadrons spread,
Strange their attire, their aspect firm and dread.
The holy cross their ensigns bold display,
To Salem's aid they plough'd the wat'ry way:
Yet first, the cause the same, on Tago's shore
They dye their maiden swords in pagan gore.
Proud stood the Moor on Lisbon's warlike towers,
From Lisbon's walls they drive the Moorish powers:
Amid the thickest of the glorious fight,
Lo, Henry falls, a gallant German knight,
A martyr falls: that holy tomb behold,
There waves the blossom'd palm, the boughs of gold:
O'er Henry's grave the sacred plant arose,
And from the leaves,[514] Heav'n's gift, gay health redundant flows.

"Aloft, unfurl!" the valiant Paulus cries.
Instant, new wars on new-spread ensigns rise
"In robes of white behold a priest advance![515]
His sword in splinters smites the Moorish lance:
Arronchez won revenges Lira's fall:
And lo, on fair Savilia's batter'd wall,
How boldly calm, amid the crashing spears,
That hero-form the Lusian standard rears.
There bleeds the war on fair Vandalia's plain:
Lo, rushing through the Moors, o'er hills of slain
The hero rides, and proves by genuine claim
The son of Egas,[516] and his worth the same.
Pierc'd by his dart the standard-bearer dies;
Beneath his feet the Moorish standard lies:
High o'er the field, behold the glorious blaze!
The victor-youth the Lusian flag displays.
Lo, while the moon through midnight azure rides,
From the high wall adown his spear-staff glides
The dauntless Gerald:[517] in his left he bears
Two watchmen's heads, his right the falchion rears:
The gate he opens, swift from ambush rise
His ready bands, the city falls his prize:

Evora still the grateful honour pays,
Her banner'd flag the mighty deed displays:
There frowns the hero; in his left he bears
The two cold heads, his right the falchion rears.
Wrong'd by his king,[518] and burning for revenge,
Behold his arms that proud Castilian change;
The Moorish buckler on his breast he bears,
And leads the fiercest of the pagan spears.
Abrantes falls beneath his raging force,
And now to Tagus bends his furious course.
Another fate he met on Tagus' shore,
Brave Lopez from his brows the laurels tore;
His bleeding army strew'd the thirsty ground,
And captive chains the rageful leader bound.
Resplendent far that holy chief behold!
Aside he throws the sacred staff of gold,
And wields the spear of steel. How bold advance
The num'rous Moors, and with the rested lance
Hem round the trembling Lusians. Calm and bold
Still towers the priest, and lo, the skies unfold:[519]
Cheer'd by the vision, brighter than the day,
The Lusians trample down the dread array
Of Hagar's legions: on the reeking plain
Low, with their slaves, four haughty kings lie slain.
In vain Alcazar rears her brazen walls,
Before his rushing host Alcazar falls.
There, by his altar, now the hero shines,
And, with the warrior's palm, his mitre twines.
That chief behold: though proud Castilia's host
He leads, his birth shall Tagus ever boast.
As a pent flood bursts headlong o'er the strand
So pours his fury o'er Algarbia's land:
Nor rampir'd town, nor castled rock afford
The refuge of defence from Payo's sword.
By night-veil'd art proud Sylves falls his prey,
And Tavila's high, walls, at middle day,
Fearless he scales: her streets in blood deplore
The seven brave hunters murder'd by the Moor.[520]
These three bold knights how dread![521] Thro' Spain and France
At joust and tourney with the tilted lance
Victors they rode: Castilia's court beheld
Her peers o'erthrown; the peers with rancour swell'd:
The bravest of the three their swords surround;
Brave Ribeir strews them vanquish'd o'er the ground.
Now let thy thoughts, all wonder and on fire,
That darling son of warlike Fame admire.
Prostrate at proud Castilia's monarch's feet
His land lies trembling: lo, the nobles meet:

Softly they seem to breathe, and forward bend
The servile neck; each eye distrusts his friend;
Fearful each tongue to speak; each bosom cold:
When, colour'd with stern rage, erect and bold,
The hero rises: 'Here no foreign throne
Shall fix its base; my native king alone
Shall reign.' Then, rushing to the fight, he leads;
Low, vanquish'd in the dust, Castilia bleeds.
Where proudest hope might deem it vain to dare,
God led him on, and crown'd the glorious war.
Though fierce, as num'rous, are the hosts that dwell
By Betis' stream, these hosts before him fell.
The fight behold: while absent from his bands,
Press'd on the step of flight his army stands,
To call the chief a herald speeds away:
Low, on his knees, the gallant chief survey!
He pours his soul, with lifted hands implores,
And Heav'n's assisting arm, inspir'd, adores.
Panting, and pale, the herald urges speed:
With holy trust of victory decreed,
Careless he answers, 'Nothing urgent calls:'
And soon the bleeding foe before him falls.
To Numa, thus, the pale patricians fled—
'The hostile squadrons o'er the kingdom spread!'
They cry; unmov'd, the holy king replies—
'And I, behold, am off'ring sacrifice!'[522]
Earnest, I see thy wond'ring eyes inquire
Who this illustrious chief, his country's sire?
The Lusian Scipio well might speak his fame,
But nobler Nunio shines a greater name:[523]
On earth's green bosom, or on ocean grey,
A greater never shall the sun survey.

"Known by the silver cross, and sable shield,
Two Knights of Malta[524] there command the field;
From Tago's banks they drive the fleecy prey,
And the tir'd ox lows on his weary way:
When, as the falcon through the forest glade
Darts on the lev'ret, from the brown-wood shade
Darts Roderic on their rear; in scatter'd flight
They leave the goodly herds the victor's right.
Again, behold, in gore he bathes his sword;
His captive friend,[525] to liberty restor'd,
Glows to review the cause that wrought his woe,
The cause, his loyalty, as taintless snow.
Here treason's well-earn'd meed allures thine eyes,[526]
Low, grovelling in the dust, the traitor dies;
Great Elvas gave the blow. Again, behold,

Chariot and steed in purple slaughter roll'd:
Great Elvas triumphs; wide o'er Xeres' plain
Around him reeks the noblest blood of Spain.

"Here Lisbon's spacious harbour meets the view:
How vast the foe's, the Lusian fleet how few!
Castile's proud war-ships, circling round, enclose
The Lusian galleys; through their thund'ring rows,
Fierce pressing on, Pereira fearless rides,
His hook'd irons grasp the adm'ral's sides:
Confusion maddens: on the dreadless knight
Castilia's navy pours its gather'd might:
Pereira dies, their self-devoted prey,
And safe the Lusian galleys speed away.[527]

"Lo, where the lemon-trees from yon green hill
Throw their cool shadows o'er the crystal rill;
There twice two hundred fierce Castilian foes
Twice eight, forlorn, of Lusian race enclose;
Forlorn they seem; but taintless flow'd their blood
From those three hundred who of old withstood;
Withstood, and from a thousand Romans tore
The victor-wreath, what time the shepherd[528] bore
The leader's staff of Lusus: equal flame
Inspir'd these few,[529] their victory the same.
Though twenty lances brave each single spear,
Never the foes superior might to fear
Is our inheritance, our native right,
Well tried, well prov'd in many a dreadful fight.

"That dauntless earl behold; on Libya's coast,
Far from the succour of the Lusian host,[530]
Twice hard besieg'd, he holds the Ceutan towers
Against the banded might of Afric's powers.
That other earl;[531]—behold the port he bore,
So, trod stern Mars on Thracia's hills of yore.
What groves of spears Alcazar's gates surround!
There Afric's nations blacken o'er the ground.
A thousand ensigns, glitt'ring to the day,
The waning moon's slant silver horns display.
In vain their rage; no gate, no turret falls,
The brave De Vian guards Alcazar's walls.
In hopeless conflict lost his king appears;
Amid the thickest of the Moorish spears
Plunges bold Vian: in the glorious strife
He dies, and dying saves his sov'reign's life.

"Illustrious, lo, two brother-heroes shine,[532]

Their birth, their deeds, adorn the royal line;
To ev'ry king of princely Europe known,
In ev'ry court the gallant Pedro shone.
The glorious Henry[533]—kindling at his name
Behold my sailors' eyes all sparkle flame!
Henry the chief, who first, by Heav'n inspir'd,
To deeds unknown before, the sailor fir'd,
The conscious sailor left the sight of shore,
And dar'd new oceans, never plough'd before.
The various wealth of ev'ry distant land
He bade his fleets explore, his fleets command.
The ocean's great discoverer he shines;
Nor less his honours in the martial lines:
The painted flag the cloud-wrapt siege displays,
There Ceuta's rocking wall its trust betrays.
Black yawns the breach; the point of many a spear
Gleams through the smoke; loud shouts astound the ear.
Whose step first trod the dreadful pass? Whose sword
Hew'd its dark way, first with the foe begor'd?
'Twas thine, O glorious Henry, first to dare
The dreadful pass, and thine to close the war.
Taught by his might, and humbled in her gore,
The boastful pride of Afric tower'd no more.

"Num'rous though these, more num'rous warriors shine
Th' illustrious glory of the Lusian line.
But ah, forlorn, what shame to barb'rous pride![534]
Friendless the master of the pencil died;
Immortal fame his deathless labours gave;
Poor man, he sunk neglected to the grave!"

The gallant Paulus faithful thus explain'd
The various deeds the pictur'd flags contain'd.
Still o'er and o'er, and still again untir'd,
The wond'ring regent of the wars inquir'd:
Still wond'ring, heard the various pleasing tale,
Till o'er the decks cold sigh'd the ev'ning gale:
The falling darkness dimm'd the eastern shore,
And twilight hover'd o'er the billows hoar
Far to the west, when, with his noble band,
The thoughtful regent sought his native strand.

O'er the tall mountain-forest's waving boughs
Aslant, the new moon's slender horns arose;
Near her pale chariot shone a twinkling star,
And, save the murm'ring of the wave afar,
Deep-brooding silence reign'd; each labour clos'd,
In sleep's soft arms the sons of toil repos'd.

And now, no more the moon her glimpses shed,
A sudden, black-wing'd cloud the sky o'erspread,
A sullen murmur through the woodland groan'd,
In woe-swoll'n sighs the hollow winds bemoan'd:
Borne on the plaintive gale, a patt'ring shower
Increas'd the horrors of the evil hour.
Thus, when the God of earthquakes rocks the ground,
He gives the prelude in a dreary sound;
O'er nature's face a horrid gloom he throws,
With dismal note the cock unusual crows,
A shrill-voic'd howling trembles thro' the air,
As passing ghosts were weeping in despair;
In dismal yells the dogs confess their fear,
And shiv'ring, own some dreadful presence near.
So, lower'd the night, the sullen howl the same,
And, 'mid the black-wing'd gloom, stern Bacchus came;
The form, and garb of Hagar's son he took,
The ghost-like aspect, and the threat'ning look.[535]
Then, o'er the pillow of a furious priest,
Whose burning zeal the Koran's lore profess'd,
Reveal'd he stood, conspicuous in a dream,
His semblance shining, as the moon's pale gleam:
"And guard," he cries, "my son, O timely guard,
Timely defeat the dreadful snare prepar'd:
And canst thou, careless, unaffected, sleep,
While these stern, lawless rovers of the deep
Fix on thy native shore a foreign throne,
Before whose steps thy latest race shall groan!"
He spoke; cold horror shook the Moorish priest;
He wakes, but soon reclines in wonted rest:
An airy phantom of the slumb'ring brain
He deem'd the vision; when the fiend again,
With sterner mien, and fiercer accent spoke:
"Oh faithless! worthy of the foreign yoke!
And know'st thou not thy prophet sent by Heav'n,
By whom the Koran's sacred lore was giv'n,
God's chiefest gift to men: and must I leave
The bowers of Paradise, for you to grieve,
For you to watch, while, thoughtless of your woe,
Ye sleep, the careless victims of the foe;
The foe, whose rage will soon with cruel joy,
If unoppos'd, my sacred shrines destroy?
Then, while kind Heav'n th'auspicious hour bestows,
Let ev'ry nerve their infant strength oppose.
When, softly usher'd by the milky dawn,
The sun first rises[536] o'er the daisied lawn,
His silver lustre, as the shining dew
Of radiance mild, unhurt the eye may view:

But, when on high the noon-tide flaming rays
Give all the force of living fire to blaze,
A giddy darkness strikes the conquer'd sight,
That dares, in all his glow, the lord of light.
Such, if on India's soil the tender shoot
Of these proud cedars fix the stubborn root,
Such, shall your power before them sink decay'd.
And India's strength shall wither in their shade."

He spoke; and, instant from his vot'ry's bed
Together with repose, the demon fled;
Again cold horror shook the zealot's frame,
And all his hatred of Messiah's name
Burn'd in his venom'd heart, while, veil'd in night,
Right to the palace sped the demon's flight.
Sleepless the king he found, in dubious thought;
His conscious fraud a thousand terrors brought:
All gloomy as the hour, around him stand,
With haggard looks, the hoary Magi band:[537]
To trace what fates on India's wide domain
Attend the rovers from unheard-of Spain,
Prepar'd, in dark futurity, to prove
The hell-taught rituals of infernal Jove:
Mutt'ring their charms, and spells of dreary sound,
With naked feet they beat the hollow ground;
Blue gleams the altar's flame along the walls,
With dismal, hollow groans the victim falls;
With earnest eyes the priestly band explore
The entrails, throbbing in the living gore.
And lo, permitted by the power divine,
The hov'ring demon gives the dreadful sign.[538]
Here furious War her gleamy falchion draws,
Here lean-ribb'd Famine writhes her falling jaws;
Dire as the fiery pestilential star
Darting his eyes, high on his trophied car,
Stern Tyranny sweeps wide o'er India's ground;
On vulture-wings fierce Rapine hovers round;
Ills after ills, and India's fetter'd might,
Th'eternal yoke.[539] Loud shrieking at the sight,
The starting wizards from the altar fly,
And silent horror glares in ev'ry eye:
Pale stands the monarch, lost in cold dismay,
And, now impatient, waits the ling'ring day.

With gloomy aspect rose the ling'ring dawn,
And dropping tears flow'd slowly o'er the lawn;
The Moorish priest, with fear and vengeance fraught,
Soon as the light appear'd his kindred sought;

Appall'd, and trembling with ungen'rous fear,
In secret council met, his tale they hear;
As, check'd by terror or impell'd by hate,
Of various means they ponder and debate,
Against the Lusian train what arts employ,
By force to slaughter, or by fraud destroy;
Now black, now pale, their bearded cheeks appear,
As boiling rage prevails, or boding fear;
Beneath their shady brows, their eye-balls roll,
Nor one soft gleam bespeaks the gen'rous soul;
Through quiv'ring lips they draw their panting breath.
While their dark fraud decrees the works of death;
Nor unresolv'd the power of gold to try
Swift to the lordly catual's gate they hie.—
Ah, what the wisdom, what the sleepless care
Efficient to avoid the traitor's snare;
What human power can give a king to know
The smiling aspect of the lurking foe!
So let the tyrant plead.[540]—The patriot king
Knows men, knows whence the patriot virtues spring;
From inward worth, from conscience firm and bold,
(Not from the man whose honest name is sold),
He hopes that virtue, whose unalter'd weight
Stands fix'd, unveering with the storms of state.

Lur'd was the regent with the Moorish gold,
And now agreed their fraudful course to hold,
Swift to the king the regent's steps they tread;
The king they found o'erwhelm'd in sacred dread.
The word they take, their ancient deeds relate,
Their ever faithful service of the state;[541]
"For ages long, from shore to distant shore
For thee our ready keels the traffic bore:
For thee we dar'd each horror of the wave;
Whate'er thy treasures boast our labours gave.
And wilt thou now confer our long-earn'd due,
Confer thy favour on a lawless crew?
The race they boast, as tigers of the wold
Bear that proud sway, by justice uncontroll'd.
Yet, for their crimes, expell'd that bloody home,
These, o'er the deep, rapacious plund'rers roam.
Their deeds we know; round Afric's shores they came,
And spread, where'er they pass'd, devouring flame;
Mozambique's towers, enroll'd in sheets of fire,
Blaz'd to the sky, her own funereal pyre.
Imperial Calicut shall feel the same,
And these proud state-rooms feed the funeral flame;
While many a league far round, their joyful eyes

Shall mark old ocean reddening to the skies.
Such dreadful fates, o'er thee, O king, depend,
Yet, with thy fall our fate shall never blend:
Ere o'er the east arise the second dawn
Our fleets, our nation from thy land withdrawn,
In other climes, beneath a kinder reign
Shall fix their port: yet may the threat be vain!
If wiser thou with us thy powers employ,
Soon shall our powers the robber-crew destroy.
By their own arts and secret deeds o'ercome,
Here shall they meet the fate escaped at home."

While thus the priest detain'd the monarch's ear,
His cheeks confess'd the quiv'ring pulse of fear.
Unconscious of the worth that fires the brave,
In state a monarch, but in heart a slave,
He view'd brave VASCO, and his gen'rous train,
As his own passions stamp'd the conscious stain:
Nor less his rage the fraudful regent fir'd;
And valiant GAMA'S fate was now conspir'd.

Ambassadors from India GAMA sought,
And oaths of peace, for oaths of friendship brought;
The glorious tale, 'twas all he wish'd, to tell;
So Ilion's[542] fate was seal'd when Hector fell.

Again convok'd before the Indian throne,
The monarch meets him with a rageful frown;
"And own," he cries, "the naked truth reveal,
Then shall my bounteous grace thy pardon seal.
Feign'd is the treaty thou pretend'st to bring:
No country owns thee, and thou own'st no king.
Thy life, long roving o'er the deep, I know—
A lawless robber, every man thy foe.
And think'st thou credit to thy tale to gain?
Mad were the sov'reign, and the hope were vain,
Through ways unknown, from utmost western shore,
To bid his fleets the utmost east explore.
Great is thy monarch, so thy words declare;
But sumptuous gifts the proof of greatness bear:
Kings thus to kings their empire's grandeur show;
Thus prove thy truth, thus we thy truth allow.
If not, what credence will the wise afford?
What monarch trust the wand'ring seaman's word?
No sumptuous gift thou bring'st.[543]—Yet, though some crime
Has thrown thee, banish'd from thy native clime,
(Such oft of old the hero's fate has been),
Here end thy toils, nor tempt new fates unseen:

Each land the brave man nobly calls his home:
Or if, bold pirates, o'er the deep you roam,
Skill'd the dread storm to brave, O welcome here!
Fearless of death, or shame, confess sincere:
My name shall then thy dread protection be,
My captain thou, unrivall'd on the sea."

Oh now, ye Muses, sing what goddess fir'd
GAMA'S proud bosom, and his lips inspir'd.
Fair Acidalia, love's celestial queen,[544]
The graceful goddess of the fearless mien,
Her graceful freedom on his look bestow'd,
And all collected in his bosom glow'd.
"Sov'reign," he cries, "oft witness'd, well I know
The rageful falsehood of the Moorish foe:
Their fraudful tales, from hatred bred, believ'd,
Thine ear is poison'd, and thine eye deceiv'd.
What light, what shade the courtier's mirror gives,
That light, that shade the guarded king receives.
Me hast thou view'd in colours not mine own,
Yet, bold I promise shall my truth be known.
If o'er the seas a lawless pest I roam,
A blood-stain'd exile from my native home,
How many a fertile shore and beauteous isle,
Where Nature's gifts, unclaim'd, unbounded, smile,
Mad have I left, to dare the burning zone,
And all the horrors of the gulfs unknown
That roar beneath the axle of the world.
Where ne'er before was daring sail unfurl'd!
And have I left these beauteous shores behind,
And have I dar'd the rage of ev'ry wind,
That now breath'd fire, and now came wing'd with frost,
Lur'd by the plunder of an unknown coast?
Not thus the robber leaves his certain prey
For the gay promise of a nameless day.
Dread and stupendous, more than death-doom'd man
Might hope to compass, more than wisdom plan,
To thee my toils, to thee my dangers rise:
Ah! Lisbon's kings behold with other eyes.
Where virtue calls, where glory leads the way,
No dangers move them, and no toils dismay.
Long have the kings of Lusus' daring race
Resolv'd the limits of the deep to trace,
Beneath the morn to ride the furthest waves,
And pierce the farthest shore old Ocean laves.
Sprung from the prince,[545] before whose matchless power
The strength of Afric wither'd as a flower
Never to bloom again, great Henry shone,

Each gift of nature and of art his own;
Bold as his sire, by toils on toils untir'd,
To find the Indian shore his pride aspir'd.
Beneath the stars that round the Hydra shine,
And where fam'd Argo hangs the heav'nly sign,
Where thirst and fever burn on ev'ry gale
The dauntless Henry rear'd the Lusian sail.
Embolden'd by the meed that crown'd his toils,
Beyond the wide-spread shores and num'rous isles,
Where both the tropics pour the burning day,
Succeeding heroes forc'd th' exploring way;
That race which never view'd the Pleiad's car,
That barb'rous race beneath the southern star,
Their eyes beheld.—Dread roar'd the blast—the wave
Boils to the sky, the meeting whirlwinds rave
O'er the torn heav'ns; loud on their awe-struck ear
Great Nature seem'd to call, 'Approach not here!'
At Lisbon's court they told their dread escape,
And from her raging tempests, nam'd the Cape.[546]
'Thou southmost point,' the joyful king exclaim'd,
'Cape of Good Hope, be thou for ever nam'd!
Onward my fleets shall dare the dreadful way,
And find the regions of the infant day.'
In vain the dark and ever-howling blast
Proclaim'd, 'This ocean never shall be past;'
Through that dread ocean, and the tempests' roar,
My king commanded, and my course I bore.
The pillar thus of deathless fame, begun
By other chiefs,[547] beneath the rising sun
In thy great realm, now to the skies I raise,
The deathless pillar of my nation's praise.
Through these wild seas no costly gift I brought;
Thy shore alone and friendly peace I sought.
And yet to thee the noblest gift I bring
The world can boast—the friendship of my king.
And mark the word, his greatness shall appear
When next my course to India's strand I steer,
Such proofs I'll bring as never man before
In deeds of strife, or peaceful friendship bore.
Weigh now my words, my truth demands the light,
For truth shall ever boast, at last, resistless might."

Boldly the hero spake with brow severe,
Of fraud alike unconscious, as of fear:
His noble confidence with truth impressed
Sunk deep, unwelcome, in the monarch's breast,
Nor wanting charms his avarice to gain
Appear'd the commerce of illustrious Spain.

Yet, as the sick man loathes the bitter draught,
Though rich with health he knows the cup comes fraught;
His health without it, self-deceiv'd, he weighs,
Now hastes to quaff the drug, and now delays;
Reluctant thus, as wav'ring passion veer'd,
The Indian lord the dauntless GAMA heard:
The Moorish threats yet sounding in his ear,
He acts with caution, and is led by fear.
With solemn pomp he bids his lords prepare
The friendly banquet; to the regent's care
Commends brave GAMA, and with pomp retires:
The regent's hearths awake the social fires;
Wide o'er the board the royal feast is spread,
And, fair embroidered, shines DE GAMA'S bed.
The regent's palace high o'erlook'd the bay
Where GAMA'S black-ribb'd fleet at anchor lay.[548]

Ah, why the voice of ire and bitter woe
O'er Tago's banks, ye nymphs of Tagus, show?
The flow'ry garlands from your ringlets torn,
Why wand'ring wild with trembling steps forlorn?
The demon's rage you saw, and mark'd his flight
To the dark mansions of eternal night:
You saw how, howling through the shades beneath,
He wak'd new horrors in the realms of death.
What trembling tempests shook the thrones of hell,
And groan'd along her caves, ye muses, tell.
The rage of baffled fraud, and all the fire
Of powerless hate, with tenfold flames conspire;
From ev'ry eye the tawny lightnings glare,
And hell, illumin'd by the ghastly flare,
(A drear blue gleam), in tenfold horror shows
Her darkling caverns; from his dungeon rose
Hagar's stern son: pale was his earthy hue,
And from his eye-balls flash'd the lightnings blue;
Convuls'd with rage the dreadful shade demands
The last assistance of th' infernal bands.
As when the whirlwinds, sudden bursting, bear
Th' autumnal leaves high floating through the air;
So, rose the legions of th' infernal state,
Dark Fraud, base Art, fierce Rage, and burning Hate:
Wing'd by the Furies to the Indian strand
They bend; the demon leads the dreadful band,
And, in the bosoms of the raging Moors
All their collected, living strength he pours.
One breast alone against his rage was steel'd,
Secure in spotless Truth's celestial shield.

One evening past, another evening clos'd,
The regent still brave GAMA'S suit oppos'd;
The Lusian chief his guarded guest detain'd,
With arts on arts, and vows of friendship feign'd.
His fraudful art, though veil'd in deep disguise,
Shone bright to GAMA'S manner-piercing eyes.
As in the sun's bright[549] beam the gamesome boy
Plays with the shining steel or crystal toy,
Swift and irregular, by sudden starts,
The living ray with viewless motion darts,
Swift o'er the wall, the floor, the roof, by turns
The sun-beam dances, and the radiance burns:
In quick succession, thus, a thousand views
The sapient Lusian's lively thought pursues;
Quick as the lightning ev'ry view revolves,
And, weighing all, fix'd are his dread resolves.
O'er India's shore the sable night descends,
And GAMA, now, secluded from his friends,
Detain'd a captive in the room of state,
Anticipates in thought to-morrow's fate;
For just Mozaide no gen'rous care delays,
And VASCO'S trust with friendly toils repays.

END OF THE EIGHTH BOOK

BOOK IX

THE ARGUMENT

The liberation of Gama's factors is effected by a great victory over the Moorish fleet, and by the
bombardment of Calicut. Gama returns in consequence to his ships, and weighs anchor to return to
Europe with the news of his great discoveries. Camoëns then introduces a very singular, but agreeable
episode, recounting the love adventures of his heroes in one of the islands of the ocean. Venus, in
search of her son, journeys through all his realms to implore his aid, and at length arrives at the spot
where Love's artillery and arms are forged. Venus intercedes with her son in favour of the Portuguese.
The island of Love, like that of Delos, floats on the ocean. It is then explained by the poet that these
seeming realities are only allegorical.

Red[550] rose the dawn; roll'd o'er the low'ring sky,
The scattering clouds of tawny purple fly.
While yet the day-spring struggled with the gloom,
The Indian monarch sought the regent's dome.
In all the luxury of Asian state,
High on a star-gemm'd couch the monarch sat:
Then on th' illustrious captive, bending down

His eyes, stern darken'd with a threat'ning frown,
"Thy truthless tale," he cries, "thy art appears,
Confess'd inglorious by thy cautious fears.
Yet, still if friendship, honest, thou implore,
Yet now command thy vessels to the shore:
Gen'rous, as to thy friends, thy sails resign,
My will commands it, and the power is mine:
In vain thy art, in vain thy might withstands,
Thy sails, and rudders too, my will demands:[551]
Such be the test, thy boasted truth to try,
Each other test despis'd, I fix'd deny.
And has my regent sued two days in vain!
In vain my mandate, and the captive chain!
Yet not in vain, proud chief, ourself shall sue
From thee the honour to my friendship due:
Ere force compel thee, let the grace be thine,
Our grace permits it, freely to resign,
Freely to trust our friendship, ere too late
Our injur'd honour fix thy dreadful fate."

While thus he spake, his changeful look declar'd
In his proud breast what starting passions warr'd.
No feature mov'd on GAMA'S face was seen;
Stern he replies, with bold yet anxious mien,
"In me my sov'reign represented see,
His state is wounded, and he speaks in me;
Unaw'd by threats, by dangers uncontroll'd,
The laws of nations bid my tongue be bold.
No more thy justice holds the righteous scale,
The arts of falsehood and the Moors prevail;
I see the doom my favour'd foes decree,
Yet, though in chains I stand, my fleet is free.
The bitter taunts of scorn the brave disdain;
Few be my words, your arts, your threats are vain.
My sov'reign's fleet I yield not to your sway;[552]
Safe shall my fleet to Lisboa's strand convey
The glorious tale of all the toils I bore,
Afric surrounded, and the Indian shore
Discover'd. These I pledg'd my life to gain,
These to my country shall my life maintain.
One wish alone my earnest heart desires,
The sole impassion'd hope my breast respires;
My finish'd labours may my sov'reign hear!
Besides that wish, nor hope I know, nor fear.
And lo, the victim of your rage I stand,
And bare my bosom to the murd'rer's hand."

With lofty mien he spake. In stern disdain,

"My threats," the monarch cries, "were never vain:
Swift give the sign."—Swift as he spake, appear'd
The dancing streamer o'er the palace rear'd;
Instant another ensign distant rose,
Where, jutting through the flood, the mountain throws
A ridge enormous, and on either side
Defends the harbours from the furious tide.
Proud on his couch th' indignant monarch sat,
And awful silence fill'd the room of state.
With secret joy the Moors, exulting, glow'd,
And bent their eyes where GAMA'S navy rode,
Then, proudly heav'd with panting hope, explore
The wood-crown'd upland of the bending shore.
Soon o'er the palms a mast's tall pendant flows,
Bright to the sun the purple radiance glows;
In martial pomp, far streaming to the skies,
Vanes after vanes in swift succession rise,
And, through the opening forest-boughs of green,
The sails' white lustre moving on is seen;
When sudden, rushing by the point of land
The bowsprits nod, and wide the sails expand;
Full pouring on the sight, in warlike pride,
Extending still the rising squadrons ride:
O'er every deck, beneath the morning rays,
Like melted gold, the brazen spear-points blaze;
Each prore surrounded with a hundred oars,
Old Ocean boils around the crowded prores:
And, five times now in number GAMA'S might,
Proudly their boastful shouts provoke the fight;
Far round the shore the echoing peal rebounds,
Behind the hill an answ'ring shout resounds:
Still by the point new-spreading sails appear,
Till seven times GAMA'S fleet concludes the rear.
Again the shout triumphant shakes the bay;
Form'd as a crescent, wedg'd in firm array,
Their fleet's wide horns the Lusian ships enclasp,
Prepar'd to crush them in their iron grasp.
Shouts echo shouts.—With stern, disdainful eyes
The Indian king to manly GAMA cries,
"Not one of thine on Lisboa's shore shall tell
The glorious tale, how bold thy heroes fell."
With alter'd visage, for his eyes flash'd fire,
"God sent me here, and God's avengeful ire
Shall blast thy perfidy," great VASCO cried,
"And humble in the dust thy wither'd pride."
A prophet's glow inspir'd his panting breast,
Indignant smiles the monarch's scorn confess'd.
Again deep silence fills the room of state,

And the proud Moors, secure, exulting wait:
And now inclasping GAMA'S in a ring,
Their fleet sweeps on.—Loud whizzing from the string
The black-wing'd arrows float along the sky,
And rising clouds the falling clouds supply.
The lofty crowding spears that bristling stood
Wide o'er the galleys as an upright wood,
Bend sudden, levell'd for the closing fight,
The points, wide-waving, shed a gleamy light.
Elate with joy the king his aspect rears,
And valiant GAMA, thrill'd with transport, hears
His drums' bold rattling raise the battle sound;
Echo, deep-ton'd, hoarse, vibrates far around;
The shiv'ring trumpets tear the shrill-voic'd air,
Quiv'ring the gale, the flashing lightnings flare,
The smoke rolls wide, and sudden bursts the roar,
The lifted waves fall trembling, deep the shore
Groans; quick and quicker blaze embraces blaze
In flashing arms; louder the thunders raise
Their roaring, rolling o'er the bended skies
The burst incessant; awe-struck Echo dies
Falt'ring and deafen'd; from the brazen throats,
Cloud after cloud, enroll'd in darkness, floats,
Curling their sulph'rous folds of fiery blue,
Till their huge volumes take the fleecy hue,
And roll wide o'er the sky; wide as the sight
Can measure heav'n, slow rolls the cloudy white:
Beneath, the smoky blackness spreads afar
Its hov'ring wings, and veils the dreadful war
Deep in its horrid breast; the fierce red glare,
Cheq'ring the rifted darkness, fires the air,
Each moment lost and kindled, while around,
The mingling thunders swell the lengthen'd sound.
When piercing sudden through the dreadful roar
The yelling shrieks of thousands strike the shore:
Presaging horror through the monarch's breast
Crept cold; and gloomy o'er the distant east,
Through Gata's hills[553] the whirling tempest sigh'd,
And westward sweeping to the blacken'd tide,
Howl'd o'er the trembling palace as it past,
And o'er the gilded walls a gloomy twilight cast;
Then, furious, rushing to the darken'd bay,[554]
Resistless swept the black-wing'd night away,
With all the clouds that hover'd o'er the fight,
And o'er the weary combat pour'd the light.

As by an Alpine mountain's pathless side
Some traveller strays, unfriended of a guide;

If o'er the hills the sable night descend,
And gath'ring tempest with the darkness blend,
Deep from the cavern'd rocks beneath, aghast
He hears the howling of the whirlwind's blast;
Above, resounds the crash, and down the steep
Some rolling weight groans on with found'ring sweep;
Aghast he stands, amid the shades of night,
And all his soul implores the friendly light:
It comes; the dreadful lightning's quiv'ring blaze
The yawning depth beneath his lifted step betrays;
Instant unmann'd, aghast in horrid pain,
his knees no more their sickly weight sustain;
Powerless he sinks, no more his heart-blood flows;
So sunk the monarch, and his heart-blood froze;
So sunk he down, when o'er the clouded bay
The rushing whirlwind pour'd the sudden day:
Disaster's giant arm in one wide sweep
Appear'd, and ruin blacken'd o'er the deep;
The sheeted masts drove floating o'er the tide,
And the torn hulks roll'd tumbling on the side;
Some shatter'd plank each heaving billow toss'd,
And, by the hand of Heav'n, dash'd on the coast
Groan'd prores ingulf'd; the lashing surges rave
O'er the black keels upturn'd, the swelling wave
Kisses the lofty mast's reclining head;
And, far at sea, some few torn galleys fled.
Amid the dreadful scene triumphant rode
The Lusian war-ships, and their aid bestow'd:
Their speedy boats far round assisting ply'd,
Where plunging, struggling, in the rolling tide,
Grasping the shatter'd wrecks, the vanquish'd foes
Rear'd o'er the dashing waves their haggard brows.
No word of scorn the lofty GAMA spoke,
Nor India's king the dreadful silence broke.
Slow pass'd the hour, when to the trembling shore,
In awful pomp, the victor-navy bore:
Terrific, nodding on, the bowsprits bend,
And the red streamers other war portend:
Soon bursts the roar; the bombs tremendous rise,
And trail their black'ning rainbows o'er the skies;
O'er Calicut's proud domes their rage they pour,
And wrap her temples in a sulph'rous shower.
'Tis o'er—In threat'ning silence rides the fleet:
Wild rage, and horror yell in ev'ry street;
Ten thousands pouring round the palace gate,
In clam'rous uproar wail their wretch'd fate:
While round the dome, with lifted hands, they kneel'd,
"Give justice, justice to the strangers yield—

Our friends, our husbands, sons, and fathers slain!
Happier, alas, than these that yet remain—
Curs'd be the counsels, and the arts unjust—
Our friends in chains—our city in the dust—
Yet, yet prevent—"
The silent VASCO saw
The weight of horror, and o'erpowering awe
That shook the Moors, that shook the regent's knees,
And sunk the monarch down. By swift degrees
The popular clamour rises. Lost, unmann'd,
Around the king the trembling council stand;
While, wildly glaring on each other's eyes,
Each lip in vain the trembling accent tries;
With anguish sicken'd, and of strength bereft,
Earnest each look inquires, What hope is left!
In all the rage of shame and grief aghast,
The monarch, falt'ring, takes the word at last:
"By whom, great chief, are these proud war-ships sway'd,
Are there thy mandates honour'd and obey'd?
Forgive, great chief, let gifts of price restrain
Thy just revenge. Shall India's gifts be vain!—
Oh spare my people and their doom'd abodes—
Prayers, vows, and gifts appease the injur'd gods:
Shall man deny? Swift are the brave to spare:
The weak, the innocent confess their care—
Helpless, as innocent of guile, to thee
Behold these thousands bend the suppliant knee—
Thy navy's thund'ring sides black to the land
Display their terrors—yet mayst thou command—"

O'erpower'd he paus'd. Majestic and serene
Great VASCO rose, then, pointing to the scene
Where bled the war, "Thy fleet, proud king, behold
O'er ocean and the strand in carnage roll'd!
So, shall this palace, smoking in the dust,
And yon proud city, weep thy arts unjust.
The Moors I knew, and, for their fraud prepar'd,
I left my fix'd command my navy's guard:[555]
Whate'er from shore my name or seal convey'd
Of other weight, that fix'd command forbade;
Thus, ere its birth destroy'd, prevented fell
What fraud might dictate, or what force compel.
This morn the sacrifice of Fraud I stood,
But hark, there lives the brother of my blood,
And lives the friend, whose cares conjoin'd control
These floating towers, both brothers of my soul.
'If thrice,' I said, 'arise the golden morn,
Ere to my fleet you mark my glad return,

Dark Fraud with all her Moorish arts withstands,
And force, or death withholds me from my bands:
Thus judge, and swift unfurl the homeward sail,
Catch the first breathing of the eastern gale,
Unmindful of my fate on India's shore:[556]
Let but my monarch know, I wish no more.'
Each, panting while I spoke, impatient cries,
The tear-drop bursting in their manly eyes,
'In all but one thy mandates we obey,
In one we yield not to thy gen'rous sway:
Without thee, never shall our sails return;
India shall bleed, and Calicut shall burn—
Thrice shall the morn arise; a flight of bombs
Shall then speak vengeance to their guilty domes:
Till noon we pause; then, shall our thunders roar,
And desolation sweep the treach'rous shore.'
Behold, proud king, their signal in the sky,
Near his meridian tower the sun rides high.
O'er Calicut no more the ev'ning shade
Shall spread her peaceful wings, my wrath unstaid;
Dire through the night her smoking dust shall gleam,
Dire thro' the night shall shriek the female scream."

"Thy worth, great chief," the pale-lipp'd regent cries,
"Thy worth we own: oh, may these woes suffice!
To thee each proof of India's wealth we send;
Ambassadors, of noblest race, attend—"
Slow as he falter'd, GAMA caught the word,
"On terms I talk not, and no truce afford:
Captives enough shall reach the Lusian shore:
Once you deceiv'd me, and I treat no more.
E'en now my faithful sailors, pale with rage,
Gnaw their blue lips, impatient to engage;
Rang'd by their brazen tubes, the thund'ring band
Watch the first movement of my brother's hand;
E'en now, impatient, o'er the dreadful tire
They wave their eager canes betipp'd with fire;
Methinks my brother's anguish'd look I see,
The panting nostril and the trembling knee,
While keen he eyes the sun. On hasty strides,
Hurried along the deck, Coello chides
His cold, slow ling'ring, and impatient cries,
'Oh, give the sign, illume the sacrifice,
A brother's vengeance for a brother's blood—"

He spake; and stern the dreadful warrior stood;
So seem'd the terrors of his awful nod,
The monarch trembled as before a god;

The treach'rous Moors sank down in faint dismay,
And speechless at his feet the council lay:
Abrupt, with outstretched arms, the monarch cries,
"What yet—" but dar'd not meet the hero's eyes,
"What yet may save!"[557]—Great VASCO stern rejoins,
"Swift, undisputing, give th' appointed signs:
High o'er thy loftiest tower my flag display,
Me and my train swift to my fleet convey:
Instant command—behold the sun rides high—"
He spake, and rapture glow'd in ev'ry eye;
The Lusian standard o'er the palace flow'd,
Swift o'er the bay the royal barges row'd.
A dreary gloom a sudden whirlwind threw;
Amid the howling blast, enrag'd, withdrew
The vanquish'd demon. Soon, in lustre mild
As April smiles, the sun auspicious smil'd:
Elate with joy, the shouting thousands trod,
And GAMA to his fleet triumphant rode.

Soft came the eastern gale on balmy wings:
Each joyful sailor to his labour springs;
Some o'er the bars their breasts robust recline,
And, with firm tugs, the rollers[558] from the brine,
Reluctant dragg'd, the slime-brown'd anchors raise;
Each gliding rope some nimble hand obeys;
Some bending o'er the yard-arm's length, on high,
With nimble hands, the canvas wings untie;
The flapping sails their wid'ning folds distend,
And measur'd, echoing shouts their sweaty toils attend.
Nor had the captives lost the leader's care,
Some to the shore the Indian barges bear;
The noblest few the chief detains, to own
His glorious deeds before the Lusian throne;
To own the conquest of the Indian shore:
Nor wanted ev'ry proof of India's store.
What fruits in Ceylon's fragrant woods abound,
With woods of cinnamon her hills are crown'd:
Dry'd in its flower, the nut of Banda's grove,
The burning pepper, and the sable clove;
The clove, whose odour on the breathing gale,
Far to the sea, Molucca's plains exhale;
All these, provided by the faithful Moor,
All these, and India's gems, the navy bore:
The Moor attends, Mozaide, whose zealous care
To GAMA'S eyes unveil'd each treach'rous snare:[559]
So burn'd his breast with Heav'n-illumin'd flame,
And holy rev'rence of Messiah's name.
O, favour'd African, by Heaven's own light

Call'd from the dreary shades of error's night!
What man may dare his seeming ills arraign,
Or what the grace of Heaven's designs explain!
Far didst thou from thy friends a stranger roam,
There wast thou call'd to thy celestial home.[560]

With rustling sound now swell'd the steady sail;
The lofty masts reclining to the gale,
On full-spread wings the navy springs away,
And, far behind them, foams the ocean grey:
Afar the less'ning hills of Gata fly,
And mix their dim blue summits with the sky:
Beneath the wave low sinks the spicy shore,
And, roaring through the tide, each nodding prore
Points to the Cape, great Nature's southmost bound,
The Cape of Tempests, now of Hope renown'd.
Their glorious tale on Lisboa's shore to tell
Inspires each bosom with a rapt'rous swell;
Now through their breasts the chilly tremors glide,
To dare once more the dangers dearly tried.—
Soon to the winds are these cold fears resign'd,
And all their country rushes on the mind;
How sweet to view their native land, how sweet
The father, brother, and the bride to greet!
While list'ning round the hoary parent's board
The wond'ring kindred glow at ev'ry word;
How sweet to tell what woes, what toils they bore,
The tribes, and wonders of each various shore!
These thoughts, the traveller's lov'd reward, employ,
And swell each bosom with unutter'd joy.[561]

The queen of love, by Heaven's eternal grace,
The guardian goddess of the Lusian race;
The queen of love, elate with joy, surveys
Her heroes, happy, plough the wat'ry maze:
Their dreary toils revolving in her thought,
And all the woes by vengeful Bacchus wrought;
These toils, these woes, her yearning cares employ,
To bathe, and balsam in the streams of joy.
Amid the bosom of the wat'ry waste,
Near where the bowers of Paradise were plac'd,[562]
An isle, array'd in all the pride of flowers,
Of fruits, of fountains, and of fragrant bowers,
She means to offer to their homeward prows,
The place of glad repast and sweet repose;
And there, before their raptur'd view, to raise
The heav'n-topp'd column of their deathless praise.

The goddess now ascends her silver car,
(Bright was its hue as love's translucent star);
Beneath the reins the stately birds,[563] that sing
Their sweet-ton'd death-song spread the snowy wing;
The gentle winds beneath her chariot sigh,
And virgin blushes purple o'er the sky:
On milk-white pinions borne, her cooing doves
Form playful circles round her as she moves;
And now their beaks in fondling kisses join,
In am'rous nods their fondling necks entwine.
O'er fair Idalia's bowers the goddess rode,
And by her altars sought Idalia's god:
The youthful bowyer of the heart was there;
His falling kingdom claim'd his earnest care.[564]
His bands he musters, through the myrtle groves
On buxom wings he trains the little loves.
Against the world, rebellious and astray,
He means to lead them, and resume his sway:
For base-born passions, at his shrine, 'twas told,
Each nobler transport of the breast controll'd.
A young Actæon,[565] scornful of his lore,
Morn after morn pursues the foamy boar,
In desert wilds, devoted to the chase;
Each dear enchantment of the female face
Spurn'd, and neglected. Him, enrag'd, he sees,
And sweet, and dread his punishment decrees.
Before his ravish'd sight, in sweet surprise,
Naked in all her charms, shall Dian rise;
With love's fierce flames his frozen heart shall burn,[566]
Coldly his suit, the nymph, unmov'd, shall spurn.
Of these lov'd dogs that now his passions sway,
Ah, may he never fall the hapless prey!

Enrag'd, he sees a venal herd, the shame
Of human race, assume the titled name;[567]
And each, for some base interest of his own,
With Flatt'ry's manna'd lips assail the throne.
He sees the men, whom holiest sanctions bind
To poverty, and love of human kind;
While, soft as drop the dews of balmy May,
Their words preach virtue, and her charms display,
He sees with lust of gold their eyes on fire,
And ev'ry wish to lordly state aspire;
He sees them trim the lamp at night's mid hour,
To plan new laws to arm the regal power;
Sleepless, at night's mid hour, to raze the laws,
The sacred bulwarks of the people's cause,
Fram'd ere the blood of hard-earn'd victory

On their brave fathers' helm-hack'd swords was dry.

Nor these alone; each rank, debas'd and rude,
Mean objects, worthless of their love, pursued:
Their passions thus rebellious to his lore,
The god decrees to punish and restore.
The little loves, light hov'ring in the air,
Twang their silk bow-strings, and their aims prepare:
Some on th' immortal anvils point the dart,
With power resistless to inflame the heart;
Their arrow heads they tip with soft desires,
And all the warmth of love's celestial fires;
Some sprinkle o'er the shafts the tears of woe,
Some store the quiver, some steel-spring the bow;
Each chanting as he works the tuneful strain
Of love's dear joys, of love's luxurious pain;
Charm'd was the lay to conquer and refine,
Divine the melody, the song divine.

Already, now, began the vengeful war,
The witness of the god's benignant care;
On the hard bosoms of the stubborn crowd[568]
An arrowy shower the bowyer train bestow'd;
Pierced by the whizzing shafts, deep sighs the air,
And answering sighs the wounds of love declare.
Though various featur'd, and of various hue,
Each nymph seems loveliest in her lover's view;
Fir'd by the darts, by novice archers sped,
Ten thousand wild, fantastic loves are bred:
In wildest dreams the rustic hind aspires,
And haughtiest lords confess the humblest fires.

The snowy swans of love's celestial queen
Now land her chariot on the shore of green;
One knee display'd, she treads the flow'ry strand,
The gather'd robe falls loosely from her hand;
Half-seen her bosom heaves the living snow,
And on her smiles the living roses glow.
The bowyer god,[569] whose subtle shafts ne'er fly
Misaim'd, in vain, in vain on earth or sky,
With rosy smiles the mother power receives;
Around her climbing, thick as ivy leaves,
The vassal loves in fond contention join
Who, first and most, shall kiss her hand divine.
Swift in her arms she caught her wanton boy,
And, "Oh, my son," she cries, "my pride, my joy!
Against thy might the dreadful Typhon fail'd,
Against thy shaft nor heav'n, nor Jove prevail'd;

Unless thine arrow wake the young desires,
My strength, my power, in vain each charm expires:
My son, my hope, I claim thy powerful aid,
Nor be the boon thy mother sues delay'd:
Where'er—so will th' eternal fates—where'er
The Lusian race the victor standards rear,
There shall my hymns resound, my altars flame,
And heav'nly Love her joyful lore proclaim.
My Lusian heroes, as my Romans, brave,
Long toss'd, long hopeless on the storm-torn wave,
Wearied and weak, at last on India's shore
Arriv'd, new toils, repose denied, they bore;
For Bacchus there with tenfold rage pursued
My dauntless sons, but now his might subdued,
Amid these raging seas, the scene of woes,
Theirs shall be now the balm of sweet repose;
Theirs ev'ry joy the noblest heroes claim,
The raptur'd foretaste of immortal fame.
Then, bend thy bow and wound the Nereid train,
The lovely daughters of the azure main;
And lead them, while they pant with am'rous fire,
Right to the isle which all my smiles inspire:
Soon shall my care that beauteous isle supply,
Where Zephyr, breathing love, on Flora's lap shall sigh.
There let the nymphs the gallant heroes meet,
And strew the pink and rose beneath their feet:
In crystal halls the feast divine prolong,
With wine nectareous and immortal song:
Let every nymph the snow-white bed prepare,
And, fairer far, resign her bosom there;
There, to the greedy riotous embrace
Resign each hidden charm with dearest grace.
Thus, from my native waves a hero line
Shall rise, and o'er the East illustrious shine;[570]
Thus, shall the rebel world thy prowess know,
And what the boundless joys our friendly powers bestow."

She said; and smiling view'd her mighty boy;
Swift to the chariot springs the god of joy;
His ivory bow, and arrows tipp'd with gold,
Blaz'd to the sun-beam as the chariot roll'd:
Their silver harness shining to the day,
The swans, on milk-white pinions, spring away,
Smooth gliding o'er the clouds of lovely blue;
And Fame[571] (so will'd the god) before them flew:
A giant goddess, whose ungovern'd tongue
With equal zeal proclaims or right or wrong;
Oft had her lips the god of love blasphem'd,

And oft with tenfold praise his conquests nam'd:
A hundred eyes she rolls with ceaseless care,
A thousand tongues what these behold declare:
Fleet is her flight, the lightning's wing she rides,   }
And, though she shifts her colours swift as glides   }
The April rainbow, still the crowd she guides.   }
And now, aloft her wond'ring voice she rais'd,
And, with a thousand glowing tongues, she prais'd
The bold discoverers of the eastern world—
In gentle swells the list'ning surges curl'd,
And murmur'd to the sounds of plaintive love
Along the grottoes where the Nereids rove.
The drowsy power on whose smooth easy mien
The smiles of wonder and delight are seen,
Whose glossy, simp'ring eye bespeaks her name,
Credulity, attends the goddess Fame.
Fir'd by the heroes' praise, the wat'ry gods,[572]
With ardent speed forsake their deep abodes;
Their rage by vengeful Bacchus rais'd of late,
Now stung remorse, and love succeeds to hate.
Ah, where remorse in female bosom bleeds,
The tend'rest love in all its glow succeeds.
When fancy glows, how strong, O Love, thy power!
Nor slipp'd the eager god the happy hour;
Swift fly his arrows o'er the billowy main,
Wing'd with his fires, nor flies a shaft in vain:
Thus, ere the face the lover's breast inspires,
The voice of fame awakes the soft desires.
While from the bow-string start the shafts divine,
His ivory moon's wide horns incessant join,
Swift twinkling to the view: and wide he pours,
Omnipotent in love, his arrowy showers.
E'en Thetis' self confess'd the tender smart,
And pour'd the murmurs of the wounded heart:
Soft o'er the billows pants the am'rous sigh;
With wishful languor melting on each eye
The love-sick nymphs explore the tardy sails
That waft the heroes on the ling'ring gales.

Give way, ye lofty billows, low subside,
Smooth as the level plain, your swelling pride,
Lo, Venus comes! Oh, soft, ye surges, sleep,
Smooth be the bosom of the azure deep,
Lo, Venus comes! and in her vig'rous train
She brings the healing balm of love-sick pain.
White as her swans,[573] and stately as they rear
Their snowy crests when o'er the lake they steer,
Slow moving on, behold, the fleet appears,

And o'er the distant billow onward steers.
The beauteous Nereids, flush'd in all their charms,
Surround the goddess of the soft alarms:
Right to the isle she leads the smiling train,
And all her arts her balmy lips explain;
The fearful languor of the asking eye,
The lovely blush of yielding modesty,
The grieving look, the sigh, the fav'ring smile,
And all th' endearments of the open wile,
She taught the nymphs—in willing breasts that heav'd
To hear her lore, her lore the nymphs receiv'd.

As now triumphant to their native shore
Through the wide deep the joyful navy bore,
Earnest the pilot's eyes sought cape or bay,
For long was yet the various wat'ry way;
Sought cape or isle, from whence their boats might bring
The healthful bounty of the crystal spring:
When sudden, all in nature's pride array'd,
The Isle of Love its glowing breast display'd.
O'er the green bosom of the dewy lawn
Soft blazing flow'd the silver of the dawn,
The gentle waves the glowing lustre share,
Arabia's balm was sprinkled o'er the air.
Before the fleet, to catch the heroes' view,
The floating isle fair Acidalia drew:
Soon as the floating verdure caught their sight,[574]
She fix'd, unmov'd, the island of delight.
So when in child-birth of her Jove-sprung load,
The sylvan goddess and the bowyer god,
In friendly pity of Latona's woes,[575]
Amid the waves the Delian isle arose.
And now, led smoothly o'er the furrow'd tide,
Right to the isle of joy the vessels glide:
The bay they enter, where on ev'ry hand,
Around them clasps the flower-enamell'd land;
A safe retreat, where not a blast may shake
Its flutt'ring pinions o'er the stilly lake.
With purple shells, transfus'd as marble veins,
The yellow sands celestial Venus stains.
With graceful pride three hills of softest green
Rear their fair bosoms o'er the sylvan scene;
Their sides embroider'd boast the rich array
Of flow'ry shrubs in all the pride of May;
The purple lotus and the snowy thorn,
And yellow pod-flowers ev'ry slope adorn.
From the green summits of the leafy hills
Descend, with murm'ring lapse, three limpid rills:

Beneath the rose-trees loit'ring, slow they glide,
Now, tumbles o'er some rock their crystal pride;
Sonorous now, they roll adown the glade,
Now, plaintive tinkle in the secret shade,
Now, from the darkling grove, beneath the beam
Of ruddy morn, like melted silver stream,
Edging the painted margins of the bowers,
And breathing liquid freshness on the flowers.
Here, bright reflected in the pool below,
The vermeil apples tremble on the bough;
Where o'er the yellow sands the waters sleep
The primros'd banks, inverted, dew-drops weep;
Where murm'ring o'er the pebbles purls the stream
The silver trouts in playful curvings gleam.
Long thus, and various, ev'ry riv'let strays,
Till closing, now, their long meand'ring maze,
Where in a smiling vale the mountains end,
Form'd in a crystal lake the waters blend:[576]
Fring'd was the border with a woodland shade,
In ev'ry leaf of various green array'd,
Each yellow-ting'd, each mingling tint between
The dark ash-verdure and the silv'ry green.
The trees, now bending forward, slowly shake
Their lofty honours o'er the crystal lake;
Now, from the flood the graceful boughs retire
With coy reserve, and now again admire
Their various liv'ries, by the summer dress'd,
Smooth-gloss'd and soften'd in the mirror's breast.
So, by her glass the wishful virgin stays,
And, oft retiring, steals the ling'ring gaze.
A thousand boughs aloft to heav'n display
Their fragrant apples, shining to the day;
The orange here perfumes the buxom air,
And boasts the golden hue of Daphne's hair.[577]
Near to the ground each spreading bough descends,
Beneath her yellow load the citron bends;
The fragrant lemon scents the cooly grove;
Fair as (when rip'ning for the days of love)
The virgin's breasts the gentle swell avow,
So, the twin fruitage swell on every bough.
Wild forest-trees the mountain sides array'd
With curling foliage and romantic shade:
Here spreads the poplar, to Alcides dear;
And dear to Phœbus, ever verdant here,
The laurel joins the bowers for ever green,
The myrtle bowers belov'd of beauty's queen.
To Jove the oak his wide-spread branches rears;
And high to heav'n the fragrant cedar bears;

Where through the glades appear the cavern'd rocks,
The lofty pine-tree waves her sable locks;
Sacred to Cybĕlē the whisp'ring pine
Loves the wild grottoes where the white cliffs shine;
Here towers the cypress, preacher to the wise,
Less'ning from earth her spiral honours rise,
Till, as a spear-point rear'd, the topmost spray
Points to the Eden of eternal day.
Here round her fost'ring elm the smiling vine,
In fond embraces, gives her arms to twine,
The num'rous clusters pendant from the boughs,
The green here glistens, here the purple glows;
For, here the genial seasons of the year
Danc'd hand in hand, no place for winter here;
His grisly visage from the shore expell'd,
United sway the smiling seasons held.
Around the swelling fruits of deep'ning red,
Their snowy hues the fragrant blossoms spread;
Between the bursting buds of lucid green
The apple's ripe vermilion blush is seen;
For here each gift Pomona's hand bestows
In cultur'd garden, free, uncultur'd flows,
The flavour sweeter, and the hue more fair,
Than e'er was foster'd by the hand of care.
The cherry here in shining crimson glows;
And, stain'd with lover's blood,[578] in pendent rows,
The bending boughs the mulberries o'erload;
The bending boughs caress'd by Zephyr nod.
The gen'rous peach, that strengthens in exile
Far from his native earth, the Persian soil,
The velvet peach, of softest glossy blue,
Hangs by the pomegranate of orange hue,
Whose open heart a brighter red displays
Than that which sparkles in the ruby's blaze.
Here, trembling with their weight, the branches bear,
Delicious as profuse, the tap'ring pear.
For thee, fair fruit, the songsters of the grove
With hungry bills from bower to arbour rove.
Ah, if ambitious thou wilt own the care
To grace the feast of heroes and the fair,
Soft let the leaves, with grateful umbrage, hide
The green-tinged orange of thy mellow side.
A thousand flowers of gold, of white and red,
Far o'er the shadowy vale[579] their carpets spread,
Of fairer tap'stry, and of richer bloom,
Than ever glow'd in Persia's boasted loom:
As glitt'ring rainbows o'er the verdure thrown,
O'er every woodland walk th' embroid'ry shone.

Here o'er the wat'ry mirror's lucid bed
Narcissus, self-enamour'd, hangs the head;
And here, bedew'd with love's celestial tears,
The woe-mark'd flower of slain Adonis rears[580]
Its purple head, prophetic of the reign
When lost Adonis shall revive again.
At strife appear the lawns and purpled skies,
Which from each other stole the beauteous dyes:[581]
The lawn in all Aurora's lustre glows,
Aurora steals the blushes of the rose,
The rose displays the blushes that adorn
The spotless virgin on the nuptial morn.
Zephyr and Flora emulous conspire
To breathe their graces o'er the field's attire;
The one gives healthful freshness, one the hue
Fairer than e'er creative pencil drew.
Pale as the love-sick hopeless maid they dye
The modest violet; from the curious eye
The modest violet turns her gentle head,
And, by the thorn, weeps o'er her lowly bed.
Bending beneath the tears of pearly dawn
The snow-white lily glitters o'er the lawn;
Low from the bough reclines the damask rose,
And o'er the lily's milk-white bosom glows.
Fresh in the dew, far o'er the painted dales,
Each fragrant herb her sweetest scent exhales.
The hyacinth bewrays the doleful Ai,[582]
And calls the tribute of Apollo's sigh;
Still on its bloom the mournful flower retains
The lovely blue that dy'd the stripling's veins.
Pomona, fir'd with rival envy, views
The glaring pride of Flora's darling hues;
Where Flora bids the purple iris spread,
She hangs the wilding's blossom white and red;
Where wild-thyme purples, where the daisy snows
The curving slopes, the melon's pride she throws;
Where by the stream the lily of the vale,
Primrose, and cowslip meek, perfume the gale,
Beneath the lily, and the cowslip's bell,
The scarlet strawberries luxurious swell.
Nor these alone the teeming Eden yields,
Each harmless bestial crops the flow'ry fields;
And birds of ev'ry note, and ev'ry wing,
Their loves responsive thro' the branches sing:
In sweet vibrations thrilling o'er the skies,
High pois'd in air, the lark his warbling tries;
The swan, slow sailing o'er the crystal lake,
Tunes his melodious note; from ev'ry brake

The glowing strain the nightingale returns,
And, in the bowers of love, the turtle mourns.
Pleas'd to behold his branching horns appear,
O'er the bright fountain bends the fearless deer;
The hare starts trembling from the bushy shade,
And, swiftly circling, crosses oft the glade.
Where from the rocks the bubbling founts distil,
The milk-white lambs come bleating down the hill;
The dappled heifer seeks the vales below,
And from the thicket springs the bounding doe.
To his lov'd nest, on fondly flutt'ring wings,
In chirping bill the little songster brings
The food untasted; transport thrills his breast;
'Tis nature's touch, 'tis instinct's heav'n-like feast.
Thus bower and lawn were deck'd with Eden's flowers,
And song and joy imparadis'd the bowers.

And soon the fleet their ready anchors threw:
Lifted on eager tip-toe at the view,
On nimble feet that bounded to the strand
The second Argonauts[583] elance to land.
Wide o'er the beauteous isle[584] the lovely fair
Stray through the distant glades, devoid of care.
From lowly valley and from mountain grove
The lovely nymphs renew the strains of love.
Here from the bowers that crown the plaintive rill
The solemn harp's melodious warblings thrill;
Here from the shadows of the upland grot
The mellow lute renews the swelling note.
As fair Diana, and her virgin train,
Some gaily ramble o'er the flow'ry plain,
In feign'd pursuit of hare or bounding roe,
Their graceful mien and beauteous limbs to show;
Now seeming careless, fearful now and coy,
(So, taught the goddess of unutter'd joy),
And, gliding through the distant glades, display
Each limb, each movement, naked as the day.
Some, light with glee, in careless freedom take
Their playful revels in the crystal lake;
One trembling stands no deeper than the knee
To plunge reluctant, while in sportful glee
Another o'er her sudden laves the tide;
In pearly drops the wishful waters glide,
Reluctant dropping from her breasts of snow;
Beneath the wave another seems to glow;
The am'rous waves her bosom fondly kiss'd,
And rose and fell, as panting, on her breast.
Another swims along with graceful pride,

Her silver arms the glist'ning waves divide,
Her shining sides the fondling waters lave,
Her glowing cheeks are brighten'd by the wave,
Her hair, of mildest yellow, flows from side
To side, as o'er it plays the wanton tide,
And, careless as she turns, her thighs of snow
Their tap'ring rounds in deeper lustre show.

Some gallant Lusians sought the woodland prey,
And, thro' the thickets, forc'd the pathless way;
Where some, in shades impervious to the beam,
Supinely listen'd to the murm'ring stream:
When sudden, through the boughs, the various dyes
Of pink, of scarlet, and of azure rise,
Swift from the verdant banks the loit'rers spring,
Down drops the arrow from the half-drawn string:
Soon they behold 'twas not the rose's hue,
The jonquil's yellow, nor the pansy's blue:
Dazzling the shades the nymphs appear—the zone
And flowing scarf in gold and azure shone.
Naked as Venus stood in Ida's bower,
Some trust the dazzling charms of native power;
Through the green boughs and darkling shades they show
The shining lustre of their native snow,
And every tap'ring, every rounded swell
Of thigh, of bosom, as they glide, reveal.
As visions, cloth'd in dazzling white, they rise,
Then steal unnoted from the flurried eyes:
Again apparent, and again, withdrawn,
They shine and wanton o'er the smiling lawn.
Amaz'd and lost in rapture of surprise,
"All joy, my friends!" the brave VELOSO cries,
"Whate'er of goddesses old fable told,
Or poet sung of sacred groves, behold.
Sacred to goddesses divinely bright
These beauteous forests own their guardian might.
From eyes profane, from ev'ry age conceal'd,
To us, behold, all Paradise reveal'd!
Swift let us try if phantoms of the air,
Or living charms, appear divinely fair!"
Swift at the word the gallant Lusians bound,
Their rapid footsteps scarcely touch the ground;
Through copse, through brake, impatient of their prey,
Swift as the wounded deer, they spring away:
Fleet through the winding shades, in rapid flight,
The nymphs, as wing'd with terror, fly their sight;
Fleet though they fled, the mild reverted eye
And dimpling smile their seeming fear deny.

Fleet through the shades in parted rout they glide:
If winding path the chosen pairs divide,
Another path by sweet mistake betrays,
And throws the lover on the lover's gaze:
If dark-brow'd bower conceal the lovely fair,
The laugh, the shriek, confess the charmer there.

Luxurious here the wanton zephyrs toy,
And ev'ry fondling fav'ring art employ.
Fleet as the fair ones speed, the busy gale
In wanton frolic lifts the trembling veil;
White though the veil, in fairer brighter glow,
The lifted robe displays the living snow:
Quick flutt'ring on the gale the robe conceals,
Then instant to the glance each charm reveals;
Reveals, and covers from the eyes on fire,
Reveals, and with the shade inflames desire.
One, as her breathless lover hastens on,
With wily stumble sudden lies o'erthrown;
Confus'd, she rises with a blushing smile;
The lover falls the captive of her guile:
Tripp'd by the fair, he tumbles on the mead,
The joyful victim of his eager speed.

Afar, where sport the wantons in the lake,
Another band of gallant youths betake;
The laugh, the shriek, the revel and the toy,
Bespeak the innocence of youthful joy.
The laugh, the shriek, the gallant Lusians hear
As through the forest glades they chase the deer;
For, arm'd, to chase the bounding roe they came,
Unhop'd the transport of a nobler game.
The naked wantons, as the youths appear,
Shrill through the woods resound the shriek of fear.
Some feign such terror of the forc'd embrace,
Their virgin modesty to this gives place,
Naked they spring to land, and speed away
To deepest shades unpierc'd by glaring day;
Thus, yielding freely to the am'rous eyes
What to the am'rous hands their fear denies.
Some well assume Diana's virgin shame,
When on her naked sports the hunter[585] came
Unwelcome—plunging in the crystal tide,
In vain they strive their beauteous limbs to hide;
The lucid waves ('twas all they could) bestow
A milder lustre and a softer glow.
As, lost in earnest care of future need,
Some to the banks, to snatch their mantles, speed,

Of present view regardless; ev'ry wile
Was yet, and ev'ry net of am'rous guile.
Whate'er the terror of the feign'd alarm,
Display'd, in various force, was ev'ry charm.
Nor idle stood the gallant youth; the wing
Of rapture lifts them, to the fair they spring;
Some to the copse pursue their lovely prey;
Some, cloth'd and shod, impatient of delay,
Impatient of the stings of fierce desire,
Plunge headlong in the tide to quench the fire.
So, when the fowler to his cheek uprears
The hollow steel, and on the mallard bears,
His eager dog, ere bursts the flashing roar,
Fierce for the prey, springs headlong from the shore,
And barking, cuts the wave with furious joy:
So, mid the billow springs each eager boy,
Springs to the nymph whose eyes from all the rest
By singling him her secret wish confess'd.

A son of Mars was there, of gen'rous race,
His ev'ry elegance of manly grace;
Am'rous and brave, the bloom of April youth
Glow'd on his cheek, his eye spoke simplest truth;
Yet love, capricious to th' accomplish'd boy,
Had ever turn'd to gall each promis'd joy,
Had ever spurn'd his vows; yet still his heart
Would hope, and nourish still the tender smart:
The purest delicacy fann'd his fires,
And proudest honour nurs'd his fond desires.
Not on the first that fair before him glow'd,
Not on the first the youth his love bestow'd.
In all her charms the fair Ephyre came,
And Leonardo's heart was all on flame.
Affection's melting transport o'er him stole,
And love's all gen'rous glow entranced his soul;
Of selfish joy unconscious, ev'ry thought
On sweet delirium's ocean stream'd afloat.
Pattern of beauty did Ephyre shine,
Nor less she wish'd these beauties to resign:
More than her sisters long'd her heart to yield,
Yet, swifter fled she o'er the smiling field.
The youth now panting with the hopeless chase,
"Oh turn," he cries, "oh turn thy angel face:
False to themselves, can charms like these conceal
The hateful rigour of relentless steel?
And, did the stream deceive me, when I stood
Amid my peers reflected in the flood?
The easiest port and fairest bloom I bore—

False was the stream—while I in vain deplore,
My peers are happy; lo, in ev'ry shade,
In ev'ry bower, their love with love repaid!
I, I alone through brakes, through thorns pursue
A cruel fair. Ah, still my fate proves true,
True to its rigour—who, fair nymph, to thee
Reveal'd 'twas I that sued! unhappy me!
Born to be spurn'd though honesty inspire.
Alas, I faint, my languid sinews tire;
Oh stay thee—powerless to sustain their weight
My knees sink down, I sink beneath my fate!"
He spoke; a rustling urges thro' the trees,
Instant new vigour strings his active knees,
Wildly he glares around, and raging cries,
"And must another snatch my lovely prize!
In savage grasp thy beauteous limbs constrain!
I feel, I madden while I feel the pain!
Oh lost, thou fli'st the safety of my arms,
My hand shall guard thee, softly seize thy charms,
No brutal rage inflames me, yet I burn!
Die shall thy ravisher. O goddess, turn,
And smiling view the error of my fear;
No brutal force, no ravisher is near;
A harmless roebuck gave the rustling sounds,
Lo, from the thicket swift as thee he bounds!
Ah, vain the hope to tire thee in the chase!
I faint, yet hear, yet turn thy lovely face.
Vain are thy fears; were ev'n thy will to yield
The harvest of my hope, that harvest field
My fate would guard, and walls of brass would rear
Between my sickle and the golden ear.
Yet fly me not; so may thy youthful prime
Ne'er fly thy cheek on the grey wing of time.
Yet hear, the last my panting breath can say,
Nor proudest kings, nor mightiest hosts can sway
Fate's dread decrees; yet thou, O nymph, divine,
Yet thou canst more, yet thou canst conquer mine.
Unmov'd each other yielding nymph I see;
Joy to their lovers, for they touch not thee!
But thee!—oh, every transport of desire,
That melts to mingle with its kindred fire,
For thee respires—alone I feel for thee
The dear wild rage of longing ecstasy:
By all the flames of sympathy divine
To thee united, thou by right art mine.
From thee, from thee the hallow'd transport flows
That sever'd rages, and for union glows:
Heav'n owns the claim. Hah, did the lightning glare:

Yes, I beheld my rival, though the air
Grew dim; ev'n now I heard him softly tread.
Oh rage, he waits thee on the flow'ry bed!
I see, I see thee rushing to his arms,
And sinking on his bosom, all thy charms
To him resigning in an eager kiss,
All I implor'd, the whelming tide of bliss!
And shall I see him riot on thy charms,
Dissolv'd in joy, exulting in thine arms?
Oh burst, ye lightnings, round my destin'd head,
Oh pour your flashes—" Madd'ning as he said,[586]
Amid the windings of the bow'ry wood
His trembling footsteps still the nymph pursued.
Woo'd to the flight she wing'd her speed to hear
His am'rous accents melting on her ear.
And now, she turns the wild walk's serpent maze;
A roseate bower its velvet couch displays;
The thickest moss its softest verdure spread,
Crocus and mingling pansy fring'd the bed,
The woodbine dropp'd its honey from above,
And various roses crown'd the sweet alcove.
Here, as she hastens, on the hopeless boy
She turns her face, all bath'd in smiles of joy;
Then, sinking down, her eyes suffused with love
Glowing on his, one moment lost reprove.
Here was no rival, all he wish'd his own;
Lock'd in her arms soft sinks the stripling down.
Ah, what soft murmurs panting thro' the bowers
Sigh'd to the raptures of the paramours!
The wishful sigh, and melting smile conspire,
Devouring kisses fan the fiercer fire;
Sweet violence, with dearest grace, assails,
Soft o'er the purpos'd frown the smile prevails,
The purpos'd frown betrays its own deceit,
In well-pleas'd laughter ends the rising threat;
The coy delay glides off in yielding love,
And transport murmurs thro' the sacred grove.
The joy of pleasing adds its sacred zest,
And all is love, embracing and embraced.

The golden morn beheld the scenes of joy;
Nor, sultry noon, mayst thou the bowers annoy;
The sultry noon-beam shines the lover's aid,
And sends him glowing to the secret shade.
O'er evr'y shade, and ev'ry nuptial bower
The love-sick strain the virgin turtles pour;
For nuptial faith and holy rites combin'd,
The Lusian heroes and the nymphs conjoin'd.

With flow'ry wreaths, and laurel chaplets, bound
With ductile gold, the nymphs the heroes crown'd:
By ev'ry spousal holy ritual tied,
No chance, they vow, shall e'er their hands divide,
In life, in death, attendant as their fame;
Such was the oath of ocean's sov'reign dame:
The dame (from heav'n and holy Vesta sprung,
For ever beauteous and for ever young),
Enraptur'd, views the chief whose deathless name
The wond'ring world and conquer'd seas proclaim.
With stately pomp she holds the hero's hand,
And gives her empire to his dread command,
By spousal ties confirm'd; nor pass'd untold
What Fate's unalter'd page had will'd of old:
The world's vast globe in radiant sphere she show'd,
The shores immense, and seas unknown, unplough'd;
The seas, the shores, due to the Lusian keel
And Lusian sword, she hastens to reveal.
The glorious leader by the hand she takes,
And, dim below, the flow'ry bower forsakes.
High on a mountain's starry top divine
Her palace walls of living crystal shine;
Of gold and crystal blaze the lofty towers;
Here, bath'd in joy, they pass the blissful hours:
Engulf'd in tides on tides of joy, the day
On downy pinions glides unknown away.
While thus the sov'reigns in the palace reign,
Like transport riots o'er the humbler plain,
Where each, in gen'rous triumph o'er his peers,
His lovely bride to ev'ry bride prefers.

"Hence, ye profane!"[587]—the song melodious rose,
By mildest zephyrs wafted through the boughs,
Unseen the warblers of the holy strain—
"Far from these sacred bowers, ye lewd profane!
Hence each unhallow'd eye, each vulgar ear;
Chaste and divine are all the raptures here.
The nymphs of ocean, and the ocean's queen,
The isle angelic, ev'ry raptur'd scene,
The charms of honour and its meed confess,
These are the raptures, these the wedded bliss:
The glorious triumph and the laurel crown,
The ever blossom'd palms of fair renown,
By time unwither'd, and untaught to cloy;
These are the transports of the Isle of Joy.
Such was Olympus and the bright abodes;
Renown was heav'n, and heroes were the gods.
Thus, ancient times, to virtue ever just,

To arts and valour rear'd the worshipp'd bust.
High, steep, and rugged, painful to be trod,
With toils on toils immense is virtue's road;
But smooth at last the walks umbrageous smile,
Smooth as our lawns, and cheerful as our isle.
Up the rough road Alcides, Hermes, strove,
All men like you, Apollo, Mars, and Jove:
Like you to bless mankind Minerva toil'd;
Diana bound the tyrants of the wild;
O'er the waste desert Bacchus spread the vine;
And Ceres taught the harvest-field to shine.
Fame rear'd her trumpet; to the blest abodes
She rais'd, and hail'd them gods, and sprung of gods.

"The love of fame, by heav'n's own hand impress'd,
The first, and noblest passion of the breast,
May yet mislead.—Oh guard, ye hero train,
No harlot robes of honours false and vain,
No tinsel yours, be yours all native gold,
Well-earn'd each honour, each respect you hold:
To your lov'd king return a guardian band,
Return the guardians of your native land;
To tyrant power be dreadful; from the jaws
Of fierce oppression guard the peasant's cause.
If youthful fury pant for shining arms,
Spread o'er the eastern world the dread alarms;[588]
There bends the Saracen the hostile bow,
The Saracen thy faith, thy nation's foe;
There from his cruel gripe tear empire's reins,
And break his tyrant-sceptre o'er his chains.
On adamantine pillars thus shall stand
The throne, the glory of your native land;
And Lusian heroes, an immortal line,
Shall ever with us share our isle divine."

DISSERTATION ON THE FICTION OF THE ISLAND OF VENUS.

From the earliest ages, and in the most distant nations, palaces, forests and gardens, have been the favourite themes of poets. And though, as in Homer's island of Rhadamanthus, the description is sometimes only cursory; at other times they have lavished all their powers, and have vied with each other in adorning their edifices and landscapes. The gardens of Alcinous in the Odyssey, and Elysium in the Æneid, have excited the ambition of many imitators. Many instances of these occur in the later writers. These subjects, however, it must be owned, are so natural to the genius of poetry, that it is scarcely fair to attribute to an imitation of the classics, the innumerable descriptions of this kind which abound in the old romances. In these, under different allegorical names, every passion, every virtue and vice, had its palace, its enchanted bower, or its dreary cave. Among the Italians, on the revival of letters,

Pulci, Boiardo, and others, borrowed these fictions from the Gothic romancers; Ariosto borrowed from them, and Spenser has copied Ariosto and Tasso. In the sixth and seventh books of the Orlando Furioso, there is a fine description of the island and palace of Alcina, or Vice; and in the tenth book (but inferior to the other in poetical colouring), we have a view of the country of Logistilla, or Virtue. The passage, of this kind, however, where Ariosto has displayed the richest poetical painting, is in the xxxiv. book, in the description of Paradise, whither he sends Astolpho, the English duke, to ask the help of St. John to recover the wits of Orlando. The whole is most admirably fanciful. Astolpho mounts the clouds on the winged horse, sees Paradise, and, accompanied by the Evangelist, visits the moon; the adventures in which orb are almost literally translated in Milton's Limbo. But the passage which may be said to bear the nearest resemblance to the descriptive part of the island of Venus, is the landscape of Paradise, of which the ingenious Mr. Hoole, to whose many acts of friendship I am proud to acknowledge myself indebted, has obliged me with this translation, though only ten books of his Ariosto are yet published.

"O'er the glad earth the blissful season pours
The vernal beauties of a thousand flowers
In varied tints: there show'd the ruby's hue,
The yellow topaz, and the sapphire blue.
The mead appears one intermingled blaze
Where pearls and diamonds dart their trembling rays.
Not emerald here so bright a verdure yields
As the fair turf of those celestial fields.
On ev'ry tree the leaves unfading grow,
The fruitage ripens and the flow'rets blow!
The frolic birds, gay-plum'd, of various wing
Amid the boughs their notes melodious sing:
Still lakes, and murm'ring streams, with waters clear,
Charm the fix'd eye, and lull the list'ning ear.
A soft'ning genial air, that ever seems
In even tenor, cools the solar beams
With fanning breeze; while from the enamell'd field,
Whate'er the fruits, the plants, the blossoms yield
Of grateful scent, the stealing gales dispense
The blended sweets to feed th' immortal sense.

"Amid the plain a palace dazzling bright,
Like living flame, emits a streamy light,
And, wrapp'd in splendour of refulgent day,
Outshines the strength of ev'ry mortal ray.

"Astolpho gently now directs his speed
To where the spacious pile enfolds the mead
In circuit wide, and views with eager eyes
Each nameless charm that happy soil supplies.
With this compar'd, he deems the world below
A dreary desert and a seat of woe!
By Heaven and Nature, in their wrath bestow'd,
In evil hour, for man's unblest abode.

"Near and more near the stately walls he drew,
In steadfast gaze transported at the view:
They seem'd one gem entire, of purer red
Than deep'ning gleams transparent rubies shed.
Stupendous work! by art Dædalian rais'd,
Transcending all by feeble mortals prais'd!
No more henceforth let boasting tongues proclaim
Those wonders of the world, so chronicled by fame!"

Camoëns read and admired Ariosto; but it by no means follows that he borrowed the hint of his island of
Venus from that poet. The luxury of flowery description is as common in poetry as are the tales of love.
The heroes of Ariosto meet beautiful women in the palace of Alcina:—

"Before the threshold wanton damsels wait,
Or, sport between the pillars of the gate:
But, beauty more had brighten'd in their face
Had modesty attemper'd ev'ry grace;
In vestures green each damsel swept the ground,
Their temples fair, with leafy garlands crown'd.
These, with a courteous welcome, led the knight
To this sweet Paradise of soft delight....
Enamour'd youths and tender damsels seem
To chant their loves beside a purling stream.
Some by a branching tree, or mountain's shade,
In sports and dances press the downy glade,
While one discloses to his friend, apart,
The secret transport of his am'rous heart."—BOOK vi.

But these descriptions also, which bring the homes of knight-errantry into the way of beautiful wantons,
are as common in the old romance as the use of the alphabet: and indeed the greatest part of these
love-adventures are evidently borrowed from the fable of Circe. Astolpho, who was transformed into a
myrtle by Alcina, thus informs Rogero:—

"Her former lovers she esteem'd no more,
For many lovers she possess'd before;
I was her joy—
Too late, alas, I found her wav'ring mind
In love inconstant as the changing wind!
Scarce had I held two months the fairy's grace,
When a new youth was taken to my place:
Rejected, then, I join'd the banish'd herd
That lost her love, as others were preferr'd ...
Some here, some there, her potent charms retain,
In diverse forms imprison'd to remain;
In beeches, olives, palms, or cedars clos'd,
Or, such as me, you here behold expos'd;
In fountains some, and some in beasts confin'd,
As suits the wayward fairy's cruel mind."

When incidents, character, and conduct confess the resemblance, we may, with certainty, pronounce from whence the copy is taken. Where only a similar stroke of passion or description occurs, it belongs alone to the arrogance of dulness, to tell us on what passage the poet had his eye. Every great poet has been persecuted in this manner: Milton in particular. His commentators have not left him a flower of his own growth. Yet, like the creed of the atheist, their system is involved in the deepest absurdity. It is easy to suppose that men of poetical feelings, in describing the same thing, should give us the same picture.

But, that the Paradise Lost, which forms one animated whole of the noblest poetry, is a mere cento, compiled from innumerable authors, ancient and modern, is a supposition which gives Milton a cast of talents infinitely more extraordinary and inexplicable than the greatest poetical genius. When Gaspar Poussin painted clouds and trees in his landscapes, he did not borrow the green and the blue of the leaf and the sky from Claude Lorraine. Neither did Camoëns, when he painted his island of Venus, spend the half of his life in collecting his colours from all his predecessors who had described the beauties of the vernal year, or the stages of passion. Camoëns knew how others had painted the flowery bowers of love; these formed his taste, and corrected his judgment. He viewed the beauties of nature with poetical eyes, from thence he drew his landscapes; he had felt all the allurements of love, and from thence he describes the agitations of that passion.

Nor is the description of fairy bowers and palaces, though most favourite topics, peculiar to the romances of chivalry. The poetry of the orientals also abounds with them, yet, with some characteristic differences. Like the constitutions and dress of the Asiatics, the landscapes of the eastern muse are warm and feeble, brilliant and slight, and, like the manners of the people, wear an eternal sameness. The western muse, on the contrary, is nervous as her heroes, sometimes flowery as her Italian or English fields, sometimes majestically great as her Runic forests of oak and pine; and always various, as the character of her inhabitants. Yet, with all those differences of feature, several oriental fictions greatly resemble the island of Circe, and the flowery dominions of Alcina. In particular, the adventures of Prince Agib, or the third Calender, in the Arabian Tales, afford a striking likeness of painting and catastrophe.

If Ariosto's, however, seem to resemble any eastern fiction, the island of Venus in Camoëns bears a more striking resemblance to a passage in Chaucer. The following beautiful piece of poetical painting occurs inthe Assembly of the Fowles:—

"The bildir oak, and eke the hardie ashe,
The pillir elme, the coffir unto caraine,
The boxe pipetre, the holme to whippis lasshe,
The sailing firre, the cypres deth to plaine,
The shortir ewe, the aspe for shaftis plaine,
The olive of pece, and eke the dronkin vine,
The victor palme, the laurir to divine.
A gardein sawe I full of blossomed bowis,
Upon a river, in a grené mede
There as sweetness evirmore inough is,
With flouris white, and blewe, yelowe, and rede,
And colde and clere wellestremis, nothing dede,
That swommin full of smale fishis light,

With finnis rede, and scalis silver bright.

On every bough the birdis herd I syng
With voice of angell, in ther harmonie
That busied 'hem, ther birdis forthe to bryng,
And little pretie conies to ther plaie gan hie;
And furthir all about I gan espie
The dredful roe, the buck, the hart and hind,
Squirils, and bestis smal of gentle kind.
Of instrumentes of stringis, in accorde
Herd I so plaie a ravishyng swetnesse,
That God, that makir is of all and Lorde,
Ne herd nevir a better, as I gesse,
There with a winde, unneth it might be lesse,
Made in the levis grene a noisé soft
Accordant to the foulis song en loft.

The aire of the place so attempre was,
That ner was there grevaunce of hot ne cold—

Under a tre beside a well I seye
Cupid our lorde his arrowes forge and file,
And at his fete his bowe all redie laye,
And well his doughtir temprid all the while
The heddis in the well, and with her wile
She couchid 'hem aftir as thei should serve,
Some for to flea, and some to wound and carve.

And upon pillirs grete of Jaspir long
I saw a temple of Brasse ifoundid strong.

And about the temple dauncid alwaie
Women inow, of which some there ywere
Faire of 'hemself, and some of 'hem were gaie,
In kirtils all disheveled went thei there,
That was ther office or from yere to yere,
And on the temple sawe I white and faire
Of dovis sittyng many a thousande paire."

Here we have Cupid forging his arrows, the woodland, the streams, the music of instruments and birds, the frolics of deer and other animals; and women enow. In a word, the island of Venus is here sketched out, yet Chaucer was never translated into Latin or any language of the continent, nor did Camoëns understand a line of English. The subject was common, and the same poetical feelings in Chaucer and Camoëns pointed out to each what were the beauties of landscapes and of bowers devoted to pleasure.

Yet, though the fiction of bowers, of islands, and palaces, was no novelty in poetry, much, however, remains to be attributed to the poetical powers and invention of Camoëns. The island of Venus contains, of all others, by much the completest gradation, and fullest assemblage of that species of luxuriant painting. Nothing in the older writers is equal to it in fulness. Nor can the island of Armida, in Tasso, be compared to it, in poetical embroidery or passionate expression; though Tasso as undoubtedly built upon the model of Camoëns, as Spenser appropriated the imagery of Tasso when he described the bower of Acrasia, part of which he has literally translated from the Italian poet. The beautiful fictions of Armida and Acrasia, however, are much too long to be here inserted, and they are well known to every reader of taste.

But the chief praise of our poet is yet unmentioned. The introduction of so beautiful a fiction as an essential part of the conduct and machinery of an epic poem, does the greatest honour to the invention of Camoëns. The machinery of the former part of the poem not only acquires dignity, but is completed by it. And the conduct of Homer and Virgil has, in this, not only received a fine imitation, but a masterly contrast. In the finest allegory the heroes of the Lusiad receive their reward: and, by means of this allegory, our poet gives a noble imitation of the noblest part of the Æneid. In the tenth Lusiad, GAMA and his heroes hear the nymphs in the divine palace of Thetis sing the triumphs of their countrymen in the conquest of India: after this the goddess shows GAMA a view of the eastern world, from the Cape of Good Hope to the furthest islands of Japan. She poetically describes every region, and the principal islands, and concludes, "All these are given to the western world by you." It is impossible any poem can be summed up with greater sublimity. The Fall of Troy is nothing to this. Nor is this all: the most masterly fiction, finest compliment, and ultimate purpose of the Æneid is not only nobly imitated, but the conduct of Homer, in concluding the Iliad, as already observed, is paralleled, without one circumstance being borrowed. Poetical conduct cannot possibly bear a stronger resemblance, than the reward of the heroes of the Lusiad, the prophetic song, and the vision shown to GAMA bear to the games at the funeral of Patroclus and the redemption of the body of Hector, considered as the completion of the anger of Achilles, the subject of the Iliad. Nor is it a greater honour to resemble a Homer and a Virgil, than it is to be resembled by a Milton. Milton certainly heard of Fanshaw's translation of the Lusiad, though he might never have seen the original, for it was published fourteen years before he gave his Paradise Lost to the world. But, whatever he knew of it, had the last book of the Lusiad been two thousand years known to the learned, every one would have owned that the two last boots of the Paradise Lost were evidently formed upon it. But whether Milton borrowed any hint from Camoëns is of little consequence. That the genius of the great Milton suggested the conclusion of his immortal poem in the manner and with the machinery of the Lusiad, is enough. It is enough that the part of Michael and Adam in the two last books of the Paradise Lost are, in point of conduct, exactly the same with the part of Thetis and GAMA in the conclusion of the Lusiad. Yet, this difference must be observed; in the narrative of his last book, Milton has flagged, as Addison calls it, and fallen infinitely short of the untired spirit of the Portuguese poet.

END OF THE NINTH BOOK

BOOK X

THE ARGUMENT

In the opening of this, the last canto, the poet resumes the allegory of the Isle of Joy, or of Venus: the fair nymphs conduct their lovers to their radiant palaces, where delicious wines sparkle in every cup. Before the poet describes the song of a prophetic siren, who celebrates the praise of the heroes who are destined in ennoble the name of their country, he addresses himself to his muse in a tone of sorrow, which touches us the more deeply when we reflect upon the unhappy situation to which this great poet was at last reduced. In the song of the siren, which follows, is afforded a prophetic view from the period of Gama's expedition down to Camoëns' own times, in which Pacheco, and other heroes of Portugal, pass in review before the eye of the reader. When the siren has concluded her prophetic song, Thetis conducts Gama to the top of a mountain and addresses him in a set speech. The poem concludes with the poet's apostrophe to King Sebastian.

Far o'er the western ocean's distant bed
Apollo now his fiery coursers sped;
Far o'er the silver lake of Mexic[589] roll'd
His rapid chariot wheels of burning gold:
The eastern sky was left to dusky grey,
And o'er the last hot breath of parting day,
Cool o'er the sultry noon's remaining flame,
On gentle gales the grateful twilight came.
Dimpling the lucid pools, the fragrant breeze
Sighs o'er the lawns, and whispers thro' the trees;
Refresh'd, the lily rears the silver head,
And opening jasmines o'er the arbours spread.
Fair o'er the wave that gleam'd like distant snow,
Graceful arose the moon, serenely slow;
Not yet full orb'd, in clouded splendour dress'd,
Her married arms embrace her pregnant breast.
Sweet to his mate, recumbent o'er his young,
The nightingale his spousal anthem sung;
From ev'ry bower the holy chorus rose,
From ev'ry bower the rival anthem flows.
Translucent, twinkling through the upland grove,
In all her lustre shines the star of love;
Led by the sacred ray from ev'ry bower,
A joyful train, the wedded lovers pour:
Each with the youth above the rest approv'd,
Each with the nymph above the rest belov'd,
They seek the palace of the sov'reign dame;
High on a mountain glow'd the wondrous frame:
Of gold the towers, of gold the pillars shone,
The walls were crystal, starr'd with precious stone.
Amid the hall arose the festive board,
With nature's choicest gifts promiscuous stor'd:
So will'd the goddess to renew the smile
Of vital strength, long worn by days of toil.
On crystal chairs, that shin'd as lambent flame,
Each gallant youth attends his lovely dame;
Beneath a purple canopy of state

The beauteous goddess and the leader sat:
The banquet glows—Not such the feast, when all
The pride of luxury in Egypt's hall
Before the love-sick Roman[590] spread the boast
Of ev'ry teeming sea and fertile coast.
Sacred to noblest worth and Virtue's ear,
Divine, as genial, was the banquet here;
The wine, the song, by sweet returns inspire,
Now wake the lover's, now the hero's fire.
On gold and silver from th' Atlantic main,
The sumptuous tribute of the sea's wide reign,
Of various savour, was the banquet pil'd;
Amid the fruitage mingling roses smil'd.
In cups of gold that shed a yellow light,
In silver, shining as the moon of night,
Amid the banquet flow'd the sparkling wine,
Nor gave Falernia's fields the parent vine:
Falernia's vintage, nor the fabled power
Of Jove's ambrosia in th' Olympian bower
To this compare not; wild, nor frantic fires,
Divinest transport this alone inspires.
The bev'rage, foaming o'er the goblet's breast,
The crystal fountain's cooling aid confess'd;[591]
The while, as circling flow'd the cheerful bowl,
Sapient discourse, the banquet of the soul,
Of richest argument and brightest glow,
Array'd in dimpling smiles, in easiest flow
Pour'd all its graces: nor in silence stood
The powers of music, such as erst subdued
The horrid frown of hell's profound domains,[592]
And sooth'd the tortur'd ghosts to slumber on their chains.
To music's sweetest chords, in loftiest vein,
An angel siren joins the vocal strain;
The silver roofs resound the living song,
The harp and organ's lofty mood prolong
The hallow'd warblings; list'ning Silence rides
The sky, and o'er the bridled winds presides;
In softest murmurs flows the glassy deep,
And each, lull'd in his shade, the bestials sleep.
The lofty song ascends the thrilling skies,
The song of godlike heroes yet to rise;
Jove gave the dream, whose glow the siren fir'd,
And present Jove the prophecy inspir'd.
Not he, the bard of love-sick Dido's board,
Nor he, the minstrel of Phæacia's lord,
Though fam'd in song, could touch the warbling string,
Or, with a voice so sweet, melodious sing.
And thou, my muse, O fairest of the train,

Calliope, inspire my closing strain.
No more the summer of my life remains,[593]
My autumn's length'ning ev'nings chill my veins;
Down the black stream of years by woes on woes
Wing'd on, I hasten to the tomb's repose,
The port whose deep, dark bottom shall detain
My anchor, never to be weigh'd again,
Never on other sea of life to steer
The human course.—Yet thou, O goddess, hear,
Yet let me live, though round my silver'd head
Misfortune's bitt'rest rage unpitying shed
Her coldest storms; yet, let me live to crown
The song that boasts my nation's proud renown.

Of godlike heroes sung the nymph divine,
Heroes whose deeds on GAMA'S crest shall shine;
Who through the seas, by GAMA first explor'd,
Shall bear the Lusian standard and the sword,
Till ev'ry coast where roars the orient main,
Blest in its sway, shall own the Lusian reign;
Till ev'ry pagan king his neck shall yield,
Or vanquish'd, gnaw the dust on battle-field.

"High Priest of Malabar," the goddess sung,
"Thy faith repent not, nor lament thy wrong;[594]
Though, for thy faith to Lusus' gen'rous race,
The raging zamoreem thy fields deface:
From Tagus, lo, the great Pacheco sails
To India, wafted on auspicious gales.
Soon as his crooked prow the tide shall press,
A new Achilles shall the tide confess;
His ship's strong sides shall groan beneath his weight,
And deeper waves receive the sacred freight.[595]
Soon as on India's strand he shakes his spear,
The burning east shall tremble, chill'd with fear;
Reeking with noble blood, Cambalao's stream
Shall blaze impurpled on the ev'ning beam;
Urg'd on by raging shame, the monarch brings,
Banded with all their powers, his vassal kings:
Narsinga's rocks their cruel thousands pour,
Bipur's stern king attends, and thine, Tanore:
To guard proud Calicut's imperial pride
All the wide North sweeps down its peopled tide:
Join'd are the sects that never touch'd before,
By land the pagan, and by sea the Moor.
O'er land, o'er sea the great Pacheco strews
The prostrate spearmen, and the founder'd proas.[596]
Submiss and silent, palsied with amaze,

Proud Malabar th' unnumber'd slain surveys:
Yet burns the monarch; to his shrine he speeds;
Dire howl the priests, the groaning victim bleeds;
The ground they stamp, and, from the dark abodes,
With tears and vows, they call th' infernal gods.
Enrag'd with dog-like madness, to behold
His temples and his towns in flames enroll'd,
Secure of promis'd victory, again
He fires the war, the lawns are heap'd with slain.
With stern reproach he brands his routed Nayres,
And for the dreadful field himself prepares;
His harness'd thousands to the fight he leads;
And rides exulting where the combat bleeds:
Amid his pomp his robes are sprinkled o'er,
And his proud face dash'd, with his menials' gore:[597]
From his high couch he leaps, and speeds to flight
On foot inglorious, in his army's sight.
Hell then he calls, and all the powers of hell,
The secret poison, and the chanted spell;
Vain as the spell the poison'd rage is shed,
For Heav'n defends the hero's sacred head.
Still fiercer from each wound the tyrant burns,
Still to the field with heavier force returns;
The seventh dread war he kindles; high in air
The hills dishonour'd lift their shoulders bare;
Their woods, roll'd down, now strew the river's side,
Now rise in mountain turrets o'er the tide;
Mountains of fire, and spires of bick'ring flame,
While either bank resounds the proud acclaim,
Come floating down, round Lusus' fleet to pour
Their sulph'rous entrails[598] in a burning shower.
Oh, vain the hope.—Let Rome her boast resign;
Her palms, Pacheco, never bloom'd like thine;
Nor Tiber's bridge,[599] nor Marathon's red field,   }
Nor thine, Thermopylæ, such deeds beheld;   }
Nor Fabius' arts such rushing storms repell'd.   }
Swift as, repuls'd, the famish'd wolf returns
Fierce to the fold, and, wounded, fiercer burns;
So swift, so fierce, seven times, all India's might
Returns unnumber'd to the dreadful fight;
One hundred spears, seven times in dreadful stower,
Strews in the dust all India's raging power."

The lofty song (for paleness o'er her spread)
The nymph suspends, and bows the languid head;
Her falt'ring words are breathed on plaintive sighs:
"Ah, Belisarius, injur'd chief," she cries,
"Ah, wipe thy tears; in war thy rival see,

Injur'd Pacheco falls despoil'd like thee;
In him, in thee dishonour'd Virtue bleeds,
And Valour weeps to view her fairest deeds,—
Weeps o'er Pacheco, where, forlorn he lies
Low on an alms-house bed, and friendless dies.
Yet shall the muses plume his humble bier,
And ever o'er him pour th' immortal tear;
Though by the king, alone to thee unjust,
Thy head, great chief, was humbled in the dust,
Loud shall the muse indignant sound thy praise—
'Thou gav'st thy monarch's throne its proudest blaze.'
While round the world the sun's bright car shall ride,
So bright shall shine thy name's illustrious pride;
Thy monarch's glory, as the moon's pale beam,
Eclips'd by thine, shall shed a sickly gleam.
Such meed attends when soothing flatt'ry sways,
And blinded State its sacred trust betrays!"

Again the nymph exalts her brow, again
Her swelling voice resounds the lofty strain:
"Almeyda comes, the kingly name he bears,
Deputed royalty his standard rears:
In all the gen'rous rage of youthful fire
The warlike son attends the warlike sire.
Quiloa's blood-stain'd tyrant now shall feel
The righteous vengeance of the Lusian steel.
Another prince, by Lisbon's throne belov'd,
Shall bless the land, for faithful deeds approv'd.
Mombaz shall now her treason's meed behold,
When curling flames her proudest domes enfold:
Involv'd in smoke, loud crashing, low shall fall
The mounded temple and the castled wall.
O'er India's seas the young Almeyda pours,
Scorching the wither'd air, his iron show'rs;
Torn masts and rudders, hulks and canvas riv'n,
Month after month before his prows are driv'n;
But Heav'n's dread will, where clouds of darkness rest,
That awful will, which knows alone the best,
Now blunts his spear: Cambaya's squadrons join'd
With Egypt's fleets, in pagan rage combin'd,
Engrasp him round; red boils the stagg'ring flood,
Purpled with volleying flames and hot with blood:
Whirl'd by the cannon's rage, in shivers torn,
His thigh, far scattered, o'er the wave is borne.
Bound to the mast the godlike hero stands,[600]
Waves his proud sword, and cheers his woful bands.
Though winds and seas their wonted aid deny,
To yield he knows not, but he knows to die:

Another thunder tears his manly breast:
Oh fly, blest spirit, to thy heav'nly rest!
Hark! rolling on the groaning storm I hear,
Resistless vengeance thund'ring on the rear.
I see the transports of the furious sire,
As o'er the mangled corse his eyes flash fire.
Swift to the fight, with stern though weeping eyes,
Fix'd rage fierce burning in his breast, he flies;
Fierce as the bull that sees his rival rove
Free with the heifers through the mounded grove,
On oak or beech his madd'ning fury pours;
So pours Almeyda's rage on Dabul's towers.
His vanes wide waving o'er the Indian sky,
Before his prows the fleets of India fly;[601]
On Egypt's chief his mortars' dreadful tire
Shall vomit all the rage of prison'd fire:
Heads, limbs, and trunks shall choke the struggling tide,
Till, ev'ry surge with reeking crimson dy'd,
Around the young Almeyda's hapless urn
His conqueror's naked ghosts shall howl and mourn.
As meteors flashing through the darken'd air
I see the victors' whirling falchions glare;
Dark rolls the sulph'rous smoke o'er Dio's skies,
And shrieks of death, and shouts of conquest rise,
In one wide tumult blended. The rough roar
Shakes the brown tents on Ganges' trembling shore;
The waves of Indus from the banks recoil;
And matrons, howling on the strand of Nile,
By the pale moon, their absent sons deplore:
Long shall they wail; their sons return no more.

"Ah, strike the notes of woe!" the siren cries;
"A dreary vision swims before my eyes.
To Tagus' shore triumphant as he bends,
Low in the dust the hero's glory ends:
Though bended bow, nor thund'ring engine's hail,
Nor Egypt's sword, nor India's spear prevail,
Fall shall the chief before a naked foe,
Rough clubs and rude-hurl'ed stones shall strike the blow;
The Cape of Tempests shall his tomb supply,
And in the desert sands his bones shall lie,
No boastful trophy o'er his ashes rear'd:
Such Heav'n's dread will, and be that will rever'd!

"But lo, resplendent shines another star,"
Loud she resounds, "in all the blaze of war!
Great Cunia[602] guards Melinda's friendly shore,
And dyes her seas with Oja's hostile gore;

Lamo and Brava's tow'rs his vengeance tell:
Green Madagascar's flow'ry dales shall swell
His echo'd fame, till ocean's southmost bound
On isles and shores unknown his name resound.

"Another blaze, behold, of fire and arms!
Great Albuquerque awakes the dread alarms:
O'er Ormuz' walls his thund'ring flames he pours,
While Heav'n, the hero's guide, indignant show'rs
Their arrows backwards[603] on the Persian foe,
Tearing the breasts and arms that twang'd the bow.
Mountains of salt and fragrant gums in vain
Were spent untainted to embalm the slain.
Such heaps shall strew the seas and faithless strand
Of Gerum, Mazcate,[604] and Calayat's land,
Till faithless Ormuz own the Lusian sway,
And Barem's[605] pearls her yearly safety pay.

"What glorious palms on Goa's isle I see,[606]
Their blossoms spread, great Albuquerque, for thee!
Through castled walls the hero breaks his way,
And opens with his sword the dread array
Of Moors and pagans; through their depth he rides,
Through spears and show'ring fire the battle guides.
As bulls enrag'd, or lions smear'd with gore,
His bands sweep wide o'er Goa's purpled shore.
Nor eastward far though fair Malacca[607] lie,
Her groves embosom'd in the morning sky;
Though with her am'rous sons the valiant line
Of Java's isle in battle rank combine,
Though poison'd shafts their pond'rous quivers store;
Malacca's spicy groves and golden ore,
Great Albuquerque, thy dauntless toils shall crown!
Yet art thou stain'd."[608] Here, with a sighful frown,
The goddess paus'd, for much remain'd unsung,
But blotted with a humble soldier's wrong.
"Alas," she cries, "when war's dread horrors reign,
And thund'ring batteries rock the fiery plain,
When ghastly famine on a hostile soil,
When pale disease attends on weary toil,
When patient under all the soldier stands,
Detested be the rage which then demands
The humble soldier's blood, his only crime
The am'rous frailty of the youthful prime!
Incest's cold horror here no glow restrain'd,
Nor sacred nuptial bed was here profan'd,
Nor here unwelcome force the virgin seiz'd;
A slave, lascivious, in his fondling pleas'd,

Resigns her breast. Ah, stain to Lusian fame!
('Twas lust of blood, perhaps 'twas jealous flame;)
The leader's rage, unworthy of the brave,
Consigns the youthful soldier to the grave.
Not Ammon[609] thus Apelles' love repaid,
Great Ammon's bed resign'd the lovely maid;
Nor Cyrus thus reprov'd Araspas' fire;
Nor haughtier Carlo thus assum'd the sire,
Though iron Baldwin to his daughter's bower,
An ill-match'd lover, stole in secret hour:
With nobler rage the lofty monarch glow'd,
And Flandria's earldom on the knight bestow'd."[610]

Again the nymph the song of fame resounds:
"Lo, sweeping wide o'er Ethiopia's bounds,
Wide o'er Arabia's purple shore, on high
The Lusian ensigns blaze along the sky:
Mecca, aghast, beholds the standards shine,
And midnight horror shakes Medina's shrine;[611]
Th' unhallow'd altar bodes th' approaching foe,
Foredoom'd in dust its prophet's tomb to strew.
Nor Ceylon's isle, brave Soarez, shall withhold
Its incense, precious as the burnish'd gold,
What time o'er proud Columbo's loftiest spire
Thy flag shall blaze: Nor shall th' immortal lyre
Forget thy praise, Sequeyra! To the shore
Where Sheba's sapient queen the sceptre bore,[612]
Braving the Red Sea's dangers shalt thou force
To Abyssinia's realm thy novel course;
And isles, by jealous Nature long conceal'd,
Shall to the wond'ring world be now reveal'd.
Great Menez next the Lusian sword shall bear;
Menez, the dread of Afric, high shall rear
His victor lance, till deep shall Ormuz groan,
And tribute doubled her revolt atone.

"Now shines thy glory in meridian height"—
And loud her voice she rais'd—"O matchless knight!
Thou, thou, illustrious GAMA, thou shalt bring
The olive bough of peace, deputed king!
The lands by thee discover'd shall obey
Thy sceptred power, and bless thy regal sway.
But India's crimes, outrageous to the skies,
A length of these Saturnian days denies:
Snatch'd from thy golden throne,[613] the heav'ns shall claim
Thy deathless soul, the world thy deathless name.

"Now o'er the coast of faithless Malabar

Victorious Henry[614] pours the rage of war;
Nor less the youth a nobler strife shall wage,
Great victor of himself though green in age;
No restless slave of wanton am'rous fire,
No lust of gold shall taint his gen'rous ire.
While youth's bold pulse beats high, how brave the boy
Whom harlot-smiles nor pride of power decoy!
Immortal be his name! Nor less thy praise,
Great Mascarene,[615] shall future ages raise:
Though power, unjust, withhold the splendid ray
That dignifies the crest of sov'reign sway,
Thy deeds, great chief, on Bintam's humbled shore
(Deeds such as Asia never view'd before)
Shall give thy honest fame a brighter blaze
Than tyrant pomp in golden robes displays.
Though bold in war the fierce usurper shine,
Though Cutial's potent navy o'er the brine
Drive vanquish'd: though the Lusian Hector's sword
For him reap conquest, and confirm him lord;
Thy deeds, great peer, the wonder of thy foes,
Thy glorious chains unjust, and gen'rous woes,
Shall dim the fierce Sampayo's fairest fame,
And o'er his honours thine aloud proclaim.
Thy gen'rous woes! Ah gallant injur'd chief,
Not thy own sorrows give the sharpest grief.
Thou seest the Lusian name her honours stain,
And lust of gold her heroes' breasts profane;
Thou seest ambition lift the impious head,
Nor God's red arm, nor ling'ring justice dread;
O'er India's bounds thou seest these vultures prowl,
Full gorged with blood, and dreadless of control;
Thou seest and weepst thy country's blotted name,
The gen'rous sorrow thine, but not the shame.
Nor long the Lusian ensigns stain'd remain:
Great Nunio[616] comes, and razes every stain.
Though lofty Calè's warlike towers he rear;
Though haughty Melic groan beneath his spear;
All these, and Diu yielded to his name,
Are but th' embroid'ry of his nobler fame.
Far haughtier foes of Lusian race he braves;
The awful sword of justice high he waves:
Before his bar the injur'd Indian stands,
And justice boldly on his foe demands,
The Lusian foe; in wonder lost, the Moor
Beholds proud rapine's vulture grip restore;
Beholds the Lusian hands in fetters bound
By Lusian hands, and wound repaid for wound.
Oh, more shall thus by Nunio's worth be won,

Than conquest reaps from high-plum'd hosts o'erthrown.
Long shall the gen'rous Nunio's blissful sway
Command supreme. In Dio's hopeless day
The sov'reign toil the brave Noronha takes,   }
Awed by his fame[617] the fierce-soul'd Rumien shakes,   }
And Dio's open'd walls in sudden flight forsakes.   }
A son of thine, O GAMA,[618] now shall hold
The helm of empire, prudent, wise, and bold:
Malacca sav'd and strengthen'd by his arms,
The banks of Tor shall echo his alarms;
His worth shall bless the kingdoms of the morn,
For all thy virtues shall his soul adorn.
When fate resigns thy hero to the skies,
A vet'ran, fam'd on Brazil's shore[619] shall rise:
The wide Atlantic and the Indian main,
By turns, shall own the terrors of his reign.
His aid the proud Cambayan king implores,
His potent aid Cambaya's king restores.
The dread Mogul with all his thousands flies,
And Dio's towers are Souza's well-earn'd prize.
Nor less the zamorim o'er blood-stain'd ground[620]
Shall speed his legions, torn with many a wound,
In headlong rout. Nor shall the boastful pride
Of India's navy, though the shaded tide
Around the squadron'd masts appear the down
Of some wide forest, other fate renown.
Loud rattling through the hills of Cape Camore[621]
I hear the tempest of the battle roar!
Clung to the splinter'd masts I see the dead
Badala's shore with horrid wreck bespread;
Baticala inflam'd by treach'rous hate,
Provokes the horrors of Badala's fate:
Her seas in blood, her skies enwrapt in fire,
Confess the sweeping storm of Souza's ire.
No hostile spear now rear'd on sea or strand,
The awful sceptre graces Souza's hand;
Peaceful he reigns, in counsel just and wise;
And glorious Castro now his throne supplies:
Castro, the boast of gen'rous fame, afar
From Dio's strand shall sway the glorious war.
Madd'ning with rage to view the Lusian band,
A troop so few, proud Dio's towers command,
The cruel Ethiop Moor to heav'n complains,
And the proud Persian's languid zeal arraigns.
The Rumien fierce, who boasts the name of Rome,[622]
With these conspires, and vows the Lusians' doom.
A thousand barb'rous nations join their powers
To bathe with Lusian blood the Dion towers.

Dark rolling sheets, forth belch'd from brazen wombs,
And bor'd, like show'ring clouds, with hailing bombs,
O'er Dio's sky spread the black shades of death;
The mine's dread earthquakes shake the ground beneath.
No hope, bold Mascarene,[623] mayst thou respire,
A glorious fall alone, thy just desire.
When lo, his gallant son brave Castro sends—
Ah heav'n, what fate the hapless youth attends!
In vain the terrors of his falchion glare:
The cavern'd mine bursts, high in pitchy air
Rampire and squadron whirl'd convulsive, borne
To heav'n, the hero dies in fragments torn.
His loftiest bough though fall'n, the gen'rous sire
His living hope devotes with Roman ire.
On wings of fury flies the brave Alvar
Through oceans howling with the wintry war,
Through skies of snow his brother's vengeance bears;
And, soon in arms, the valiant sire appears:
Before him vict'ry spreads her eagle wing
Wide sweeping o'er Cambaya's haughty king.
In vain his thund'ring coursers shake the ground,
Cambaya bleeding of his might's last wound
Sinks pale in dust: fierce Hydal-Kan[624] in vain
Wakes war on war; he bites his iron chain.
O'er Indus' banks, o'er Ganges' smiling vales,
No more the hind his plunder'd field bewails:
O'er ev'ry field, O Peace, thy blossoms glow,
The golden blossoms of thy olive bough;
Firm bas'd on wisest laws great Castro crowns,
And the wide East the Lusian empire owns.

"These warlike chiefs, the sons of thy renown,
And thousands more, O VASCO, doom'd to crown
Thy glorious toils, shall through these seas unfold
Their victor-standards blaz'd with Indian gold;
And in the bosom of our flow'ry isle,
Embath'd in joy shall o'er their labours smile.
Their nymphs like yours, their feast divine the same,
The raptur'd foretaste of immortal fame."

So sang the goddess, while the sister train
With joyful anthem close the sacred strain:
"Though Fortune from her whirling sphere bestow
Her gifts capricious in unconstant flow,
Yet laurell'd honour and immortal fame
Shall ever constant grace the Lusian name."
So sung the joyful chorus, while around
The silver roofs the lofty notes resound.

The song prophetic, and the sacred feast,
Now shed the glow of strength through ev'ry breast.
When with the grace and majesty divine,
Which round immortals when enamour'd shine,
To crown the banquet of their deathless fame,
To happy GAMA thus the sov'reign dame:
"O lov'd of Heav'n, what never man before,
What wand'ring science never might explore,
By Heav'n's high will, with mortal eyes to see
Great nature's face unveil'd, is given to thee.
Thou and thy warriors follow where I lead:
Firm be your steps, for arduous to the tread,
Through matted brakes of thorn and brier, bestrew'd
With splinter'd flint, winds the steep slipp'ry road."
She spake, and smiling caught the hero's hand,
And on the mountain's summit soon they stand;
A beauteous lawn with pearl enamell'd o'er,
Emerald and ruby, as the gods of yore
Had sported here. Here in the fragrant air
A wondrous globe appear'd, divinely fair!
Through ev'ry part the light transparent flow'd,
And in the centre, as the surface, glow'd.
The frame ethereal various orbs compose,
In whirling circles now they fell, now rose;
Yet never rose nor fell,[625] for still the same
Was ev'ry movement of the wondrous frame;
Each movement still beginning, still complete,
Its author's type, self-pois'd, perfection's seat.

Great VASCO, thrill'd with reverential awe,
And rapt with keen desire, the wonder saw.
The goddess mark'd the language of his eyes,
"And here," she cried, "thy largest wish suffice."
Great nature's fabric thou dost here behold,
Th' ethereal, pure, and elemental mould
In pattern shown complete, as nature's God
Ordain'd the world's great frame, His dread abode;
For ev'ry part the Power Divine pervades,
The sun's bright radiance, and the central shades;
Yet, let not haughty reason's bounded line
Explore the boundless God, or where define,
Where in Himself, in uncreated light
(While all His worlds around seem wrapp'd in night),
He holds His loftiest state.[626] By primal laws
Impos'd on Nature's birth (Himself the cause),
By her own ministry, through ev'ry maze,
Nature in all her walks, unseen, He sways.
These spheres behold;[627] the first in wide embrace

Surrounds the lesser orbs of various face;
The Empyrean this, the holiest heav'n
To the pure spirits of the bless'd is giv'n:
No mortal eye its splendid rays may bear,
No mortal bosom feel the raptures there.
The earth, in all her summer pride array'd,
To this might seem a drear sepulchral shade.
Unmov'd it stands; within its shining frame,
In motion swifter than the lightning's flame,
Swifter than sight the moving parts may spy,
Another sphere whirls round its rapid sky.
Hence motion darts its force,[628] impulsive draws,
And on the other orbs impresses laws;
The sun's bright car attentive to its force
Gives night and day, and shapes his yearly course;
Its force stupendous asks a pond'rous sphere
To poise its fury, and its weight to bear:
Slow moves that pond'rous orb; the stiff, slow pace
One step scarce gains, while wide his annual race
Two hundred times the sun triumphant rides;
The crystal heav'n is this, whose rigour guides
And binds the starry sphere:[629] That sphere behold,
With diamonds spangled, and emblaz'd with gold!
What radiant orbs that azure sky adorn,
Fair o'er the night in rapid motion borne!
Swift as they trace the heav'n's wide circling line,
Whirl'd on their proper axles, bright they shine.
Wide o'er this heav'n a golden belt displays
Twelve various forms; behold the glitt'ring blaze!
Through these the sun in annual journey towers,
And o'er each clime their various tempers pours;
In gold and silver of celestial mine
How rich far round the constellations shine!
Lo, bright emerging o'er the polar tides,
In shining frost the Northern Chariot rides;[630]
Mid treasur'd snows here gleams the grisly Bear,
And icy flakes incrust his shaggy hair.
Here fair Andromeda, of heav'n belov'd;
Her vengeful sire, and, by the gods reprov'd,
Beauteous Cassiope. Here, fierce and red,   }
Portending storms, Orion lifts his head;   }
And here the Dogs their raging fury shed.   }
The Swan, sweet melodist, in death he sings,
The milder Swan here spreads his silver wings.
Here Orpheus' Lyre, the melancholy Hare,
And here the watchful Dragon's eye-balls glare;
And Theseus' ship, oh, less renown'd than thine,
Shall ever o'er these skies illustrious shine.

Beneath this radiant firmament behold
The various planets in their orbits roll'd:
Here, in cold twilight, hoary Saturn rides;
Here Jove shines mild, here fiery Mars presides;
Apollo here, enthron'd in light, appears
The eye of heav'n, emblazer of the spheres;
Beneath him beauteous glows the Queen of Love—
The proudest hearts her sacred influence prove;
Here Hermes, fam'd for eloquence divine,
And here Diana's various faces shine;
Lowest she rides, and, through the shadowy night,
Pours on the glist'ning earth her silver light.
These various orbs, behold, in various speed
Pursue the journeys at their birth decreed.
Now, from the centre far impell'd they fly,
Now, nearer earth they sail a lower sky,
A shorten'd course: Such are their laws impress'd
By God's dread will,[631] that will for ever best.

"The yellow earth, the centre of the whole,
There lordly rests sustain'd on either pole.
The limpid air enfolds in soft embrace
The pond'rous orb, and brightens o'er her face.
Here, softly floating o'er th' aërial blue,
Fringed with the purple and the golden hue,
The fleecy clouds their swelling sides display;
From whence, fermented by the sulph'rous ray,
The lightnings blaze, and heat spreads wide and rare;
And now, in fierce embrace with frozen air,
Their wombs, compress'd, soon feel parturient throws,
And white wing'd gales bear wide the teeming snows.
Thus, cold and heat their warring empires hold,
Averse yet mingling, each by each controll'd,
The highest air and ocean's bed they pierce,
And earth's dark centre feels their struggles fierce.

"The seat of man, the earth's fair breast, behold;
Here wood-crown'd islands wave their locks of gold.
Here spread wide continents their bosoms green,
And hoary Ocean heaves his breast between.
Yet, not th' inconstant ocean's furious tide
May fix the dreadful bounds of human pride.
What madd'ning seas between these nations roar!
Yet Lusus' hero-race shall visit ev'ry shore.
What thousand tribes, whom various customs sway,
And various rites, these countless shores display!
Queen of the world, supreme in shining arms,
Hers ev'ry art, and hers all wisdom's charms,

Each nation's tribute round her foot-stool spread,
Here Christian Europe[632] lifts the regal head.
Afric behold,[633] alas, what alter'd view!
Her lands uncultur'd, and her son's untrue;
Ungraced with all that sweetens human life,
Savage and fierce they roam in brutal strife;
Eager they grasp the gifts which culture yields,
Yet, naked roam their own neglected fields.
Lo, here enrich'd with hills of golden ore,
Monomotapa's empire hems the shore.
There round the Cape, great Afric's dreadful bound,
Array'd in storms (by you first compass'd round),
Unnumber'd tribes as bestial grazers stray,
By laws unform'd, unform'd by reason's sway:
Far inward stretch the mournful sterile dales,
Where, on the parch'd hill-side, pale Famine wails.
On gold in vain the naked savage treads;
Low, clay-built huts, behold, and reedy sheds,
Their dreary towns. Gonzalo's zeal shall glow[634]
To these dark minds the path of light to show:
His toils to humanize the barb'rous mind
Shall, with the martyr's palms, his holy temples bind.
Great Naya,[635] too, shall glorious here display
His God's dread might: behold, in black array,
Num'rous and thick as when in evil hour
The feather'd race whole harvest fields devour,
So thick, so num'rous round Sofála's towers
Her barb'rous hordes remotest Africa pours:
In vain; Heav'n's vengeance on their souls impress'd,
They fly, wide scatter'd as the driving mist.
Lo, Quama there, and there the fertile Nile
Curs'd with that gorging fiend, the crocodile,
Wind their long way: the parent lake behold,
Great Nilus' fount, unseen, unknown of old,
From whence, diffusing plenty as he glides,
Wide Abyssinia's realm the stream divides.
In Abyssinia Heav'n's own altars blaze,[636]
And hallow'd anthems chant Messiah's praise.
In Nile's wide breast the isle of Měrŏē see!
Near these rude shores a hero sprung from thee,
Thy son, brave GAMA,[637] shall his lineage show
In glorious triumphs o'er the paynim[638] foe.
There by the rapid Ob her friendly breast
Melinda spreads, thy place of grateful rest.
Cape Aromata there the gulf defends,
Where by the Red Sea wave great Afric ends.
Illustrious Suez, seat of heroes old,
Fam'd Hierapolis, high-tower'd, behold.

Here Egypt's shelter'd fleets at anchor ride,
And hence, in squadrons, sweep the eastern tide.
And lo, the waves that aw'd by Moses' rod,
While the dry bottom Israel's armies trod,
On either hand roll'd back their frothy might,
And stood, like hoary rocks, in cloudy height.
Here Asia, rich in ev'ry precious mine,
In realms immense, begins her western line.
Sinai behold, whose trembling cliffs of yore
In fire and darkness, deep pavilion'd, bore
The Hebrews' God, while day, with awful brow,
Gleam'd pale on Israel's wand'ring tents below.
The pilgrim now the lonely hill ascends,
And, when the ev'ning raven homeward bends,
Before the virgin-martyr's tomb[639] he pays
His mournful vespers, and his vows of praise.
Jidda behold, and Aden's parch'd domain
Girt by Arzira's rock, where never rain
Yet fell from heav'n; where never from the dale
The crystal riv'let murmur'd to the vale.
The three Arabias here their breasts unfold,
Here breathing incense, here a rocky wold;
O'er Dofar's plain the richest incense breathes,
That round the sacred shrine its vapour wreathes;
Here the proud war-steed glories in his force,
As, fleeter than the gale, he holds the course.
Here, with his spouse and household lodg'd in wains,
The Arab's camp shifts, wand'ring o'er the plains,
The merchant's dread, what time from eastern soil
His burthen'd camels seek the land of Nile.
Here Rosalgate and Farthac stretch their arms,
And point to Ormuz, fam'd for war's alarms;
Ormuz, decreed full oft to quake with dread
Beneath the Lusian heroes' hostile tread,
Shall see the Turkish moons,[640] with slaughter gor'd,
Shrink from the lightning of De Branco's sword.[641]
There on the gulf that laves the Persian shore,
Far through the surges bends Cape Asabore.
There Barem's isle;[642] her rocks with diamonds blaze,
And emulate Aurora's glitt'ring rays.
From Barem's shore Euphrates' flood is seen,
And Tigris' waters, through the waves of green
In yellowy currents many a league extend,
As with the darker waves averse they blend.
Lo, Persia there her empire wide unfolds!
In tented camp his state the monarch holds:
Her warrior sons disdain the arms of fire,[643]
And, with the pointed steel, to fame aspire;

Their springy shoulders stretching to the blow,
Their sweepy sabres hew the shrieking foe.
There Gerum's isle the hoary ruin wears
Where Time has trod:[644] there shall the dreadful spears
Of Sousa and Menezes strew the shore
With Persian sabres, and embathe with gore.
Carpella's cape, and sad Carmania's strand,
There, parch'd and bare, their dreary wastes expand.
A fairer landscape here delights the view;
From these green hills beneath the clouds of blue,
The Indus and the Ganges roll the wave,
And many a smiling field propitious lave.
Luxurious here, Ulcinda's harvests smile,
And here, disdainful of the seaman's toil,
The whirling tides of Jaquet furious roar;
Alike their rage when swelling to the shore,
Or, tumbling backward to the deep, they force
The boiling fury of their gulfy course:
Against their headlong rage nor oars nor sails,
The stemming prow alone, hard toil'd, prevails.
Cambaya here begins her wide domain;
A thousand cities here shall own the reign
Of Lisboa's monarchs. He who first shall crown
Thy labours, GAMA,[645] here shall boast his own.
The length'ning sea that washes India's strand
And laves the cape that points to Ceylon's land
(The Taprobanian isle,[646] renown'd of yore),
Shall see his ensigns blaze from shore to shore.
Behold how many a realm, array'd in green,
The Ganges' shore and Indus' bank between!
Here tribes unnumber'd, and of various lore,
With woful penance fiend-like shapes adore;
Some Macon's orgies;[647] all confess the sway
Of rites that shun, like trembling ghosts, the day.
Narsinga's fair domain behold; of yore
Here shone the gilded towers of Meliapore.
Here India's angels, weeping o'er the tomb
Where Thomas sleeps,[648] implore the day to come,
The day foretold, when India's utmost shore
Again shall hear Messiah's blissful lore.
By Indus' banks the holy prophet trod,
And Ganges heard him preach the Saviour-God;
Where pale disease erewhile the cheek consum'd,
Health, at his word, in ruddy fragrance bloom'd;
The grave's dark womb his awful voice obey'd,
And to the cheerful day restor'd the dead;
By heavenly power he rear'd the sacred shrine,
And gain'd the nations by his life divine.

The priests of Brahma's hidden rites beheld,
And envy's bitt'rest gall their bosom's swell'd.
A thousand deathful snares in vain they spread;
When now the chief who wore the triple thread,[649]
Fir'd by the rage that gnaws the conscious breast
Of holy fraud, when worth shines forth confess'd,
Hell he invokes, nor hell in vain he sues;
His son's life-gore his wither'd hands imbrues;
Then, bold assuming the vindictive ire,
And all the passions of the woful sire,
Weeping, he bends before the Indian throne,
Arraigns the holy man, and wails his son:
A band of hoary priests attest the deed,
And India's king condemns the seer to bleed.
Inspir'd by Heav'n the holy victim stands,
And o'er the murder'd corse extends his hands:
'In God's dread power, thou slaughter'd youth, arise,
And name,thy murderer,' aloud he cries.
When, dread to view, the deep wounds instant close,
And, fresh in life, the slaughter'd youth arose,
And nam'd his treach'rous sire. The conscious air
Quiver'd, and awful horror raised the hair
On ev'ry head. From Thomas India's king
The holy sprinkling of the living spring
Receives, and wide o'er all his regal bounds
The God of Thomas ev'ry tongue resounds.
Long taught the holy seer the words of life;
The priests of Brahma still to deeds of strife
(So boil'd their ire) the blinded herd impell'd,
And high, to deathful rage, their rancour swell'd.
'Twas on a day, when melting on his tongue
Heav'n's offer'd mercies glow'd, the impious throng,
Rising in madd'ning tempest, round him shower'd
The splinter'd flint; in vain the flint was pour'd:
But Heav'n had now his finish'd labours seal'd;
His angel guards withdraw the etherial shield;
A Brahmin's javelin tears his holy breast—
Ah Heav'n, what woes the widow'd land express'd!
Thee, Thomas, thee, the plaintive Ganges mourn'd,[650]
And Indus' banks the murm'ring moan return'd;
O'er ev'ry valley where thy footsteps stray'd,
The hollow winds the gliding sighs convey'd.
What woes the mournful face of India wore,
These woes in living pangs his people bore.
His sons, to whose illumin'd minds he gave
To view the ray that shines beyond the grave,
His pastoral sons bedew'd his corse with tears,
While high triumphant through the heav'nly spheres,

With songs of joy, the smiling angels wing
His raptur'd spirit to the eternal King.
O you, the followers of the holy seer,
Foredoom'd the shrines of Heav'n's own lore to rear,
You, sent by Heav'n his labours to renew,
Like him, ye Lusians, simplest Truth pursue.[651]
Vain is the impious toil, with borrow'd grace,
To deck one feature of her angel face;
Behind the veil's broad glare she glides away,
And leaves a rotten form, of lifeless, painted clay.

"Much have you view'd of future Lusian reign;
Broad empires yet, and kingdoms wide, remain,
Scenes of your future toils and glorious sway—
And lo, how wide expands the Gangic bay!
Narsinga here in num'rous legions bold,
And here Oryxa boasts her cloth of gold.
The Ganges here in many a stream divides,   }
Diffusing plenty from his fatt'ning tides,   }
As through Bengala's rip'ning vales he glides;   }
Nor may the fleetest hawk, untir'd, explore
Where end the ricy groves that crown the shore.
There view what woes demand your pious aid!
On beds and litters, o'er the margin laid,
The dying[652] lift their hollow eyes, and crave
Some pitying hand to hurl them in the wave.
Thus Heav'n (they deem), though vilest guilt they bore
Unwept, unchanged, will view that guilt no more.
There, eastward, Arracan her line extends;
And Pegu's mighty empire southward bends:
Pegu, whose sons (so held old faith) confess'd
A dog their sire;[653] their deeds the tale attest.
A pious queen their horrid rage restrain'd;[654]
Yet, still their fury Nature's God arraign'd.
Ah, mark the thunders rolling o'er the sky;
Yes, bath'd in gore, shall rank pollution lie.

"Where to the morn the towers of Tava shine,
Begins great Siam's empire's far-stretch'd line.
On Queda's fields the genial rays inspire
The richest gust of spicery's fragrant fire.
Malacca's castled harbour here survey,
The wealthful seat foredoom'd of Lusian sway.
Here to their port the Lusian fleets shall steer,
From ev'ry shore far round assembling here
The fragrant treasures of the eastern world:
Here from the shore by rolling earthquakes hurl'd,
Through waves all foam, Sumatra's isle was riv'n,

And, mid white whirlpools, down the ocean driv'n.[655]
To this fair isle, the golden Chersonese,
Some deem the sapient monarch plough'd the seas;
Ophir its Tyrian name.[656] In whirling roars
How fierce the tide boils down these clasping shores!
High from the strait the length'ning coast afar
Its moonlike curve points to the northern star,
Opening its bosom to the silver ray
When fair Aurora pours the infant day.
Patane and Pam, and nameless nations more,
Who rear their tents on Menam's winding shore,
Their vassal tribute yield to Siam's throne;
And thousands more,[657] of laws, of names unknown,
That vast of land inhabit. Proud and bold,
Proud of their numbers, here the Laos hold
The far-spread lawns; the skirting hills obey
The barb'rous Avas', and the Brahma's sway.
Lo, distant far, another mountain chain
Rears its rude cliffs, the Guio's dread domain;
Here brutaliz'd the human form is seen,
The manners fiend-like as the brutal mien:
With frothing jaws they suck the human blood,
And gnaw the reeking limbs,[658] their sweetest food;
Horrid, with figur'd seams of burning steel,
Their wolf-like frowns their ruthless lust reveal.
Cambaya there the blue-tinged Mecon laves,
Mecon the eastern Nile, whose swelling waves,
'Captain of rivers' nam'd, o'er many a clime,
In annual period, pour their fatt'ning slime.
The simple natives of these lawns believe
That other worlds the souls of beasts receive;[659]
Where the fierce murd'rer-wolf, to pains decreed,
Sees the mild lamb enjoy the heav'nly mead.
Oh gentle Mecon,[660] on thy friendly shore
Long shall the muse her sweetest off'rings pour!
When tyrant ire, chaf'd by the blended lust
Of pride outrageous, and revenge unjust,
Shall on the guiltless exile burst their rage,
And madd'ning tempests on their side engage,
Preserv'd by Heav'n the song of Lusian fame,
The song, O VASCO, sacred to thy name,
Wet from the whelming surge, shall triumph o'er
The fate of shipwreck on the Mecon's shore,
Here rest secure as on the muse's breast!
Happy the deathless song, the bard, alas, unblest!

"Chiampa there her fragrant coast extends,
There Cochin-China's cultur'd land ascends:

From Anam Bay begins the ancient reign
Of China's beauteous art-adorn'd domain;
Wide from the burning to the frozen skies,
O'erflow'd with wealth, the potent empire lies.
Here, ere the cannon's rage in Europe roar'd,[661]
The cannon's thunder on the foe was pour'd:
And here the trembling needle sought the north,
Ere Time in Europe brought the wonder forth.
No more let Egypt boast her mountain pyres;
To prouder fame yon bounding wall aspires,
A prouder boast of regal power displays
Than all the world beheld in ancient days.
Not built, created seems the frowning mound;   }
O'er loftiest mountain tops, and vales profound   }
Extends the wondrous length, with warlike castles crown'd.   }
Immense the northern wastes their horrors spread;[662]
In frost and snow the seas and shores are clad.
These shores forsake, to future ages due:
A world of islands claims thy happier view,
Where lavish Nature all her bounty pours,
And flowers and fruits of ev'ry fragrance showers.
Japan behold; beneath the globe's broad face
Northward she sinks, the nether seas embrace
Her eastern bounds; what glorious fruitage there,
Illustrious GAMA, shall thy labours bear!
How bright a silver mine![663] when Heav'n's own lore
From pagan dross shall purify her ore.

"Beneath the spreading wings of purple morn,
Behold what isles these glist'ning seas adorn!
'Mid hundreds yet unnam'd, Ternate behold!
By day, her hills in pitchy clouds inroll'd,
By night, like rolling waves, the sheets of fire
Blaze o'er the seas, and high to heav'n aspire.
For Lusian hands here blooms the fragrant clove,
But Lusian blood shall sprinkle ev'ry grove.
The golden birds that ever sail the skies
Here to the sun display their shining dyes,
Each want supplied, on air they ever soar;
The ground they touch not[664] till they breathe no more.
Here Banda's isles their fair embroid'ry spread
Of various fruitage, azure, white, and red;
And birds of ev'ry beauteous plume display
Their glitt'ring radiance, as, from spray to spray,
From bower to bower, on busy wings they rove,
To seize the tribute of the spicy grove.
Borneo here expands her ample breast,
By Nature's hand in woods of camphor dress'd;

The precious liquid, weeping from the trees,
Glows warm with health, the balsam of disease.
Fair are Timora's dales with groves array'd,
Each riv'let murmurs in the fragrant shade,
And, in its crystal breast, displays the bowers
Of Sanders, blest with health-restoring powers.
Where to the south the world's broad surface bends,
Lo, Sunda's realm her spreading arms extends.
From hence the pilgrim brings the wondrous tale,[665]
A river groaning through a dreary dale
(For all is stone around) converts to stone
Whate'er of verdure in its breast is thrown.
Lo, gleaming blue, o'er fair Sumatra's skies,
Another mountain's trembling flames arise;
Here from the trees the gum[666] all fragrance swells,
And softest oil a wondrous fountain wells.
Nor these alone the happy isle bestows,
Fine is her gold, her silk resplendent glows.
Wide forests there beneath Maldivia's tide[667]
From with'ring air their wondrous fruitage hide.
The green-hair'd Nereids, tend the bow'ry dells,
Whose wondrous fruitage poison's rage expels.
In Ceylon, lo, how high yon mountain's brows!
The sailing clouds its middle height enclose.
Holy the hill is deem'd, the hallow'd tread
Of sainted footstep[668] marks its rocky head.
Lav'd by the Red Sea gulf, Socotra's bowers
There boast the tardy aloe's beauteous flowers.
On Afric's strand, foredoom'd to Lusian sway,
Behold these isles, and rocks of dusky gray;
From cells unknown here bounteous ocean pours
The fragrant amber on the sandy shores.
And lo, the Island of the Moon[669] displays
Her vernal lawns, and num'rous peaceful bays:
The halcyons[670] hov'ring o'er the bays are seen,
And lowing herds adorn the vales of green.

"Thus, from the cape where sail was ne'er unfurl'd,
Till thine, auspicious, sought the eastern world,
To utmost wave, where first the morning star
Sheds the pale lustre of her silver car,
Thine eyes have view'd the empires and the isles,
The world immense, that crowns thy glorious toils—
That world where ev'ry boon is shower'd from Heav'n,
Now to the West, by thee, great chief, is giv'n.[671]

"And still, O blest, thy peerless honours grow,
New op'ning views the smiling fates bestow.

With alter'd face the moving globe behold;
There ruddy ev'ning sheds her beams of gold.
While now, on Afric's bosom faintly die
The last pale glimpses of the twilight sky,
Bright o'er the wide Atlantic rides the morn,
And dawning rays another world adorn:
To farthest north that world enormous bends,
And cold, beneath the southern pole-star ends.
Near either pole[672] the barb'rous hunter, dress'd
In skins of bears, explores the frozen waste:
Where smiles the genial sun with kinder rays,
Proud cities tower, and gold-roof'd temples blaze.
This golden empire, by the heav'n's decree,
Is due, Castile, O favour'd power, to thee!
Even now, Columbus o'er the hoary tide
Pursues the ev'ning sun, his navy's guide.
Yet, shall the kindred Lusian share the reign,
What time this world shall own the yoke of Spain.
The first bold hero[673] who to India's shores
Through vanquish'd waves thy open'd path explores,
Driv'n by the winds of heav'n from Afric's strand,
Shall fix the holy cross on yon fair land.
That mighty realm, for purple wood renown'd,
Shall stretch the Lusian empire's western bound.
Fir'd by thy fame, and with his king in ire,
To match thy deeds shall Magalhaens aspire.[674]
In all but loyalty, of Lusian soul,
No fear, no danger shall his toils control.
Along these regions, from the burning zone
To deepest south, he dares the course unknown.
While, to the kingdoms of the rising day,
To rival thee he holds the western way,
A land of giants[675] shall his eyes behold,
Of camel strength, surpassing human mould:
And, onward still, thy fame his proud heart's guide
Haunting him unappeas'd, the dreary tide
Beneath the southern star's cold gleam he braves,
And stems the whirls of land-surrounded waves.
For ever sacred to the hero's fame,
These foaming straits shall bear his deathless name.
Through these dread jaws of rock he presses on,
Another ocean's breast, immense, unknown,
Beneath the south's cold wings, unmeasur'd, wide,
Receives his vessels; through the dreary tide
In darkling shades, where never man before
Heard the waves howl, he dares the nameless shore.

"Thus far, O favour'd Lusians, bounteous Heav'n

Your nation's glories to your view has giv'n.
What ensigns, blazing to the morn, pursue
The path of heroes, open'd first by you!
Still be it yours the first in fame to shine:
Thus shall your brides new chaplets still entwine,
With laurels ever new your brows enfold,
And braid your wavy locks with radiant gold.

"How calm the waves, how mild the balmy gale!
The halcyons call; ye Lusians, spread the sail;
Old ocean, now appeas'd, shall rage no more.
Haste, point the bowsprit to your native shore:
Soon shall the transports of the natal soil
O'erwhelm, in bounding joy, the thoughts of ev'ry toil."

The goddess spake[676]; and VASCO wav'd his hand,
And soon the joyful heroes crowd the strand.
The lofty ships with deepen'd burthens prove
The various bounties of the Isle of Love.
Nor leave the youths their lovely brides behind,
In wedded bands, while time glides on, conjoin'd;
Fair as immortal fame in smiles array'd,
In bridal smiles, attends each lovely maid.
O'er India's sea, wing'd on by balmy gales
That whisper'd peace, soft swell'd the steady sails:
Smooth as on wing unmov'd the eagle flies,
When to his eyrie cliff he sails the skies,
Swift o'er the gentle billows of the tide,
So smooth, so soft, the prows of GAMA glide;
And now their native fields, for ever dear,
In all their wild transporting charms appear;
And Tago's bosom, while his banks repeat
The sounding peals of joy, receives the fleet.
With orient titles and immortal fame
The hero band adorn their monarch's name;
Sceptres and crowns beneath his feet they lay,
And the wide East is doom'd to Lusian sway.[677]

Enough, my muse, thy wearied wing no more
Must to the seat of Jove triumphant soar.
Chill'd by my nation's cold neglect, thy fires
Glow bold no more, and all thy rage expires.
Yet thou, Sebastian, thou, my king, attend;
Behold what glories on thy throne descend!
Shall haughty Gaul or sterner Albion boast
That all the Lusian fame in thee is lost!
Oh, be it thine these glories to renew,
And John's bold path and Pedro's course pursue:[678]

Snatch from the tyrant-noble's hand the sword,
And be the rights of humankind restor'd.
The statesman prelate to his vows confine,
Alone auspicious at the holy shrine;
The priest, in whose meek heart Heav'n pours its fires,
Alone to Heav'n, not earth's vain pomp, aspires.
Nor let the muse, great king, on Tago's shore,
In dying notes the barb'rous age deplore.
The king or hero to the muse unjust
Sinks as the nameless slave, extinct in dust.
But such the deeds thy radiant morn portends,
Aw'd by thy frown ev'n now old Atlas bends
His hoary head, and Ampeluza's fields
Expect thy sounding steeds and rattling shields.
And shall these deeds unsung, unknown, expire!
Oh, would thy smiles relume my fainting ire!
I, then inspir'd, the wond'ring world should see
Great Ammon's warlike son reviv'd in thee;
Reviv'd, unenvied[679] of the muse's flame
That o'er the world resounds Pelides'[680] name.
"O let th' Iambic Muse revenge that wrong
Which cannot slumber in thy sheets of lead;
Let thy abused honour crie as long
As there be quills to write, or eyes to reade:
On his rank name let thine own votes be turn'd,
Oh may that man that hath the Muses scorn'd
Alive, nor dead, be ever of a Muse adorn'd."

THE END

FOOTNOTES

The numbering continues from PART I – Books I-V

[401] Every display of eastern luxury and magnificence was lavished in the fishing parties on the Nile,
with which Cleopatra amused Mark Antony, when at any time he showed symptoms of uneasiness, or
seemed inclined to abandon the effeminate life which he led with his mistress. At one of these parties,
Mark Antony, having procured divers to put fishes upon his hooks while under the water, he very
gallantly boasted to his mistress of his great dexterity in angling. Cleopatra perceived his art, and as
gallantly outwitted him. Some other divers received her orders, and in a little while Mark Antony's line
brought up a fried fish in place of a live one, to the vast entertainment of the queen, and all the convivial
company. Octavius was at this time on his march to decide who should be master of the world.

[402] The friendship of the Portuguese and Melindians was of long continuance. Alvaro Cabral, the
second admiral who made the voyage to India, in an engagement with the Moors off the coast of Sofala,
took two ships richly freighted from the mines of that country. On finding that Xeques Fonteyma, the
commander, was uncle to the King of Melinda, he restored the valuable prize, and treated him with the

utmost courtesy. Their good offices were reciprocal. By the information of the King of Melinda, Cabral escaped the treachery of the King of Calicut. The Kings of Mombaz and Quiloa, irritated at the alliance with Portugal, made several depredations on the subjects of Melinda, who in return were effectually revenged by their European allies.

[403] A giant.

[404] Two gods contending.—According to the fable, Neptune and Minerva disputed the honour of giving a name to the city of Athens. They agreed to determine the contest by a display of their wisdom and power, in conferring the most beneficial gift on mankind. Neptune struck the earth with his trident and produced the horse, whose bounding motions are emblematical of the agitation of the sea. Pallas commanded the olive-tree, the symbol of peace, and of riches, to spring forth. The victory was adjudged to the goddess, from whom the city was named Athens. The taste of the ancient Grecians clothed almost every occurrence in mythological allegory. The founders of Athens, it is most probable, disputed whether their new city should be named from the fertility of the soil or from the marine situation of Attica. The former opinion prevailed, and the town received its name in honour of the goddess of the olive-tree—Athēnē.

[405] While Pallas here appears to wave her hand.—As Neptune struck the earth with his trident, Minerva, says the fable, struck the earth with her lance. That she waved her hand while the olive boughs spread, is a fine poetical attitude, and varies the picture from that of Neptune, which follows.

[406] Though wide, and various, o'er the sculptur'd stone.—The description of palaces is a favourite topic several times touched upon by the two great masters of epic poetry, in which they have been happily imitated by their three greatest disciples among the moderns, Camoëns, Tasso, and Milton. The description of the palace of Neptune has great merit. Nothing can be more in place than the picture of chaos and the four elements. The war of the gods, and the contest of Neptune and Minerva are touched with the true boldness of poetical colouring. To show to the English reader that the Portuguese poet is, in his manner, truly classical, is the intention of many of these notes.

[407] Bacchus.

[408] The description of Triton, who, as Fanshaw says—

"Was a great nasty clown,"

is in the style of the classics. His parentage is differently related. Hesiod makes him the son of Neptune and Amphitrité. By Triton, in the physical sense of the fable, is meant the noise, and by Salacé, the mother by some ascribed to him, the salt of the ocean. The origin of the fable of Triton, it is probable, was founded on the appearance of a sea animal, which, according to some ancient naturalists, in the upward parts resembles the human figure. Pausanias relates a wonderful story of a monstrously large one, which often came ashore on the meadows of Bœotia. Over his head was a kind of finny cartilage, which, at a distance, appeared like hair; the body covered with brown scales; the nose and ears like the human; the mouth of a dreadful width, jagged with the teeth of a panther; the eyes of a greenish hue; the hands divided into fingers, the nails of which were crooked, and of a shelly substance. This monster, whose extremities ended in a tail like a dolphin's, devoured both men and beasts as they chanced in his way. The citizens of Tanagra, at last, contrived his destruction. They set a large vessel full of wine on the sea shore. Triton got drunk with it, and fell into a profound sleep, in which condition the Tanagrians beheaded him, and afterwards, with great propriety, hung up his body in the temple of Bacchus; where, says Pausanias, it continued a long time.

[409] A shell of purple on his head he bore.—In the Portuguese—

Na cabeça por gorra tinha posta
Huma mui grandé casco de lagosta.

Thus rendered by Fanshaw—

"He had (for a montera[413]) on his crown
The shell of a red lobster overgrown."

[410] Neptune.

[411] And changeful Proteus, whose prophetic mind.—The fullest and best account of the fable of Proteus is in the fourth Odyssey.

[412] Thetis.

[413] Montera, the Spanish word for a huntsman's cap.

[414] She who the rage of Athamas to shun.—Ino, the daughter of Cadmus and Hermione, and second spouse of Athamas, king of Thebes. The fables of her fate are various. That which Camoëns follows is the most common. Athamas, seized with madness, imagined that his spouse was a lioness, and her two sons young lions. In this frenzy he slew Learchus, and drove the mother and her other son, Melicertus, into the sea. The corpse of the mother was thrown ashore on Megara and that of the son at Corinth. They were afterwards deified, the one as a sea goddess, the other as the god of harbours.

[415] And Glaucus lost to joy.—A fisherman, says the fable, who, on eating a certain herb, was turned into a sea god. Circé was enamoured of him, and in revenge of her slighted love, poisoned the fountain where his mistress usually bathed. By the force of the enchantment the favoured Scylla was changed into a hideous monster, whose loins were surrounded with the ever-barking heads of dogs and wolves. Scylla, on this, threw herself into the sea, and was metamorphosed into the rock which bears her name. The rock Scylla at a distance appears like the statue of a woman. The furious dashing of the waves in the cavities, which are level with the water, resembles the barking of wolves and dogs.

[416] Thyoneus, a name of Bacchus.

[417] High from the roof the living amber glows.—

"From the arched roof,
Pendent by subtle magic, many a row
Of starry lamps, and blazing cressets, fed
With naptha and asphaltus, yielded light
As from a sky."
MILTON.

[418] The Titans.

[419] The north wind.

[420] And rent the Mynian sails.—The sails of the Argonauts, inhabitants of Mynia.

[421] See the first note on the first book of the Lusiad.

[422]
In haughty England, where the winter spreads
His snowy mantle o'er the shining meads.—

In the original—

Là na grande Inglaterra, que de neve
Boreal sempre abunda;

that is, "In illustrious England, always covered with northern snow." Though the translator was willing to retain the manner of Homer, he thought it proper to correct the error in natural history fallen into by Camoëns. Fanshaw seems to have been sensible of the mistake of his author, and has given the following (uncountenanced by the Portuguese) in place of the eternal snows ascribed to his country:—

"In merry England, which (from cliffs that stand
Like hills of snow) once Albion's name did git."

[423] Eris, or Discordia, the goddess of contention.—VIRGIL, Æneid ii. 337.—Ed.

[424]
What knighthood asks, the proud accusers yield,
And, dare the damsels' champions to the field.—

The translator has not been able to discover the slightest vestige of this chivalrous adventure in any memoirs of the English history. It is probable, nevertheless, that however adorned with romantic ornament, it is not entirely without foundation in truth. Castera, who unhappily does not cite his authority, gives the names of the twelve Portuguese champions: Alvaro Vaz d'Almada, afterwards Count d'Avranches in Normandy; another Alvaro d'Almada, surnamed the Juster, from his dexterity at that warlike exercise; Lopez Fernando Pacheco; Pedro Homen d'Acosta; Juan Augustin Pereyra; Luis Gonfalez de Malafay; the two brothers Alvaro and Rodrigo Mendez de Cerveyra; Ruy Gomex de Sylva; Soueyro d'Acosta, who gave his name to the river Acosta in Africa; Martin Lopez d'Azevedo; and Alvaro Gonfalez de Coutigno, surnamed Magricio. The names of the English champions, and of the ladies, he confesses are unknown, nor does history positively explain the injury of which the dames complained. It must, however, he adds, have been such as required the atonement of blood; il falloit qu'elle fût sanglante, since two sovereigns allowed to determine it by the sword. "Some critics," says Castera, "may perhaps condemn this episode of Camoëns; but for my part," he continues, "I think the adventure of Olindo and Sophronia, in Tasso, is much more to be blamed. The episode of the Italian poet is totally exuberant, whereas that of the Portuguese has a direct relation to his proposed subject: the wars of his country, a vast field, in which he has admirably succeeded, without prejudice to the first rule of the epopea, the unity of the action." The severest critic must allow that the episode related by Veloso, is happily introduced. To one who has ever been at sea, the scene must be particularly pleasing. The fleet is under sail, they plough the smooth deep—

"And o'er the decks cold breath'd the midnight wind."

All but the second watch are asleep in their warm pavilions; the second watch sit by the mast, sheltered from the chilly gale by a broad sail-cloth; sleep begins to overpower them, and they tell stories to entertain one another. For beautiful, picturesque simplicity there is no sea-scene equal to this in the Odyssey, or Æneid.

[425] What time he claim'd the proud Castilian throne.—John of Gaunt, duke of Lancaster, claimed the crown of Castile in the right of his wife, Donna Constantia, daughter of Don Pedro, the late king. Assisted by his son-in-law, John I. of Portugal, he entered Galicia, and was proclaimed king of Castile at the city of St. Jago de Compostella. He afterwards relinquished his pretensions, on the marriage of his daughter, Catalina, with the infant, Don Henry of Castile.

[426] The dames by lot their gallant champions choose.—The ten champions, who in the fifth book of Tasso's Jerusalem are sent by Godfrey for the assistance of Armida, are chosen by lot. Tasso, who had read the Lusiad, and admired its author, undoubtedly had the Portuguese poet in his eye.

[427]
In that proud port half circled by the wave,
Which Portugallia to the nation gave,
A deathless name.—

Oporto, called by the Romans Calle. Hence Portugal.

[428]
Yet something more than human warms my breast,
And sudden whispers—

In the Portuguese—

Mas, se a verdade o espirito me adevinha.

Literally, "But, if my spirit truly divine." Thus rendered by Fanshaw—

But, in my aug'ring ear a bird doth sing.

[429] As Rome's Corvinus.—Valerius Maximus, a Roman tribune, who fought and slew a Gaul of enormous stature, in single combat. During the duel a raven perched on the helmet of his antagonist, sometimes pecked his face and hand, and sometimes blinded him with the flapping of his wings. The victor was thence named Corvinus, from Corvus. Vid. Livy, l. 7, c. 26.

[430] The Flandrian countess on her hero smil'd.—The princess, for whom Magricio signalized his valour, was Isabella of Portugal, and spouse to Philip the Good, duke of Burgundy, and earl of Flanders. Some Spanish chronicles relate that Charles VII. of France, having assembled the states of his kingdom, cited

Philip to appear with his other vassals. Isabella, who was present, solemnly protested that the earls of Flanders were not obliged to do homage. A dispute arose, on which she offered, according to the custom of that age, to appeal to the fate of arms. The proposal was accepted, and Magricio the champion of Isabella, vanquished a French chevalier, appointed by Charles. Though our authors do not mention this adventure, and though Emmanuel de Faria, and the best Portuguese writers treat it with doubt, nothing to the disadvantage of Camoëns is thence to be inferred. A poet is not obliged always to follow the truth of history.

[431] The Rhine another pass'd, and prov'd his might.—This was Alvaro Vaz d'Almada. The chronicle of Garibay relates, that at Basle he received from a German a challenge to measure swords, on condition that each should fight with the right side unarmed; the German by this hoping to be victorious, for he was left-handed. The Portuguese, suspecting no fraud, accepted. When the combat began he perceived the inequality. His right side unarmed was exposed to the enemy, whose left side, which was nearest to him was defended with half a cuirass. Notwithstanding all this, the brave Alvaro obtained the victory. He sprang upon the German, seized him, and, grasping him forcibly in his arms, stifled and crushed him to death; imitating the conduct of Hercules, who in the same manner slew the cruel Anteus. Here we ought to remark the address of our author; he describes at length the injury and grief of the English ladies, the voyage of the twelve champions to England, and the prowess they there displayed. When Veloso relates these, the sea is calm; but no sooner does it begin to be troubled, than the soldier abridges his recital: we see him follow by degrees the preludes of the storm, we perceive the anxiety of his mind on the view of the approaching danger, hastening his narration to an end. Behold the strokes of a master!—This note, and the one preceding, are from Castera.

[432] The halcyons, mindful of their fate, deplore.—Ceyx, king of Trachinia, son of Lucifer, married Alcyone, the daughter of Eolus. On a voyage to consult the Delphic Oracle, he was shipwrecked. His corpse was thrown ashore in the view of his spouse, who, in the agonies of her love and despair, threw herself into the sea. The gods, in pity of her pious fidelity, metamorphosed them into the birds which bear her name. The halcyon is a little bird about the size of a thrush, its plumage of a beautiful sky blue, mixed with some traits of white and carnation. It is vulgarly called the kingfisher. The halcyons very seldom appear but in the finest weather, whence they are fabled to build their nests on the waves. The female is no less remarkable than the turtle, for her conjugal affection. She nourishes and attends the male when sick, and survives his death but a few days. When the halcyons are surprised in a tempest, they fly about as in the utmost terror, with the most lamentable and doleful cries. To introduce them, therefore, in the picture of a storm is a proof, both of the taste and judgment of Camoëns.

[433] With shrill, faint voice, th' untimely ghost complains.—It may not perhaps be unentertaining to cite Madame Dacier and Mr. Pope on the voices of the dead. It will, at least, afford a critical observation which appears to have escaped them both. "The shades of the suitors," observes Dacier, "when they are summoned by Mercury out of the palace of Ulysses, emit a feeble, plaintive, inarticulate sound, τρίζουσι, strident: whereas Agamemnon, and the shades that have been long in the state of the dead, speak articulately. I doubt not but Homer intended to show, by the former description, that when the soul is separated from the organs of the body, it ceases to act after the same manner as while it was joined to it; but how the dead recover their voices afterwards is not easy to understand. In other respects Virgil paints after Homer:—

Pars tollere vocem
Exiguam: inceptus clamor frustratur hiantes."

To this Mr. Pope replies, "But why should we suppose, with Dacier, that these shades of the suitors (of Penelope) have lost the faculty of speaking? I rather imagine that the sounds they uttered were signs of complaint and discontent, and proceeded not from an inability to speak.
After Patroclus was slain he appears to Achilles, and speaks very articulately to him; yet, to express his sorrow at his departure, he acts like these suitors: for Achilles—

'Like a thin smoke beholds the spirit fly,
And hears a feeble, lamentable cry.'

Dacier conjectures that the power of speech ceases in the dead, till they are admitted into a state of rest; but Patroclus is an instance to the contrary in the Iliad, and Elpenor in the Odyssey, for they both speak before their funereal rites are performed, and consequently before they enter into a state of repose amongst the shades of the happy."

The critic, in his search for distant proofs, often omits the most material one immediately at hand. Had Madame Dacier attended to the episode of the souls of the suitors, the world had never seen her ingenuity in these mythological conjectures; nor had Mr. Pope any need to bring the case of Patroclus or Elpenor to overthrow her system. Amphimedon, one of the suitors, in the very episode which gave birth to Dacier's conjecture, tells his story very articulately to the shade of Agamemnon, though he had not received the funereal rites:—

"Our mangled bodies, now deform'd with gore,
Cold and neglected spread the marble floor:
No friend to bathe our wounds! or tears to shed
O'er the pale corse! the honours of the dead."

ODYS. XXIV.

On the whole, the defence of Pope is almost as idle as the conjectures of Dacier. The plain truth is, poetry delights in personification; everything in it, as Aristotle says of the Iliad, has manners; poetry must therefore personify according to our ideas. Thus in Milton:—

"Tears, such as angels weep, burst forth."

And thus in Homer, while the suitors are conducted to hell:—

"Trembling, the spectres glide, and plaintive vent
Thin, hollow screams, along the deep descent:"

and, unfettered with mythological distinctions, either shriek or articulately talk, according to the most poetical view of their supposed circumstances.

[434] Exod. xiv. 29.

[435] Noah.

[436] Venus.

[437] For the fable of Eolus see the tenth Odyssey.

[438]
And vow, that henceforth her Armada's sails
Should gently swell with fair propitious gales.

In innumerable instances Camoëns discovers himself a judicious imitator of the ancients. In the two great masters of the epic are several prophecies oracular of the fate of different heroes, which give an air of solemn importance to the poem. The fate of the Armada thus obscurely anticipated, resembles in particular the prophecy of the safe return of Ulysses to Ithaca, foretold by the shade of Tiresias, which was afterwards fulfilled by the Phæacians. It remains now to make some observations on the machinery used by Camoëns in this book. The necessity of machinery in the epopea, and the, perhaps, insurmountable difficulty of finding one unexceptionably adapted to a poem where the heroes are Christians, or, in other words, to a poem whose subject is modern, have already been observed in the preface. The machinery of Camoëns has also been proved, in every respect, to be less exceptionable than that of Tasso in his Jerusalem, or that of Voltaire in his Henriade. The descent of Bacchus to the palace of Neptune, in the depths of the sea, and his address to the watery gods, are noble imitations of Virgil's Juno in the first Æneid. The description of the storm is also masterly. In both instances the conduct of the Æneid is joined with the descriptive exuberance of the Odyssey. The appearance of the star of Venus through the storm is finely imagined; the influence of the nymphs of that goddess over the winds, and their subsequent nuptials, are in the spirit of the promise of Juno to Eolus:—

Sunt mihi bis septum præstanti corpore nymphæ:
Quarum, quæ forma pulcherrima; Deïopeiam
Connubio jungam stabili, propriamque dicabo:
Omnes ut tecum meritis pro talibus annos
Exigat, et pulchra faciat te prole párentem.—VIRGIL, Æn. bk. i.

And the fiction itself is an allegory, exactly in the manner of Homer. Orithia, the daughter of Erecteus, and queen of the Amazons, was ravished and carried away by Boreas.

[439] Vasco de Gama.

[440] This refers to the Catholic persecutions of Protestants whom they had previously condemned at the Diet of Spires. War was declared against the Protestants in 1546. It lasted for six years, when a treaty of peace was signed at Passau on the Danube, in 1552.—Ed.

[441] Some blindly wand'ring, holy faith disclaim.—At the time when Camoëns wrote, the German empire was plunged into all the miseries of a religious war, the Catholics using every endeavour to rivet the chains of Popery, the adherents of Luther as strenuously endeavouring to shake them off.

[442]
High sound the titles of the English crown,
King of Jerusalem.—

The title of "King of Jerusalem" was never assumed by the kings of England. Robert, duke of Normandy, son of William the Conqueror, was elected King of Jerusalem by the army in Syria, but declined it in hope of ascending the throne of England. Henry VIII. filled the throne of England when our author wrote: his luxury and conjugal brutality amply deserved the censure of the honest poet.

[443] France.

[444] What impious lust of empire steels thy breast.—The French translator very cordially agrees with the Portuguese poet in the strictures upon Germany, England, and Italy.

[445] The Mohammedans.

[446] Where Cynifio flows.—A river in Africa, near Tripoli.—VIRGIL, Georg. iii. 311.—Ed.

[447] O Italy! how fall'n, how low, how lost!—However these severe reflections on modern Italy may displease the admirers of Italian manners, the picture on the whole is too just to admit of confutation. Never did the history of any court afford such instances of villainy and all the baseness of intrigue as that of the pope's. That this view of the lower ranks in the pope's dominions is just, we have the indubitable testimony of Addison. Our poet is justifiable in his censures, for he only follows the severe reflections of the greatest of the Italian poets. It were easy to give fifty instances; two or three, however, shall suffice. Dante, in his sixth canto, del Purg.—

Ahi, serva Italia, di dolore ostello,
Nave senza nocchiero in gran tempesta,
Non donna di provincie, bordello.

"Ah, slavish Italy, the inn of dolour, a ship without a pilot in a horrid tempest:—not the mistress of provinces, but a brothel!"

Ariosto, canto 17:—

O d' ogni vitio fetida sentina
Dormi Italia imbríaco.

"O inebriated Italy, thou sleepest the sink of every filthy vice!"

And Petrarch:—

Del'empia Babilonia, ond'è fuggita
Ogni vergogna, ond'ogni bene è fuori,
Albergo di dolor, madre d'errori
Son fuggit'io per allungar la vita.

"From the impious Babylon (the Papal Court) from whence all shame and all good are fled, the inn of dolour, the mother of errors, have I hastened away to prolong my life."

[448] The fables old of Cadmus.—Cadmus having slain the dragon which guarded the fountain of Dirce, in Bœotia, sowed the teeth of the monster. A number of armed men immediately sprang up, and surrounded Cadmus, in order to kill him. By the counsel of Minerva he threw a precious stone among

them, in striving for which they slew one another. Only five survived, who afterwards assisted him to build the city of Thebes.—Vid. Ovid. Met. iv.

Terrigenæ pereunt per mutua vulnera fratres.

[449]
So fall the bravest of the Christian name,
While dogs unclean.—

Imitated from a fine passage in Lucan, beginning—

Quis furor, O Cives! quæ tanta licentia ferri,
Gentibus invisis Latium præbere cruorem?

[450] The Mohammedans.

[451] Constantinople.

[452] Beyond the Wolgian Lake.—The Caspian Sea, so called from the large river Volga, or Wolga, which empties itself into it.

[453]
Their fairest offspring from their bosoms torn,
(A dreadful tribute !)—

By this barbarous policy the tyranny of the Ottomans was long sustained. The troops of the Turkish infantry and cavalry, known by the name of Janissaries and Spahis, were thus supported. "The sons of Christians—and those the most completely furnished by nature—were taken in their childhood from their parents by a levy made every five years, or oftener, as occasion required."—SANDYS.

[454] Mohammedans.

[455]
O'er Afric's shores
The sacred shrines the Lusian heroes rear'd.—

See the note on book v. p. 137.

[456] Of deepest west.—Alludes to the discovery and conquest of the Brazils by the Portuguese.

[457] The poet, having brought his heroes to the shore of India, indulges himself with a review of the state of the western and eastern worlds; the latter of which is now, by the labour of his heroes, rendered accessible to the former. The purpose of his poem is also strictly kept in view. The west and the east he considers as two great empires; the one of the true religion, the other of a false. The professors of the true, disunited and destroying one another; the professors of the false one, all combined to extirpate the other. He upbraids the professors of the true religion for their vices, particularly for their disunion, and for deserting the interests of holy faith. His countrymen, however, he

boasts, have been its defenders and planters, and, without the assistance of their brother powers, will plant it in Asia.

"The Crusaders," according to Voltaire, "were a band of vagabond thieves, who had agreed to ramble from the heart of Europe in order to desolate a country they had no right to, and massacre, in cold blood, a venerable prince, more than fourscore years old, and his whole people, against whom they had no pretence of complaint."

To prove that the Crusades were neither so unjustifiable, so impolitic, nor so unhappy in their consequences as superficial readers of history are accustomed to regard them, would not be difficult.

Upon the whole, it will be found that the Portuguese poet talks of the political reasons of a Crusade with an accuracy in the philosophy of history as superior to that of Voltaire, as the poetical merit of the Lusiad surpasses that of the Henriade. And the critic in poetry must allow, that, to suppose the discovery of GAMA the completion of all the endeavours to overthrow the great enemies of the true religion, gives a dignity to the poem, and an importance to the hero, similar to that which Voltaire, on the same supposition, allows to the subject of the Jerusalem of Tasso.

[458] Calicut is the name of a famous sea-port town in the province of Malabar.

[459]
The herald hears
Castilia's manly tongue salute his ears.—

This in according to the truth of history. While the messenger sent ashore by GAMA was borne here and there, and carried off his feet by the throng, who understood not a word of his language, he was accosted in Spanish by a Moorish merchant, a native of Tunis, who, according to Osorius, had been the chief person with whom King Ferdinand had formerly contracted for military stores. He proved himself an honest agent, and of infinite service to GAMA; he returned to Portugal, where, according to Faria, he died in the Christian communion. He was named Monzaida.

[460] The sacred pledge of eastern faith.—To eat together was, and still is, in the east looked upon as the inviolable pledge of protection. As a Persian nobleman was one day walking in his garden, a wretch in the utmost terror prostrated himself before him, and implored to be protected from the rage of a multitude who were in pursuit of him, to take his life. The nobleman took a peach, eat part of it, and gave the rest to the fugitive, assuring him of safety. As they approached the house, they met a crowd who carried the murdered corpse of the nobleman's beloved son. The incensed populace demanded the murderer, who stood beside him, to be delivered to their fury. The father, though overwhelmed with grief and anger, replied, "We have eaten together, and I will not betray him." He protected the murderer of his son from the fury of his domestics and neighbours, and in the night facilitated his escape.

[461] i.e. crescent-shaped.—Ed.

[462] In Rhodope.—The beautiful fable of the descent of Orpheus to hell, for the recovery of his beloved wife, Eurydice, will be found in Virgil's Georgics, bk. iv., lines 460-80.—Ed.

[463]

(For now the banquet on the tented plain,
And sylvan chase his careless hours employ).—

The great Mogul, and other eastern sovereigns, attended by their courtiers, spend annually some months of the finest season in encampments in the field, in hunting parties, and military amusements.

[464] Th' enormous mountain.—The Himalaya range, which is a continuation of an immense chain of mountains girdling the northern regions of the earth and known by various names, as Caucasus, Homodus, Paropamissus, Imaus, etc., and from Imaus extended through Tartary to the sea of Kamschatka. Not the range of mountains so called in Asia Minor.—Ed.

[465] As wild traditions tell.—Pliny, imposed upon by some Greeks, who pretended to have been in India, relates this fable.—Vide Nat. Hist. lib. 12.

[466] Is fondly plac'd in Ganges' holy wave.—Almost all the Indian nations attribute to the Ganges the virtue of cleansing the soul from the stains of sin. They have such veneration for this river, that if any one in their presence were to throw any filth into the stream, an instant death would punish his audacity.

[467] Cambaya, the ancient Camanes of Ptolemy, gives name to the gulf of that name at the head of which it is situated. It is the principal seaport of Guzerat.—Ed.

[468] Porus was king of part of the Punjaub, and was conquered by Alexander the Great.—Ed.

[469] Narsinga.—The laws of Narsing oblige the women to throw themselves into the funeral pile, to be burnt with their deceased husbands. An infallible secret to prevent the desire of widowhood.—CASTERA from Barros, Dec. 4.

[470] The Canarese, who inhabit Canara, on the west coast of India.—Ed.

[471] Medina, a city of Arabia, famous as being the burial-place of Mohammed, and hence esteemed sacred.—Ed.

[472] According to tradition, Perimal, a sovereign of India, embraced Islamism about 800 years before GAMA'S voyage, divided his dominions into different kingdoms, and ended his days as a hermit at Mecca.—Ed.

[473] i.e. pariahs, outcasts.

[474] Brahma their founder as a god they boast.—Antiquity has talked much, but knew little with certainty of the Brahmins, and their philosophy. Porphyry and others esteem them the same as the Gymnosophists of the Greeks, and divide them into several sects, the Samanæi, the Germanes, the Pramnæ, the Gymnetæ, etc. Brahma is the head of the Hindu triad which consists of Brahma, Vishnu and Siva.—Ed.

[475] Almost innumerable, and sometimes as whimsically absurd as the "Arabian Nights' Entertainments," are the holy legends of India. The accounts of the god Brahma, or Brimha, are more various than those of any fable in the Grecian mythology. According to Father Bohours, in his life of

Xavier, the Brahmins hold, that the Great God having a desire to become visible, became man. In this state he produced three sons, Mayso, Visnu, and Brahma; the first, born of his mouth, the second, of his breast, the third, of his belly. Being about to return to his invisibility, he assigned various departments to his three sons. To Brahma he gave the third heaven, with the superintendence of the rites of religion. Brahma having a desire for children, begat the Brahmins, who are the priests of India, and who are believed by the other tribes to be a race of demi-gods, who have the blood of heaven running in their veins. Other accounts say, that Brahma produced the priests from his head, the more ignoble tribes from his breast, thighs, and feet.

According to the learned Kircher's account of the theology of the Brahmins, the sole and supreme god Vishnu, formed the secondary god Brahma, out of a flower that floated on the surface of the great deep before the creation. And afterwards, in reward of the virtue, fidelity, and gratitude of Brahma, gave him power to create the universe.

Hesiod's genealogy of the gods, though refined upon by the schools of Plato, is of the same class with the divine genealogies of the Brahmins. The Jewish fables, foolish questions and genealogies, reproved by Saint Paul (epist. Tit.), were probably of this kind, for the Talmudical legends were not then sprung up. Binah, or Understanding, said the cabalists, begat Kochmah, or Wisdom, etc., till at last comes Milcah, the Kingdom, who begat Shekinah, the Divine Presence. In the same manner the Christian Gnostics, of the sect of Valentinus, held their Πλήρωμα, and their thirty Æons. Ampsiu and Auraan, they tell us, i.e. Profundity and Silence, begat Bacua and Tharthuu, Mind and Truth; these begat Ubucua and Thardeadie, Word and Life, and these Merexa and Atarbarba, Man and Church. The other conjunctions of their thirty Æons are of similar ingenuity. The prevalence of the same spirit of mythological allegory in such different nations, affords the philosopher a worthy field for speculation.

Almost as innumerable as their legends are the dreadful penances to which the Hindus submit themselves for the expiation of sins. Some hold the transmigration of souls, and of consequence abstain from all animal food.{*} Yet, however austere in other respects, they freely abandon themselves to every species of debauchery, some of them esteeming the most unnatural abominations as the privilege of their sanctity. The cow they venerate as sacred. If a dying man can lay hold of a cow's tail, and expire with it in his hands, his soul is sure to be purified, and perhaps will enjoy the signal favour to transmigrate into the body of one of those animals. The temples of India, which are numerous, are filled with innumerable idols of the most horrid figures. The Brahmins are allowed to eat nothing but what is cooked by themselves. Astrology is their principal study; yet, though they are mostly a despicable set of fortune-tellers, some of them are excellent moralists, and particularly inculcate the comprehensive virtue of humanity, which is enforced by the opinion, that Divine beings often assume the habit of mendicants, in order to distinguish the charitable from the inhuman. They have several traditions of the virtuous, on these happy trials, being translated into heaven; the best designed incitement to virtue, perhaps, which their religion contains. Besides the Brahmins, the principal sect of that vast region called India, there are several others, who are divided and subdivided, according to innumerable variations, in every province. In Cambaya, the Banians, a sect who strictly abstain from all animal food, are numerous.

{*} Though from the extracts given by Mr. Dow, the philosopher Goutam appears to have been a very Duns Scotus or Aquinas in metaphysics, the Pythagorean reason why the Brahmins abstain from animal food, is a convincing proof of their ignorance in natural philosophy. Some will let vermin overrun them; some of the Banians cover their mouth with a cloth, lest they should suck in a gnat with their breath; and some carefully sweep the floor ere they tread upon it, lest they dislodge the soul of an insect. And yet *they do not know that in the water they drink, and in every salad they eat, they cause the death of innumerable living creatures.*

The sacred books of the Hindoos are written in a dead language, the Sanskrit, which none but the Brahmins are allowed to study. So strict in this are they, says Mr. Dow, that only one Mussulman was ever instructed in it, and his knowledge was obtained by fraud. Mahummud Akbar, emperor of India, though bred a Mohammedan, studied several religions. In the Christian he was instructed by a Portuguese. But, finding that of the Hindoos inaccessible, he had recourse to art. A boy named Feizi, was, as the orphan of a Brahmin, put under the care of one of the most eminent of these philosophers, and obtained full knowledge of their hidden religion. But the fraud being discovered, he was laid under the restraint of an oath, and it does not appear that he ever communicated the knowledge thus acquired.

[476] Kotwâl, the chief officer of police in a town.—FORBES' Hindustani Dictionary.

[477] The monster forms, Chimera-like, and rude.—Chimera, a monster slain by Bellerophon.

"First, dire Chimera's conquest was enjoin'd,
A mingled monster of no mortal kind;
Behind, a dragon's fiery tail was spread,
A goat's rough body bore a lion's head;
Her pitchy nostrils flaky flames expire,
Her gaping throat emits infernal fire."

POPE'S II. vi.

[478] So Titan's son.—Briareus.

[479] Before these shrines the blinded Indians bow.—In this instance, Camoëns has, with great art, deviated from the truth of history. As it was the great purpose of his hero to propagate the law of heaven in the East, it would have been highly absurd to have represented GAMA and his attendants as on their knees in a pagan temple. This, however, was the case. "GAMA, who had been told," says Osorius, "that there were many Christians in India, conjectured that the temple, to which the catual led him, was a Christian church. At their entrance they were met by four priests, who seemed to make crosses on their foreheads. The walls were painted with many images. In the middle was it little round chapel, in the wall of which, opposite to the entrance, stood an image which could hardly be discovered. The four priests ascending, some entered the chapel by a little brass door, and pointing to the benighted image, cried aloud, 'Mary, Mary!' The catual and his attendants prostrated themselves an the ground, while the Lusians on their bended knees adored the blessed virgin." Thus Osorius. Another writer says, that a Portuguese, having some doubt, exclaimed, "If this be the devil's image, I however worship God."

[480] Here India's fate.—The description of the palace of the zamorim, situated among aromatic groves, is according to history; the embellishment of the walls is in imitation of Virgil's description of the palace of King Latinus:—

Tectum augustum, ingens, centum sublime columnis,
Urbe fuit summa, etc.

"The palace built by Picus, vast and proud,   }

Supported by a hundred pillars stood,   }
And round encompass'd with a rising wood.   }
The pile o'erlook'd the town, and drew the sight,
Surprised, at once, with reverence and delight....
Above the portal, carv'd in cedar wood,
Placed in their ranks their godlike grandsires stood.
Old Saturn, with his crooked scythe on high;
And Italus, that led the colony:
And ancient Janus with his double face,
And bunch of keys, the porter of the place.
There stood Sabinus, planter of the vines,   }
On a short pruning-hook his head reclines;   }
And studiously surveys his gen'rous wines.   }
Then warlike kings who for their country fought,
And honourable wounds from battle brought.
Around the posts hung helmets, darts, and spears;   }
And captive chariots, axes, shields, and bars;   }
And broken beaks of ships, the trophies of their wars.   }
Above the rest, as chief of all the band
Was Picus plac'd, a buckler in his hand;
His other wav'd a long divining wand.
Girt in his Gabin gown the hero sate—"

DRYDEN, Æn. vii.

[481]
Behind her founder Nysa's walls were rear'd—
—at distance far
The Ganges lav'd the wide-extended war.—

This is in the perspective manner of the beautiful descriptions of the figures on the shield of Achilles.—IL. xviii.

[482] Had Semele beheld the smiling boy.—The Theban Bacchus, to whom the Greek fabulists ascribed the Indian expedition of Sesostris, king of Egypt.

[483] Semiramis.

[484] Call'd Jove his father.—The bon-mot of Olympias on this pretension of her son Alexander, was admired by the ancients. "This hot-headed youth, forsooth, cannot be at rest unless he embroil me in a quarrel with Juno."—QUINT. CURT.

[485]
The tap'stried walls with gold were pictur'd o'er,
And flow'ry velvet spread the marble floor.—

According to Osorius.

[486] A leaf.—The Betel.

[487] More now we add not.—The tenor of this first conversation between the zamorim and GAMA, is according to the truth of history.

[488] What terrors oft have thrill'd my infant breast.—The enthusiasm with which Monzaida, a Moor, talks of the Portuguese, may perhaps to some appear unnatural. Camoëns seems to be aware of this by giving a reason for that enthusiasm in the first speech of Monzaida to Gama—

Heav'n sent you here for some great work divine,
And Heav'n inspires my breast your sacred toils to join.

And, that this Moor did conceive a great affection to GAMA, whose religion he embraced, and to whom he proved of the utmost service, is according to the truth of history.

[489] The ruddy juice by Noah found.—Gen. ix. 20. "And Noah began to be an husbandman, and he planted a vineyard, and he drank of the wine,"
etc.

[490]
His faith forbade with other tribe to join
The sacred meal, esteem'd a rite divine.—

The opinion of the sacredness of the table is very ancient in the East. It is plainly to be discovered in the history of Abraham. When Melchizedek, a king and priest, blessed Abraham, it is said, "And he brought forth bread and wine and he blessed him."—Gen. xiv. 18. The patriarchs only drank wine, according to Dr. Stukely, on their more solemn festivals, when they were said to rejoice before the Lord. Other customs of the Hindoos are mentioned by Camoëns in this book. If a noble should touch a person of another tribe—

A thousand rites, and washings o'er and o'er,
Can scarce his tainted purity restore.

Nothing, says Osorius, but the death of the unhappy commoner can wipe off the pollution. Yet we are told by the same author, that Hindoo nobility cannot be forfeited, or even tarnished by the basest and greatest of crimes; nor can one of mean birth become great or noble by the most illustrious actions. The noblemen, says the same writer, adopt the children of their sisters, esteeming there can be no other certainty of the relationship of their heirs.

[491] The warlike song.—Though Camoëns began his Lusiad in Portugal, almost the whole of it was written while on the ocean, while in Africa, and in India.—See his Life.

[492] As Canace.—Daughter of Eolus. Her father, having thrown her incestuous child to the dogs, sent her a sword, with which she slew herself. In Ovid she writes an epistle to her husband-brother, where she thus describes herself:—

Dextra tenet calamum, strictum tenet altera ferrum.

[493]
Soon I beheld that wealth beneath the wave
For ever lost.—

See the Life of Camoëns.

[494] My life, like Judah's Heaven-doom'd king of yore.—Hezekiah.—See Isaiah xxxviii.

[495] And left me mourning in a dreary jail.—This, and the whole paragraph from—

Degraded now, by poverty abhorr'd,

alludes to his fortunes in India. The latter circumstance relates particularly to the base and inhuman
treatment he received on his return to Goa, after his unhappy shipwreck.—See his Life.

[496] Who spurns the muse.—Similarity of condition has produced similarity of sentiment in Camoëns
and Spenser. Each was the ornament of his country and his age, and each was cruelly neglected by the
men of power, who, in truth, were incapable to judge of their merit, or to relish their writings. We have
seen several of the strictures of Camoëns on the barbarous nobility of Portugal. The similar complaints
of Spenser will show, that neglect of genius, however, was not confined to the court of Lisbon:—

"O grief of griefs! O gall of all good hearts!
To see that virtue should despised be
Of such as first were raised for virtue's parts,
And now, broad spreading like an aged tree,
Let none shoot up that nigh them planted be.
O let not those of whom the muse is scorn'd,
Alive or dead be by the muse adorn'd."

RUINS OF TIME.

It is thought Lord Burleigh, who withheld the bounty intended by Queen Elizabeth, is here meant. But he
is more clearly stigmatized in these remarkable lines, where the misery of dependence on court favour is
painted in colours which must recall several strokes of the Lusiad to the mind of the reader:—

"Full little knowest thou that hast not tried,
What hell it is, in suing long to bide;
To lose good days, that might be better spent,
To waste long nights in pensive discontent;
To speed to-day, to be put back to-morrow,
To feed on hope, to pine with fear and sorrow;
To have thy princess' grace, yet want her peers';
To have thy asking, yet wait many years.
To fret thy soul with crosses and with cares,
To eat thy heart thro' comfortless despairs;
To fawn, to crouch, to wait, to ride, to run,
To spend, to give, to want, to be undone."

MOTHER HUBBERD'S TALE.

These lines exasperated still more the inelegant, illiberal Burleigh. So true is the observation of Mr. Hughes, that, "even the sighs of a miserable man are sometimes resented as an affront by him that is the occasion of them."

[497] Kotwâl, a sort of superintendent or inspector of police.—FORBES' Hindustani Dictionary.

[498] Lusus.

[499] His cluster'd bough, the same which Bacchus bore.—Camoëns immediately before, and in the former book, calls the ensign of Lusus a bough; here he calls it the green thyrsus of Bacchus:—

O verde Tyrso foi de Bacco usado.

The thyrsus, however, was a javelin twisted with ivy-leaves, used in the sacrifices of Bacchus.

[500] In those fair lawns the bless'd Elysium feign'd.—In this assertion our author has the authority of Strabo. a foundation sufficient for a poet. Nor are there wanting several Spanish writers, particularly Barbosa, who seriously affirm that Homer drew the fine description of Elysium, in his fourth Odyssey, from the beautiful valleys of Spain, where, in one of his voyages, they say, he arrived. Egypt, however, seems to have a better title to this honour. The fable of Charon, and the judges of hell, are evidently borrowed from the Egyptian rites of burial, and are older than Homer. After a ferryman had conveyed the corpse over a lake, certain judges examined the life of the deceased, particularly his claim to the virtue of loyalty, and, according to the report, decreed or refused the honours of sepulture. The place of the catacombs, according to Diodorus Siculus, was surrounded with deep canals, beautiful meadows, and a wilderness of groves. It is universally known that the greatest part of the Grecian fables were fabricated from the customs and opinions of Egypt. Several other nations have also claimed the honour of affording the idea of the fields of the blessed. Even the Scotch challenge it. Many Grecian fables, says an author of that country, are evidently founded on the reports of the Phœnician sailors. That these navigators traded to the coasts of Britain is certain. In the middle of summer, the season when the ancients performed their voyages, for about six weeks there is no night over the Orkney Islands; the disk of the sun, during that time, scarcely sinking below the horizon. This appearance, together with the calm which usually prevails at that season, and the beautiful verdure of the islands, could not fail to excite the admiration of the Phœnicians; and their accounts of the place naturally afforded the idea that these islands were inhabited by the spirits of the just. This, says our author, is countenanced by Homer, who places his "islands of the happy" at the extremity of the ocean. That the fables of Scylla, the Gorgones, and several others, were founded on the accounts of navigators, seems probable; and, on this supposition, the Insulæ Fortunatæ, and Purpurariæ, now the Canary and Madeira islands, also claim the honour of giving colours to the description of Elysium. The truth, however, appears to be this: That a place of happiness is reserved for the spirits of the good is the natural suggestion of that anxiety and hope concerning the future which animates the human breast. All the barbarous nations of Africa and America agree in placing their heaven in beautiful islands, at an immense distance over the ocean. The idea is universal, and is natural to every nation in a state of barbarous simplicity.

[501] The goddess Minerva.

[502] The heav'n-built towers of Troy.—Alluding to the fable of Neptune, Apollo, and Laomedon.

[503]
On Europe's strand, more grateful to the skies,
He bade th' eternal walls of Lisbon rise.—

For some account of this tradition, see the note on Lusiad, bk. iii. p. 76. Ancient traditions, however fabulous, have a good effect in poetry. Virgil has not scrupled to insert one, which required an apology:—

Prisca fides facto, sed fama perennis.

Spenser has given us the history of Brute and his descendants at full length in the Faerie Queene; and Milton, it is known, was so fond of that absurd legend, that he intended to write a poem on the subject; and by this fondness was induced to mention it as a truth in the introduction to his History of England.

[504] The brother chief.—Paulus de Gama.

[505] That gen'rous pride which Rome to Pyrrhus bore.—When Pyrrhus, king of Epirus, was at war with the Romans, his physician offered to poison him. The senate rejected the proposal, and acquainted Pyrrhus of the designed treason. Florus remarks on the infamous assassination of Viriatus, that the Roman senate did him great honour; ut videretur aliter vinci non potuisse; it was a confession that they could not otherwise conquer him,—Vid. Flor. l. 17. For a fuller account of this great man, see the note on Lusiad, bk. i. p. 9.

[506] Some deem the warrior of Hungarian race.—See the note on the Lusiad, bk. iii p. 67.

[507] Jerusalem.

[508] The first Alonzo.—King of Portugal.

[509] On his young pupil's flight.—"Some, indeed most, writers say, that the queen advancing with her army towards Guimaraez, the king, without waiting till his governor joined him, engaged them and was routed: but that afterwards the remains of his army, being joined by the troops under the command of Egaz Munitz, engaged the army of the queen a second time, and gained a complete victory."—UNIV. HIST.

[510] Egaz behold, a chief self-doom'd to death.—See the same story in bk. iii. p. 71. Though history affords no authentic document of this transaction, tradition, the poet's authority, is not silent. And the monument of Egaz in the monastery of Paço de Souza gives it countenance. Egaz and his family are there represented, in bas relief, in the attitude and garb, says Castera, as described by Camoëns.

[511] Ah Rome! no more thy gen'rous consul boast.—Sc. Posthumus, who, overpowered by the Samnites, submitted to the indignity of passing under the yoke.

[512] The Moorish king.—The Alcaydes, or tributary governors under the Miramolin{*} or Emperor of Morocco, are often by the Spanish and Portuguese writers styled kings. He who was surprised and taken prisoner by Don Fuaz Roupinho was named Gama. Fuaz, after having gained the first naval victory of the

Portuguese, also experienced their first defeat. With one and twenty sail he attacked fifty-four large galleys of the Moors. "The sea," says Brandan, "which had lately furnished him with trophies, now supplied him with a tomb."

{*} *This should be (and is evidently only a corruption of), Emir-el-Mumenin, i.e. in Arabic, Commander of the believers.—Ed.*

[513] A foreign navy brings the pious aid.—A navy of crusaders, mostly English.

[514] And from the leaves.—This legend is mentioned by some ancient Portuguese chronicles. Homer would have availed himself, as Camoëns has done, of a tradition so enthusiastic, and characteristic of the age. Henry was a native of Bonneville near Cologne. "His tomb," says Castera, "is still to be seen in the monastery of St. Vincent, but without the palm."

[515] In robes of white behold a priest advance.—Thestonius, prior of the regulars of St. Augustine of Conymbra. Some ancient chronicles relate this circumstance as mentioned by Camoëns. Modern writers assert, that he never quitted his breviary.—CASTERA.

[516] The son of Egas.—He was named Mem Moniz, and was son of Egas Moniz, celebrated for the surrender of himself and family to the King of Castile, as already mentioned.

[517] The dauntless Gerald.—"He was a man of rank, who, in order to avoid the legal punishment to which several crimes rendered him obnoxious, put himself at the head of a party of freebooters. Tiring, however, of that life, he resolved to reconcile himself to his sovereign by some noble action. Full of this idea, one evening he entered Evora, which then belonged to the Moors. In the night he killed the sentinels of one of the gates, which he opened to his companions, who soon became masters of the place. This exploit had its desired effect. The king pardoned Gerald, and made him governor of Evora. A knight with a sword in one hand, and two heads in the other, from that time became the armorial bearing of the city."—CASTERA.

[518] Wrong'd by his king.—Don Pedro Fernando de Castro, injured by the family of Lara, and denied redress by the King of Castile, took the infamous revenge of bearing arms against his native country. At the head of a Moorish army he committed several outrages in Spain; but was totally defeated in Portugal.

[519] And lo, the skies unfold.—"According to some ancient Portuguese histories, Don Matthew, bishop of Lisbon, in the reign of Alonso I, attempted to reduce Alcazar, then in possession of the Moors. His troops, being suddenly surrounded by a numerous party of the enemy, were ready to fly, when, at the prayers of the bishop, a venerable old man, clothed in white, with a red cross on his breast, appeared in the air. The miracle dispelled the fears of the Portuguese; the Moors were defeated, and the conquest of Alcazar crowned the victory."—CASTERA.

[520]
Her streets in blood deplore
The seven brave hunters murder'd by the Moor.—

"During a truce with the Moors, six cavaliers of the order of St. James were, while on a hunting party, surrounded and killed, by a numerous body of the Moors. During the fight, in which the gentlemen sold their lives dear, a common carter, named Garcias Rodrigo, who chanced to pass that way, came generously to their assistance, and lost his life along with them. The poet, in giving all seven the same title, shows us that virtue constitutes true nobility. Don Payo de Correa, grand master of the order of St. James, revenged the death of these brave unfortunates by the sack of Tavila, where his just rage put the garrison to the sword."—CASTERA.

[521] Those three bold knights how dread.—Nothing can give us a stronger picture of the romantic character of their age, than the manners of those champions, who were gentlemen of birth; and who, in the true spirit of knight-errantry, went about from court to court in quest of adventures. Their names were, Gonçalo Ribeiro; Fernando Martinez de Santarene; and Vasco Anez, foster-brother to Mary, queen of Castile, daughter of Alonzo IV. of Portugal.

[522] And I, behold, am off'ring sacrifice.—This line, the simplicity which, I think, contains great dignity, is adopted from Fanshaw—

"And I, ye see, am off'ring sacrifice;"

who has here caught the spirit of the original—

A quem lhe a dura nova estava dando,
Pois eu responde estou sacrificando;

i.e. To whom when they told the dreadful tidings, "And I," he replies "am sacrificing." The piety of Numa was crowned with victory.—Vid. 'Plut. in vit. Numæ.

[523]
The Lusian Scipio well might speak his fame,
But nobler Nunio shines a greater name.—

Castera justly observes the happiness with which Camoëns introduces the name of this truly great man. "Il va," says he, "le nommer tout à l'heure avec une adresse et une magnificence digne d'un si beau sujet."

[524] Two knights of Malta.—These knights were first named Knights Hospitalers of St. John of Jerusalem, afterwards Knights of Rhodes, from whence they were driven to Messina, ere Malta was assigned to them. By their oath of knighthood they were bound to protect the Holy Sepulchre from the profanation of infidels; immediately on taking this oath, they retired to their colleges, where they lived on their revenues in all the idleness of monkish luxury. Their original habit was black, with a white cross; their arms gules, a cross, argent.

[525] His captive friend.—Before John I. mounted the throne of Portugal, one Vasco Porcallo was governor of Villaviciosa. Roderic de Landroal and his friend, Alvarez Cuytado, having discovered that he was in the interest of the King of Castile, drove him from his town and fortress. On the establishment of King John, Porcallo had the art to obtain the favour of that prince; but, no sooner was he re-instated in the garrison, than he delivered it up to the Castilians; and plundered the house of Cuytado, whom, with his wife, he made prisoner and, under a numerous party, ordered to be sent to Olivença. Roderic de Landroal, hearing of this, attacked and defeated the escort, and set his friend at liberty.—CASTERA.

[526] Here treason's well-earn'd meed allures thine eyes.—While the kingdom of Portugal was divided, some holding with John the newly elected king, and others with the King of Castile, Roderic Marin, governor of Campo-Major, declared for the latter. Fernando d'Elvas endeavoured to gain him to the interest of his native prince, and a conference, with the usual assurances of safety, was agreed to. Marin, at this meeting, seized upon Elvas, and sent him prisoner to his castle. Elvas having recovered his liberty, a few days after met his enemy in the field, whom, in his turn, he made captive; and the traitorous Marin, notwithstanding the endeavours of their captain to save his life, met the reward of his treason from the soldiers of Elvas.—Partly from Castera.

[527] And safe the Lusian galleys speed away.—A numerous fleet of the Castilians being on their way to lay siege to Lisbon. Ruy Pereyra, the Portuguese commander, seeing no possibility of victory, boldly attacked the Spanish admiral. The fury of his onset put the Castilians in disorder, and allowed the Portuguese galleys a safe escape. In this brave piece of service the gallant Pereyra lost his life.—CASTERA.

[528] The shepherd.—Viriatus.

[529] Equal flame inspir'd these few.—The Castilians having laid siege to Almada, a fortress on a mountain near Lisbon, the garrison, in the utmost distress for water, were obliged at times to make sallies to the bottom of the hill in quest of it. Seventeen Portuguese thus employed were one day attacked by four hundred of the enemy. They made a brave defence, and effected a happy retreat into their fortress.—CASTERA.

[530] Far from the succour of the Lusian host.—When Alonzo V. took Ceuta, Don Pedro de Menezes was the only officer in the army who was willing to become governor of that fortress; which, on account of the uncertainty of succour from Portugal, and the earnest desire of the Moors to regain it, was deemed untenable. He gallantly defended his post in two severe sieges.

[531] That other earl.—He was the natural son of Don Pedro de Menezes. Alonzo V. one day, having ridden out from Ceuta with a few attendants, was attacked by a numerous party of the Moors, when De Vian, and some others under him, at the expense of their own lives, purchased the safe retreat of their sovereign.

[532] Two brother-heroes shine.—The sons of John I. Don Pedro was called the Ulysses of his age, on account both of his eloquence and his voyages. He visited almost every court of Europe, but he principally distinguished himself in Germany, where, under the standards of the Emperor Sigismond, he signalized his valour in the war against the Turks.—CASTERA.

[533] The glorious Henry.—In pursuance of the reasons assigned in the preface, the translator has here taken the liberty to make a transposition in the order of his author. In Camoëns, Don Pedro de Menezes, and his son De Vian, conclude the description of the pictured ensigns. Don Henry, the greatest man perhaps that ever Portugal produced, has certainly the best title to close this procession of the Lusian heroes. And, as he was the father of navigation, particularly of the voyage of GAMA, to sum up the narrative with his encomium has even some critical propriety.

These observations were suggested by the conduct of Camoëns, whose design, like that of Virgil, was to write a poem which might contain all the triumphs of his country. As the shield of Æneas supplies what could not be introduced in the vision of Elysium, so the ensigns of GAMA complete the purpose of the third and fourth Lusiads. The use of that long episode, the conversation with the King of Melinda, and its connection with the subject, have been already observed. The seeming episode of the pictures, while it fulfills the promise—

And all my country's wars the song adorn,

is also admirably connected with the conduct of the poem. The Hindoos naturally desire to be informed of the country, the history, and power of their foreign visitors, and Paulus sets it before their eyes. In every progression of the scenery the business of the poem advances. The regent and his attendants are struck with the warlike grandeur and power of the strangers, and to accept of their friendship, or to prevent the forerunners of so martial a nation from carrying home the tidings of the discovery of India, becomes the great object of their consideration.

[534] But ah, forlorn, what shame to barb'rous pride.—In the original.—

Mas faltamlhes pincel, faltamlhes cores,
Honra, premio, favor, que as artes criáo.

"But the pencil was wanting, colors were wanting, honour, reward, favour, the nourishers of the arts." This seemed to the translator as in impropriety, and contrary to the purpose of the whole speech of Paulus, which was to give the catual a high idea of Portugal. In the fate of the imaginary painter, the Lusian poet gives us the picture of his own, resentment wrung this impropriety from him. The spirit of the complaint, however, is preserved in the translation. The couplet—

"Immortal fame his deathless labours gave;
Poor man, he sunk neglected to the grave!"

is not in the original. It is the sigh of indignation over the unworthy fate of the unhappy Camoëns.

[535] The ghost-like aspect and the threat'ning look.—Mohammed, by some historians described as of a pale livid complexion, and trux aspectus et vox terribilis, of a fierce threatening aspect, voice, and demeanour.

[536]
When, softly usher'd by the milky dawn,
The sun first rises.—

"I deceive myself greatly," says Castera, "if this simile is not the most noble and the most natural that can be found in any poem. It has been imitated by the Spanish comedian, the illustrious Lopez de Vega, in his comedy of Orpheus and Eurydice, act i. sc. 1:—

"Como mirar puede ser
El sol al amanecer,
I quando se enciende, no."

Castera adds a very loose translation of these Spanish lines in French verse. The literal English is, As the sun may be beheld at its rising, but, when illustriously kindled, cannot. Naked, however, as this is, the imitation of Camoëns is evident. As Castera is so very bold in his encomium of this fine simile of the sun, it is but justice to add his translation of it, together with the original Portuguese, and the translation of Fanshaw. Thus the French translator:—

Les yeux peuvent soûtenir la clarté du soleil naissant, mais lorsqu'il s'est avancé dans sa carrière lumineuse, et que ses rayons répandent les ardeurs du midi, on tacherait en vain de l'envisager; un prompt aveuglement serait le prix de cette audace.

Thus elegantly in the original:—

"Em quanto he fraca a força desta gente,
Ordena como em tudo se resista,
Porque quando o Sol sahe, facilmente
Se pòde nelle por a aguda vista:
Porem despois que sobe claro, & ardente,
Se a agudeza dos olhos o conquista
Tao cega fica, quando ficareis,
Se raizes criar lhe nao tolheis."

And thus humbled by Fanshaw:—

"Now whilst this people's strength is not yet knit,
Think how ye may resist them by all ways.
For when the Sun is in his nonage yit,
Upon his morning beauty men may gaze;
But let him once up to his zenith git,
He strikes them blind with his meridian rays;
So blind will ye be, if ye look not too't,
If ye permit these cedars to take root."

[537]
Around him stand,
With haggard looks, the hoary Magi band.—

The Brahmins, the diviners of India. Ammianus Marcellinus, l. 23, says, that the Persian Magi derived their knowledge from the Brachmanes of India. And Arrianus, l. 7, expressly gives the Brahmins the name of Magi. The Magi of India, says he, told Alexander, on his pretensions to divinity, that in everything he was like other men, except that he took less rest, and did more mischief. The Brahmins are never among modern writers called Magi.

[538] The hov'ring demon gives the dreadful sign.—This has an allusion to the truth of history. Barros relates, that an anger being brought before the Zamorim, "Em hum vaso de agua l'he mostrara hunas naos, que vin ham de muy longe para a India, e que a gente d'ellas seria total destruiçam dos Mouros de aquellas partes.—In a vessel of water he showed him some ships which from a great distance came to India, the people of which would effect the utter subversion of the Moors." Camoëns has certainly chosen a more poetical method of describing this divination, a method in the spirit of Virgil; nor in this is he inferior to his great master. The supernatural flame which seizes on Lavinia while assisting at the sacrifice alone excepted, every other part of the augury of Latinus, and his dream in the Albunean forest,

whither he went to consult his ancestor, the god Faunus, in dignity and poetical colouring, cannot come in comparison with the divination of the Magi, and the appearance of the demon in the dream of the Moorish priest.

[539] Th'eternal yoke.—This picture, it may perhaps be said, is but a bad compliment to the heroes of the Lusiad, and the fruits of their discovery. A little consideration, however, will vindicate Camoëns. It is the demon and the enemies of the Portuguese who procure this divination; everything in it is dreadful, on purpose to determine the zamorim to destroy the fleet of GAMA. In a former prophecy of the conquest of India (when the catual describes the sculpture of the royal palace), our poet has been careful to ascribe the happiest effects to the discovery of his heroes:—

"Beneath their sway majestic, wise, and mild,
Proud of her victors' laws, thrice happier India smil'd."

[540] So let the tyrant plead.—In this short declamation, a seeming excrescence, the business of the poem in reality is carried on. The zamorim, and his prime minister, the catual, are artfully characterised in it; and the assertion—

Lur'd was the regent with the Moorish gold,

is happily introduced by the declamatory reflections which immediately precede it.

[541]
The Moors—their ancient deeds relate,
Their ever-faithful service of the state.—

An explanation of the word Moor is here necessary. When the East afforded no more field for the sword of the conqueror, the Saracens, assisted by the Moors, who had embraced their religion, laid the finest countries in Europe in blood and desolation. As their various embarkations were from the empire of Morocco, the Europeans gave the name of Moors to all the professors of the Mohammedan religion. In the same manner the eastern nations blended all the armies of the Crusaders under one appellation, and the Franks, of whom the army of Godfrey was mostly composed, became their common name for all the inhabitants of the West. Before the arrival of GAMA, as already observed, all the traffic of the East, from the Ethiopian side of Africa to China, was in the hands of Arabian Mohammedans, who, without incorporating with the pagan natives, had their colonies established in every country commodious for commerce. These the Portuguese called Moors; and at present the Mohammedans of India are called the Moors of Hindostan by our English writers. The intelligence these Moors gave to one another, relative to the actions of GAMA; the general terror with which they beheld the appearance of Europeans, whose rivalship they dreaded as the destruction of their power; the various frauds and arts they employed to prevent the return of one man of GAMA'S fleet to Europe, and their threat to withdraw from the dominions of the zamorim, are all according to the truth of history. The speeches of the zamorim and of GAMA, which follow, are also founded in truth.

[542] Troy.

[543] No sumptuous gift thou bring'st.—"As the Portuguese did not expect to find any people but savages beyond the Cape of Good Hope, they only brought with them some preserves and confections, with trinkets of coral, of glass, and other trifles. This opinion, however, deceived them. In Melinda and in

Calicut they found civilized nations, where the arts flourished; who wanted nothing; who were possessed of all the refinements and delicacies on which we value ourselves. The King of Melinda had the generosity to be contented with the present which GAMA made; but the zamorim, with a disdainful eye, beheld the gifts which were offered to him. The present was this: Four mantles of scarlet, six hats adorned with feathers, four chaplets of coral beads, twelve Turkey carpets, seven drinking cups of brass, a chest of sugar, two barrels of oil, and two of honey."—CASTERA.

[544] Fair Acidalia, Love's celestial queen.—Castera derives Acidalia from ἀκηδής, which, he says, implies to act without fear or restraint. Acidalia is one of the names of Venus, in Virgil; derived from Acidalus, a fountain sacred to her in Bœotia.

[545] Sprung from the prince.—John I.

[546] And from her raging tempests, nam'd the Cape.—Bartholomew Diaz, was the first who discovered the southmost point of Africa. He was driven back by the storms, which on these seas were thought always to continue, and which the learned of former ages, says Osorius, thought impassable. Diaz, when he related his voyage to John II. called the southmost point the Cape of Tempests. The expectation of the king, however, was kindled by the account, and with inexpressible joy, says the same author, he immediately named it the Cape of Good Hope.

[547]
The pillar thus of deathless fame, begun
By other chiefs, etc.—

"Till I now ending what those did begin,
The furthest pillar in thy realm advance;
Breaking the element of molten tin,
Through horrid storms I lead to thee the dance."
FANSHAW.

[548]
The regent's palace high o'erlook'd the bay,
Where Gama's black-ribb'd fleet at anchor lay.—

The resemblance of this couplet to many passages in Homer, must be obvious to the intelligent critic.

[549] As in the sun's bright beam.—Imitated from Virgil, who, by the same simile, describes the fluctuation of the thoughts of Æneas, on the eve of the Latian war:—

"Laomedontius heros
Cuncta videns, magno curarum fluctuat æstu,
Atque animum nunc huc celerem, nunc dividit illuc,
In partesque rapit varias, perque omnia versat.
Sicut aquæ tremulum labris ubi lumen ahenis
Sole repercussum, aut radiantis imagine Lunæ,
Omnia pervolitat late loca: jamque sub auras
Erigitur, summique ferit laquearia tecti."

"This way and that he turns his anxious mind,
Thinks, and rejects the counsels he design'd;
Explores himself in vain, in ev'ry part,
And gives no rest to his distracted heart:
So when the sun by day or moon by night
Strike on the polish'd brass their trembling light,
The glitt'ring species here and there divide,
And cast their dubious beams from side to side;
Now on the walls, now on the pavement play,
And to the ceiling flash the glaring day."

Ariosto has also adopted this simile in the eighth book of his Orlando Furioso:—

"Qual d'acqua chiara il tremolante lume
Dal Sol per percossa, o da' notturni rai,
Per gli ampli tetti và con lungo salto
A destra, ed a sinistra, e basso, ed alto."

"So from a water clear, the trembling light
Of Phœbus, or the silver ray of night,
Along the spacious rooms with splendour plays,
Now high, now low, and shifts a thousand ways."

HOOLE.

But the happiest circumstance belongs to Camoëns. The velocity and various shiftings of the sun-beam, reflected from a piece of crystal or polished steel in the hand of a boy, give a much stronger idea of the violent agitation and sudden shiftings of thought than the image of the trembling light of the sun or moon reflected from a vessel of water. The brazen vessel, however, and not the water, is only mentioned by Dryden. Nor must another inaccuracy pass unobserved. That the reflection of the moon flashed the glaring day is not countenanced by the original.

We have already seen the warm encomium paid by Tasso to his contemporary, Camoëns. That great poet, the ornament of Italy, has also testified his approbation by several imitations of the Lusiad. Virgil, in no instance, has more closely copied Homer, than Tasso has imitated the appearance of Bacchus, or the evil demon, in the dream of the Moorish priest. The enchanter Ismeno thus appears to the sleeping Solyman:—

"Soliman' Solimano, i tuoi silenti
Riposi à miglior tempo homai riserva:
Che sotto il giogo de straniere genti
La patria, ove regnasti, ancor' e serva.
In questa terra dormi, e non rammenti,
Ch'insepolte de' tuoi l'ossa conserva?
Ove si gran' vestigio e del tuo scorno,
Tu neghittoso aspetti il nuovo giorno?"

Thus elegantly translated by Mr. Hoole:—

"Oh! Solyman, regardless chief, awake!
In happier hours thy grateful slumber take:
Beneath a foreign yoke thy subjects bend,
And strangers o'er thy land their rule extend:
Here dost thou sleep? here close thy careless eyes,
While uninterr'd each lov'd associate lies?
Here where thy fame has felt the hostile scorn,
Canst thou, unthinking, wait the rising morn?"

The conclusion of this canto has been slightly altered by the translator. Camoëns, adhering to history, makes GAMA (when his factors are detained on shore) seize upon some of the native merchants as hostages. At the intreaty of their wives and children the zamorim liberates his captives; while GAMA, having recovered his men and the merchandise, sailed away, carrying with him the unfortunate natives, whom he had seized as hostages.

As there is nothing heroic in this dishonourable action of GAMA'S, Mickle has omitted it, and has altered the conclusion of the canto.—Ed.

[550] Mickle, in place of the first seventeen stanzas of this canto, has inserted about three hundred lines of his own composition; in this respect availing himself of the licence he had claimed in his preface.—Ed.

[551] Thy sails, and rudders too, my will demands.—According to history.

[552] My sov'reign's fleet I yield not to your sway.—The circumstance of GAMA'S refusing to put his fleet into the power of the zamorim, is thus rendered by Fanshaw:—

"The Malabar protests that he shall rot
In prison, if he send not for the ships.
He (constant, and with noble anger hot)
His haughty menace weighs not at two chips."

[553] Through Gata's hills.—The hills of Gata or Gate, mountains which form a natural barrier on the eastern side of the kingdom of Malabar.

"Nature's rude wall, against the fierce Canar
They guard the fertile walls of Malabar."

LUSIAD, vii.

[554] Then, furious, rushing to the darken'd bay.—For the circumstances of the battle, and the tempest which then happened, see the Life of GAMA.

[555] I left my fix'd command my navy's guard.—See the Life of GAMA.

[556] Unmindful of my fate on India's shore.—This most magnanimous resolution, to sacrifice his own safety or his life for the safe return of the fleet, is strictly true.—See the Life of GAMA.

[557] Abrupt—the monarch cries—"What yet may save!"—GAMA'S declaration, that no message from him to the fleet could alter the orders he had already left, and his rejection of any further treaty, have a necessary effect in the conduct of the poem. They hasten the catastrophe, and give a verisimilitude to the abrupt and full submission of the zamorim.

[558] The rollers—i.e. the capstans.—The capstan is a cylindrical windlass, worked with bars, which are moved from hole to hole as it turns round. It is used on board ship to weigh the anchors, raise the masts, etc. The versification of this passage in the original affords a most noble example of imitative harmony:—

"Mas ja nas naos os bons trabalhadores
Volvem o cabrestante, & repartidos
Pello trabalho, huns puxao pella amarra,
Outros quebrao co peito duro a barra."

STANZA X.

[559]
Mozaide, whose zealous care
To Gama's eyes reveal'd each treach'rous snare.—

Had this been mentioned sooner, the interest of the catastrophe of the poem must have languished. Though he is not a warrior, the unexpected friend of GAMA bears a much more considerable part in the action of the Lusiad than the faithful Achates, the friend of the hero, bears in the business of the Æneid.

[560] There wast thou call'd to thy celestial home.—This exclamatory address to the Moor Monzaida, however it may appear digressive, has a double propriety. The conversion of the Eastern world is the great purpose of the expedition of GAMA, and Monzaida is the first fruits of that conversion. The good characters of the victorious heroes, however neglected by the great genius of Homer, have a fine effect in making an epic poem interest us and please. It might have been said, that Monzaida was a traitor to his friends, who crowned his villainy with apostacy. Camoëns has, therefore, wisely drawn him with other features, worthy of the friendship of GAMA. Had this been neglected, the hero of the Lusiad might have shared the fate of the wise Ulysses of the Iliad, against whom, as Voltaire justly observes, every reader bears a secret ill will. Nor is the poetical character of Monzaida unsupported by history. He was not an Arab Moor, so he did not desert his countrymen. These Moors had determined on the destruction of GAMA; Monzaida admired and esteemed him, and therefore generously revealed to him his danger. By his attachment to GAMA he lost all his effects in India, a circumstance which his prudence and knowledge of affairs must have certainly foreseen. By the known dangers he encountered, by the loss he thus voluntarily sustained, and by his after constancy, his sincerity is undoubtedly proved.

[561] The joy of the fleet on the homeward departure from India.—We are now come to that part of the Lusiad, which, in the conduct of the poem, is parallel to the great catastrophe of the Iliad, when, on the death of Hector, Achilles thus addresses the Grecian army—

"Ye sons of Greece, in triumph bring
The corpse of Hector, and your pæons sing:
Be this the song, slow moving toward the shore,
'Hector is dead, and Ilion is no more.'"

Our Portuguese poet, who in his machinery, and many other instances, has followed the manner of Virgil, now forsakes him. In a very bold and masterly spirit he now models his poem by the steps of Homer. What of the Lusiad yet remains, in poetical conduct (though not in an imitation of circumstances), exactly resembles the latter part of the Iliad. The games at the funeral of Patroclus, and the redemption of the body of Hector, are the completion of the rage of Achilles. In the same manner, the reward of the heroes, and the consequences of their expedition complete the unity of the Lusiad. I cannot say it appears that Milton ever read our poet (though Fanshaw's translation was published in his time); yet no instance can be given of a more striking resemblance of plan and conduct, than may be produced in two principal parts of the poem of Camoëns, and of the Paradise Lost.—See the Dissertation which follows this book.

[562] Near where the bowers of Paradise were plac'd.—Between the mouth of the Ganges and Euphrates.

[563] Swans.

[564] His falling kingdom claim'd his earnest care.—This fiction, in poetical conduct, bears a striking resemblance to the digressive histories with which Homer enriches and adorns his poems, particularly to the beautiful description of the feast of the gods with "the blameless Ethiopians." It also contains a masterly commentary on the machinery of the Lusiad. The Divine Love conducts GAMA to India. The same Divine Love is represented as preparing to reform the corrupted world, when its attention is particularly called to bestow a foretaste of immortality on the heroes of the expedition which discovered the eastern world. Nor do the wild fantastic loves, mentioned in this little episode, afford any objection against this explanation, an explanation which is expressly given in the episode itself. These wild fantastic amours signify, in the allegory, the wild sects of different enthusiasts, which spring up under the wings of the best and most rational institutions; and which, however contrary to each other, all agree in deriving their authority from the same source.

[565] A young Actæon.—The French translator has the following characteristic note: "This passage is an eternal monument of the freedoms taken by Camoëns, and at the same time a proof of the imprudence of poets; an authentic proof of that prejudice which sometimes blinds them, notwithstanding all the light of their genius. The modern Actæon of whom he speaks, was King Sebastian. He loved the chase; but, that pleasure, which is one of the most innocent and one of the most noble we can possibly taste, did not at all interrupt his attention to the affairs of state, and did not render him savage, as our author pretends. On this point the historians are rather to be believed. And what would the lot of princes be, were they allowed no relaxation from their toils, while they allow that privilege to their people? Subjects as we are, let us venerate the amusements of our sovereigns; let us believe that the august cares for our good, which employ them, follow them often even to the very bosom of their pleasures."

Many are the strokes in the Lusiad which must endear the character of Camoëns to every reader of sensibility. The noble freedom and manly indignation with which he mentions the foible of his prince, and the flatterers of his court, would do honour to the greatest names of Greece or Rome. While the shadow of freedom remained in Portugal, the greatest men of that nation, in the days of Lusian heroism, thought and conducted themselves in the spirit of Camoëns. A noble anecdote of this brave spirit offers itself. Alonzo IV., surnamed the Brave, ascended the throne of Portugal in the vigour of his age. The pleasures of the chase engrossed all his attention. His confidants and favourites encouraged, and allured him to it. His time was spent in the forests of Cintra, while the affairs of government were neglected or executed by those whose interest it was to keep their sovereign in ignorance. His presence, at last, being necessary at Lisbon, he entered the council with all the brisk impetuosity of a young sportsman, and with great familiarity and gaiety entertained his nobles with the history of a whole month spent in hunting, in fishing, and shooting. When he had finished his narrative, a nobleman of the first rank rose up: "Courts and camps," said he, "were allotted for kings, not woods and deserts. Even the affairs of private men suffer when recreation is preferred to business. But when the whims of pleasure engross the thoughts of a king, a whole nation is consigned to ruin. We came here for other purposes than to hear the exploits of the chase, exploits which are only intelligible to grooms and falconers. If your majesty will attend to the wants, and remove the grievances of your people, you will find them obedient subjects; if not—" The king, starting with rage, interrupted him, "If not, what?" "If not," resumed the nobleman, in a firm tone, "they will look for another and a better king." Alonzo, in the highest transport of passion, expressed his resentment, and hasted out of the room. In a little while, however, he returned, calm and reconciled: "I perceive," said he, "the truth of what you say. He who will not execute the duties of a king, cannot long have good subjects. Remember, from this day, you have nothing more to do with Alonzo the sportsman, but with Alonzo the king of Portugal." His majesty was as good as his promise, and became, as a warrior and politician, one of the greatest of the Portuguese monarchs.

[566] With love's fierce flames his frozen heart shall burn.—"It is said, that upon the faith of a portrait Don Sebastian fell in love with Margaret of France, daughter of Henry II., and demanded her in marriage, but was refused. The Spaniards treated him no less unfavourably, for they also rejected his proposals for one of the daughters of Philip II. Our author considers these refusals as the punishment of Don Sebastian's excessive attachment to the chase; but this is only a consequence of the prejudice with which he viewed the amusements of his prince. The truth is, these princesses were refused for political reasons, and not with any regard to the manner in which he filled up his moments of leisure."

Thus Castera, who, with the same spirit of sagacity, starts and answers the following objections: "But here is a difficulty: Camoëns wrote during the life of Don Sebastian, but the circumstance he relates (the return of GAMA) happened several years before, under the reign of Emmanuel. How, therefore, could he say that Cupid then saw Don Sebastian at the chase, when that prince was not then born? The answer is easy: Cupid, in the allegory of this work, represents the love of God, the Holy Spirit, who is God himself. Now the Divinity admits of no distinction of time; one glance of his eye beholds the past, the present, and the future; everything is present before him."

This defence of the fiction of Actæon is not more absurd than useless. The free and bold spirit of poetry, and in particular the nature of allegory, defend it. The poet might easily have said, that Cupid foresaw; but had he said so his satire had been much less genteel. As the sentiments of Castera on this passage are extremely characteristic of French ideas, another note from him will perhaps be agreeable. "Several Portuguese writers have remarked," says he, "that the wish—

'Of these lov'd dogs that now his passions sway,
Ah! may he never fall the hapless prey!'

Had in it an air of prophecy; and fate, in effect, seemed careful to accomplish it, in making the presaged woes to fall upon Don Sebastian. If he did not fall a prey to his pack of hounds, we may, however, say that he was devoured by his favourites, who misled his youth and his great soul. But at any rate our poet has carried the similitude too far. It was certainly injurious to Don Sebastian, who nevertheless had the bounty not only not to punish this audacity, but to reward the just eulogies which the author had bestowed on him in other places. As much as the indiscretion of Camoëns ought to surprise us, as much ought we to admire the generosity of his master."

This foppery, this slavery in thinking, cannot fail to rouse the indignation of every manly breast, when the facts are fairly stated. Don Sebastian, who ascended the throne when a child, was a prince of great abilities and great spirit, but his youth was poisoned with the most romantic ideas of military glory. The affairs of state were left to his ministers (for whose character see the next note), his other studies were neglected, and military exercises, of which he not unjustly esteemed the chase a principal, were almost his sole employ. Camoëns beheld this romantic turn, and in a genteel allegorical satire foreboded its consequences. The wish, that his prince might not fall the prey of his favourite passion, was in vain. In a rash, ill-concerted expedition into Africa, Don Sebastian lost his crown in his twenty-fifth year, an event which soon after produced the fall of the Portuguese empire. Had the nobility possessed the spirit of Camoëns, had they, like him, endeavoured to check the quixotism of a young generous prince, that prince might have reigned long and happy, and Portugal might have escaped the Spanish yoke, which soon followed his defeat at Alcazar; a yoke which sunk Portugal into an abyss of misery, from which, in all probability, she will never emerge into her former splendour.

[567]
Enraged, he sees a venal herd, the shame
Of human race, assume the titled name.—

"After having ridiculed all the pleasures of Don Sebastian, the author now proceeds to his courtiers, to whom he has done no injustice. Those who are acquainted with the Portuguese history, will readily acknowledge this."—CASTERA.

[568] On the hard bosoms of the stubborn crowd.—There in an elegance in the original of this line, which the English language will not admit:—

"Nos duros coraçoens de plebe dura,"—

i.e., In the hard hearts of the hard vulgar.

[569] Cupid.

[570]
Thus from my native waves a hero line
Shall rise, and o'er the East illustrious shine.—

"By the line of heroes to be produced by the union of the Portuguese with the Nereids, is to be understood the other Portuguese, who, following the steps of GAMA, established illustrious colonies in India."—CASTERA.

[571] And Fame—a giant goddess.—This passage affords a striking instance of the judgment of Camoëns. Virgil's celebrated description of Fame is in his eye, but he copies it, as Virgil, in his best imitations, copies after Homer. He adopts some circumstances, but, by adding others, he makes a new picture, which justly may be called his own.

[572] The wat'ry gods.—To mention the gods in the masculine gender, and immediately to apply to them—

"O peito feminil, que levemente
Muda quaysquer propositos tomados."—

The ease with which the female breast changes its resolutions, may to the hypercritical appear reprehensible. The expression, however, is classical, and therefore retained. Virgil uses it, where Æneas is conducted by Venus through the flames of Troy:—

"Descendo, ac ducente Deo, flammam inter et hostes Expedior."

This is in the manner of the Greek poets, who use the word Θεός for god or goddess.

[573] White as her swans.—A distant fleet compared to swans on a lake is certainly a happy thought. The allusion to the pomp of Venus, whose agency is immediately concerned, gives it besides a peculiar propriety. This simile, however, is not in the original. It is adopted from an uncommon liberty taken by Fanshaw:—

"The pregnant sails on Neptune's surface creep,
Like her own swans, in gate, out-chest, and fether."

[574] Soon as the floating verdure caught their sight.—As the departure of GAMA from India was abrupt, he put into one of the beautiful islands of Anchediva for fresh water. "While he was here careening his ships," says Faria, "a pirate named Timoja, attacked him with eight small vessels, so linked together and covered with boughs, that they formed the appearance of a floating island." This, says Castera, afforded the fiction of the floating island of Venus. "The fictions of Camoëns," says he, "are the more marvellous, because they are all founded in history. It is not difficult to find why he makes his island of Anchediva to wander on the waves; it is an allusion to a singular event related by Barros." He then proceeds to the story of Timoja, as if the genius of Camoëns stood in need of so weak an assistance.

[575] In friendly pity of Latona's woes.—Latona, pregnant by Jupiter, was persecuted by Juno, who sent the serpent Python in pursuit of her. Neptune, in pity of her distress, raised the island of Delos for her refuge, where she was delivered of Apollo and Diana.—OVID, Met.

[576] Form'd in a crystal lake the waters blend.—Castera also attributes this to history. "The Portuguese actually found in this island," says he, "a fine piece of water ornamented with hewn stones and magnificent aqueducts; an ancient and superb work, of which nobody knew the author."

In 1505 Don Francisco Almeyda built a fort in this island. In digging among some ancient ruins he found many crucifixes of black and red colour, from whence the Portuguese conjectured, says Osorius, that the Anchedivian islands had in former ages been inhabited by Christians.—Vid. Osor. 1. iv.

[577]
The orange here perfumes the buxom air.
And boasts the golden hue of Daphne's hair.—

Frequent allusions to the fables of the ancients form a characteristic feature of the poetry of the 16th and 17th centuries. A profusion of it is pedantry; a moderate use of it, however, in a poem of those times pleases, because it discovers the stages of composition, and has in itself a fine effect, as it illustrates its subject by presenting the classical reader with some little landscapes of that country through which he has travelled. The description of forests is a favourite topic in poetry. Chaucer, Tasso, and Spenser, have been happy in it, but both have copied an admired passage in Statius:—

"Cadit ardua fagus,
Chaoniumque nemus, brumæque illæsa cupressus;
Procumbunt piceæ, flammis alimenta supremis,
Ornique, iliceæque trabes, metuandaque sulco
Taxus, et infandos belli potura cruores
Fraxinus, atque situ non expugnabile robur:
Hinc audax abies, et odoro vulnere pinus
Scinditur, acclinant intonsa cacumina terræ
Alnus amica fretis, nec inhospita vitibus ulmus."

In rural descriptions three things are necessary to render them poetical: the happiness of epithet, of picturesque arrangement, and of little landscape views. Without these, all the names of trees and flowers, though strung together in tolerable numbers, contain no more poetry than a nurseryman or a florist's catalogue. In Statius, in Tasso and Spenser's admired forests (Ger. Liber. c. 3. st. 75, 76, and F. Queen, b. 1 c. 1. st. 8, 9), the poetry consists entirely in the happiness of the epithets. In Camoëns, all the three requisites are admirably attained and blended together.

[578] And stain'd with lover's blood.—Pyramus and Thisbe:—

"Arborei fœtus aspergine cædis in atram
Vertuntur faciem: madefactaque sanguine radix
Puniceo tingit pendentia mora colore.....
At tu quo ramis arbor miserabile corpus
Nunc tegis unius, mox es tectura duorum;
Signa tene cædis: pullosque et lectibus aptos
Semper habe fœtus gemini monumenta cruoris."

OVID, Met.

[579] The shadowy vale.—Literal from the original,—O sombrio valle—which Fanshaw, however, has translated, "the gloomy valley," and thus has given us a funereal, where the author intended a festive, landscape. It must be confessed, however, that the description of the island of Venus, is infinitely the best part of all of Fanshaw's translation. And indeed the dullest prose translation might obscure, but could not possibly throw a total eclipse over, so admirable an original.

[580] The woe-mark'd flower of slain Adonis—water'd by the tears of love.—The Anemone. "This," says Castera, "is applicable to the celestial Venus, for, according to my theology, her amour with Adonis had nothing in it impure, but was only the love which nature bears to the sun." The fables of antiquity have generally a threefold interpretation, an historical allusion, a physical and a metaphysical allegory. In the latter view, the fable of Adonis is only applicable to the celestial Venus. A divine youth is outrageously slain, but shall revive again at the restoration of the golden age. Several nations, it is well known, under

different names, celebrated the Mysteries, or the death and resurrection of Adonis; among whom were the British Druids, as we are told by Dr. Stukely. In the same manner Cupid, in the fable of Psyche, is interpreted by mythologists, to signify the Divine Love weeping over the degeneracy of human nature.

[581]
At strife appear the lawns and purpled skies,
Who from each other stole the beauteous dyes.—

On this passage Castera has the following sensible, though turgid, note: "This thought," says he, "is taken from the idyllium of Ausonius on the rose:—

'Ambigeres raperetne rosis Aurora ruborem,
An daret, et flores tingere torta dies.'

Camoëns who had a genius rich of itself, still further enriched it at the expense of the ancients. Behold what makes great authors! Those who pretend to give us nothing but the fruits of their own growth, soon fail, like the little rivulets which dry up in the summer, very different from the floods, who receive in their course the tribute of a hundred and a hundred rivers, and which even in the dog-days carry their waves triumphant to the ocean."

[582] The hyacinth bewrays the doleful Ai.—Hyacinthus, a youth beloved of Apollo, by whom he was accidentally slain, and afterwards turned into a flower:—

"Tyrioque nitentior ostro
Flos oritur, formamque capit, quam lilia: si non,
Purpureus color huic, argenteus esset in illis.
Non satis hoc Phæbo est: is enim fuit auctor honoris.
Ipse suos gemitus foliis inscribit; et Ai, Ai,
Flos habet inscriptum: funestaque littera ducta est."

OVID, Met.

[583] The second Argonauts.—The expedition of the Golden Fleece was esteemed, in ancient poetry, one of the most daring adventures, the success of which was accounted miraculous. The allusions of Camoëns to this voyage, though in the spirit of his age, are by no means improper.

[584] Wide o'er the beauteous isle the lovely fair.—We now come to the passage condemned by Voltaire as so lascivious, that no nation in Europe, except the Portuguese and Italians, could bear it. The fate of Camoëns has hitherto been very peculiar. The mixture of Pagan and Christian mythology in his machinery has been anathematized, and his island of love represented as a brothel. Yet both accusations are the arrogant assertions of the most superficial acquaintance with his works. His poem itself, and a comparison of its parts with the similar conduct of the greatest modern poets, will clearly evince, that in both instances no modern epic writer of note has given less offence to true criticism.

Not to mention Ariosto, whose descriptions will often admit of no palliation, Tasso, Spenser, and Milton, have always been esteemed among the chastest of poets, yet in that delicacy of warm description, which Milton has so finely exemplified in the nuptials of our first parents, none of them can boast the continued uniformity of the Portuguese poet. Though there is a warmth in the colouring of Camoëns which even the genius of Tasso has not reached: and though the island of Armida is evidently copied from the Lusiad, yet those who are possessed of the finer feelings, will easily discover an essential difference between the love-scenes of the two poets, a difference greatly in favour of the delicacy of the former. Though the nymphs in Camoëns are detected naked in the woods, and in the stream, and though desirous to captivate, still their behaviour is that of the virgin who hopes to be the spouse. They act the part of offended modesty; even when they yield they are silent, and behave in every respect like Milton's Eve in the state of innocence, who—

"What was honour knew,"

And who displayed—

"Her virtue, and the conscience of her worth,
That would be wooed, and not unsought be won."

To sum up all, the nuptial sanctity draws its hallowed curtains, and a masterly allegory shuts up the love-scenes of Camoëns.

How different from all this is the island of Armida in Tasso, and its translation, the bower of Acrasia in Spenser! In these virtue is seduced; the scene therefore is less delicate. The nymphs, while they are bathing, in place of the modesty of the bride as in Camoëns, employ all the arts of the lascivious wanton. They stay not to be wooed; but, as Spenser gives it—

The amorous sweet spoils to greedy eyes reveal.

One stanza from our English poet, which, however, is rather fuller than the original, shall here suffice:—

"Withal she laughed and she blush'd withal,
That blushing to her laughter gave more grace,
And laughter to her blushing, as did fall.
Now when they spy'd the knight to slack his pace,
Them to behold, and in his sparkling face
The secret signs of kindled lust appear,
Their wanton merriments they did increase,
And to him beckon'd to approach more near,
And show'd him many sights, that courage cold could rear.

This and other descriptions—

"Upon a bed of roses she was laid
As faint through heat, or dight to pleasant sin"—

present every idea of lascivious voluptuousness. The allurements of speech are also added. Songs, which breathe every persuasive, are heard; and the nymphs boldly call to the beholder:—

E' dolce campo di battaglia il letto
Fiavi, e l'herbetta morbida de' prati.—TASSO.

"Our field of battle is the downy bed,
Or flow'ry turf amid the smiling mead."—HOOLE.

These, and the whole scenes in the domains of Armida and Acrasia, are in a turn of manner the reverse of the island of Venus. In these the expression and idea are meretricious. In Camoëns, though the colouring is even warmer, yet the modesty of the Venus de Medicis is still preserved. In everything he describes there is still something strongly similar to the modest attitude of the arms of that celebrated statue. Though prudery, that usual mask of the impurest minds, may condemn him, yet those of the most chaste, though less gloomy turn, will allow, that in comparison with others, he might say,—Virginibus puerisque canto.

Spenser also, where he does not follow Tasso, is often gross; and even in some instances, where the expression is most delicate, the picture is nevertheless indecently lascivious.

[585] The hunter.—Acteon.

[586] Madd'ning as he said.—At the end of his Homer Mr. Pope has given an index of the instances of imitative and sentimental harmony contained in his translations. He has also often even in his notes pointed out the adaptation of sound to sense. The translator of the Lusiad hopes he may for once say, that he has not been inattentive to this great essential of good versification: how he has succeeded the judicious only must determine. The speech of Leonard to the cursory reader may perhaps sometimes appear careless, and sometimes turgid and stiff. That speech, however, is an attempt at the imitative and sentimental harmony, and with the judicious he rests its fate. As the translation in this instance exceeds the original in length, the objection of a foreign critic requires attention. An old pursy Abbé, (and critics are apt to judge by themselves) may indeed be surprised that a man out of breath with running should be able to talk so long. But, had he consulted the experiences of others, he would have found it was no wonderful matter for a stout and young cavalier to talk twice as much, though fatigued with the chase of a couple of miles, provided the supposition be allowed, that he treads on the last steps of his flying mistress.

[587] Hence, ye profane.—We have already observed, that in every other poet the love scenes are generally described as those of guilt and remorse. The contrary character of those of Camoëns not only gives them a delicacy unknown to other moderns, but, by the fiction of the spousal rites, the allegory and machinery of the poem are most happily conducted.

[588] Spread o'er the eastern world the dread alarms.—This admonition places the whole design of the poem before us. To extirpate Mohammedanism, and propagate Christianity, were professed as the principal purpose of the discoveries of Prince Henry and King Emmanuel. In the beginning of the seventh Lusiad, the nations of Europe are upbraided for permitting the Saracens to erect and possess an empire, which alike threatened Europe and Christianity. The Portuguese, however, the patriot poet concludes, will themselves overthrow their enormous power: an event which is the proposed subject of the Lusiad, and which is represented as, in effect, completed in the last book. On this system, adopted by the poet, and which on every occasion was avowed by their kings, the Portuguese made immense conquests in the East. Yet, let it be remembered, to the honour of GAMA, and the first commanders who followed his route, that the plots of the Moors, and their various breaches of treaty, gave rise to the first wars which the Portuguese waged in Asia. On finding that all the colonies of the Moors were combined for their destruction, the Portuguese declared war against the eastern Moors, and their allies, wherever they

found them. The course of human things, however, soon took place, and the sword of victory and power soon became the sword of tyranny and rapine.

[589] Far o'er the silver lake of Mexic.—The city of Mexico is environed with an extensive lake; or, according to Cortez, in his second narration to Charles V., with two lakes, one of fresh, the other of salt water, in circuit about fifty leagues. This situation, said the Mexicans, was appointed by their God Vitzliputzli, who, according to the explanation of their picture-histories, led their forefathers a journey of fourscore years, in search of the promised land. Four of the principal priests carried the idol in a coffer of reeds. Whenever they halted they built a tabernacle for their god in the midst of their camp, where they placed the coffer and the altar. They then sowed the land, and their stay or departure, without regard to the harvest, was directed by the orders received from their idol, till at last, by his command, they fixed their abode on the site of Mexico.

[590] Before the love-sick Roman.—Mark Antony.

[591] The beverage—the fountain's cooling aid confess'd.—It was a custom of the ancients in warm climates to mix the coolest spring water with their wine, immediately before drinking; not, we may suppose, to render it less intoxicating, but on account of the cooling flavour it thereby received. Homer tells us that the wine which Ulysses gave to Polyphemus would bear twenty measures of water. Modern luxury has substituted preserved ice, in place of the more ancient mixture.

[592] Music, such as erst subdued the horrid frown of hell, etc.—Alluding to the fable of Orpheus. Fanshaw's translation, as already observed, was published fourteen years before the Paradise Lost. These lines of Milton—

"What could it less, when spirits immortal sung?
Their song was partial, but the harmony
Suspended hell, and took with ravishment
The thronging audience,"

bear a resemblance to these of Fanshaw—

"Musical instruments not wanting, such
As to the damn'd spirits once gave ease
In the dark vaults of the infernal hall."

To slumber amid their punishment, though omitted by Fanshaw, is literal:—

"Fizerao descançar da eterna pena."

[593] No more the summer of my life remains.—It is not certain when Camoëns wrote this. It seems, however, not long to have preceded the publication of his poem, at which time he was in his fifty-fifth year. This apostrophe to his muse may, perhaps, by some be blamed as another digression; but, so little does it require defence, that one need not hesitate to affirm that, had Homer, who often talks to his muse, introduced, on these favourable opportunities, any little picture or history of himself, these digressions would have been the most interesting parts of his works. Had any history of Homer complained, like this of Camoëns, it would have been bedewed with the tears of ages.

[594] Thy faith repent not, nor lament thy wrong.—P. Alvarez Cabral, the second Portuguese commander who sailed to India, entered into a treaty of alliance with Trimumpara, king of Cochin, and high priest of Malabar. The zamorim raised powerful armies to dethrone him. His fidelity to the Portuguese was unalterable, though his affairs were brought to the lowest ebb.—See the history in the Preface.

[595]
His ship's strong sides shall groan beneath his weight,
And deeper waves receive the sacred freight.—

Thus Virgil:—

"Simul accipit alveo
Ingentem Æneam. Gemuit sub pondere cymba
Sutilis, et multam accepit rimosa paludem."—ÆN. vi. 412.

That the visionary boat of Charon groaned under the weight of Æneas is a fine poetical stroke; but that the crazy rents let in the water is certainly lowering the image. The thought, however, as managed in Camoëns is much grander than in Virgil, and affords a happy instance where the hyperbole is truly poetical.

The Lusiad affords many instances which must be highly pleasing to the Portuguese, but dry to those who are unacquainted with their history. Nor need one hesitate to assert that, were we not acquainted with the Roman history from our childhood, a great part of the Æneid would appear to us intolerably uninteresting. Sensible of this disadvantage which every version of historical poetry must suffer, the translator has not only in the notes added every incident which might elucidate the subject, but has also, all along, in the episode in the third and fourth books, in the description of the painted ensigns in the eighth, and in the allusions in the present book, endeavoured to throw every historical incident into that universal language, the picturesque of poetry. When Hector storms the Grecian camp, when Achilles marches to battle, every reader understands and is affected with the bold painting. But when Nestor talks of his exploits at the funeral games of Amarynces (Iliad xxiii.) the critics themselves cannot comprehend him, and have vied with each other in inventing explanations.

[596] Proas, or paraos, Indian vessels which lie low on the water, are worked with oars, and carry 100 men and upwards apiece.

[597]
His robes are sprinkled o'er,
And his proud face dash'd, with his menials' gore.—

See the history in the Preface.

[598] Round Lusus' fleet to pour their sulph'rous entrails.—How Pacheco avoided this formidable danger, see the history in the preface.

[599] Nor Tiber's bridge.—When Porsenna besieged Rome, Horatius Cocles defended the pass of a bridge till the Romans destroyed it behind him. Having thus saved the pass, heavy armed as he was, he swam across the Tiber to his companions. Roman history, however, at this period, is often mixed with

fable. Miltiades obtained a great victory over Darius at Marathon. The stand made by Leonidas at Thermopylæ is well known. The battles of Pacheco were in defence of the fords by which alone the city of Cochin could be entered. The numbers he withstood by land and sea, and the victories he obtained, are much more astonishing than the defence of Thermopylæ.

[600] Bound to the mast the godlike hero stands.—English history affords an instance of similar resolution in Admiral Bembo, who was supported in a wooden frame, and continued the engagement after his legs and thighs were shivered in splinters. Contrary to the advice of his officers, the young Almeyda refused to bear off, though almost certain to be overpowered, and though both wind and tide were against him. His father had sharply upbraided him for a former retreat, where victory was thought impossible. He now fell the victim of his father's ideas of military glory.

[601] The fleets of India fly.—After having cleared the Indian seas, the viceroy, Almeyda, attacked the combined fleets of Egypt, Cambaya, and the zamorim, in the entrance and harbour of Diu, or Dio. The fleet of the zamorim almost immediately fled. That of Melique Yaz, Lord of Diu, suffered much; but the greatest slaughter fell upon the Egyptians and Turks, commanded by Mir-Hocem, who had defeated and killed the young Almeyda. Of 800 Mamelukes, or Turks, who fought under Mir-Hocem, only 22, says Osorius, survived this engagement. Melique Yaz, says Faria y Sousa, was born in slavery, and descended of the Christians of Roxia. The road to preferment is often a dirty one; but Melique's was much less so than that of many. As the King of Cambaya was one day riding in state, an unlucky kite dunged upon his royal head. His majesty in great wrath swore he would give all he was worth to have the offender killed. Melique, who was an expert archer, immediately despatched an arrow, which brought the audacious hawk to the ground. For the merit of this eminent service he was made Lord of Diu, or Dio, a considerable city, the strongest and the most important fortress at that time in all India.—See Faria, 1. 2, c. 2.

[602] Great Cunia.—Tristan da Cunha, or d'Acugna.

[603] Heav'n indignant showers their arrows backward.—Some writers related that, when Albuquerque besieged Ormuz, a violent wind drove the arrows of the enemy backward upon their own ranks. Osorius says, that many of the dead Persians and Moors were found to have died by arrows. But as that weapon was not used by the Portuguese he conjectures that, in their despair of victory, many of the enemy had thus killed themselves, rather than survive the defeat.

[604] Muscat.

[605] Bahrein, in the Persian Gulf.

[606] What glorious palms on Goa's isle I see.—This important place was made an archbishopric, the capital of the Portuguese empire in the east, and the seat of their viceroys; for which purposes it is advantageously situated on the coast of Dekhan. It still remains in the possession of the Portuguese.

[607] Malacca.—The conquest of this place was one of the greatest actions of Albuquerque. It became the chief port of the eastern part of Portuguese India, and second only to Goa. Besides a great many pieces of ordnance which were carried away by the Moors who escaped, 3000 large cannon remained the prize of the victors. When Albuquerque was on the way to Malacca, he attacked a large ship; but, just as his men were going to board her, she suddenly appeared all in flames, which obliged the Portuguese to bear off. Three days afterwards the same vessel sent a boat to Albuquerque, offering an

alliance, which was accepted. The flames, says Osorius, were only artificial, and did not the least damage. Another wonderful adventure immediately happened. The admiral soon after sent his long-boats to attack a ship commanded by one Nehoada Beeguea. The enemy made an obstinate resistance. Nehoada himself was pierced with several mortal wounds, but lost not one drop of blood till a bracelet was taken off his arm, when immediately the blood gushed out. According to Osorius, this was said to be occasioned by the virtue of a stone in the bracelet, taken out of an animal called Cabrisia, which, when worn on the body, could prevent the effusion of blood from the most grievous wounds.

[608] Yet art thou stain'd.—A detail of all the grant actions of Albuquerque would have been tedious and unpoetical. Camoëns has chosen the most brilliant, and has happily suppressed the rest by a display of indignation. The French translator has the following note on this passage: "Behold another instance of our author's prejudice! The action which he condemns had nothing in it blameable: but, as he was of a most amorous constitution, he thought every fault which could plead an amour in its excuse ought to be pardoned; but true heroes, such as Albuquerque, follow other maxims. This great man had in his palace a beautiful Indian slave. He viewed her with the eyes of a father, and the care of her education was his pleasure. A Portuguese soldier, named Ruy Diaz, had the boldness to enter the general's apartment, where he succeeded so well with the girl that he obtained his desire. When Albuquerque heard of it, he immediately ordered him to the gallows."

Camoëns, however, was no such undistinguishing libertine as this would represent him. In a few pages we find him praising the continence of Don Henry de Meneses, whose victory over his passions he calls the highest excellence of youth. Nor does it appear by what authority the Frenchman assures us of the chaste paternal affection which Albuquerque bore to this Indian girl. It was the great aim of Albuquerque to establish colonies in India, and, for that purpose, he encouraged his soldiers to marry with the natives. The most sightly girls were selected, and educated in the religion and household arts of Portugal, and portioned at the expense of the general. These he called his daughters, and with great pleasure he used to attend their weddings, several couples being usually joined together at one time. At one of these nuptials, says Faria, the festivity having continued late, and the brides being mixed together, several of the bridegrooms committed a blunder. The mistakes of the night, however, as they were all equal in point of honour, were mutually forgiven in the morning, and each man took his proper wife whom he had received at the altar. This delicate anecdote of Albuquerque's sons and daughters is as bad a commentary on the note of Castera as it is on the severity which the commander showed to poor Diaz. Nor does Camoëns stand alone in the condemnation of the general. The historian agrees with the poet. Mentioning the death of D. Antonio Noronha, "This gentleman," says Faria, "used to moderate the violent temper of his uncle, Albuquerque, which soon after showed itself in rigid severity. He ordered a soldier to be hanged for an amour with one of the slaves whom he called daughters, and whom he used to give in marriage. When some of his officers asked him what authority he had to take the poor man's life, he drew his sword, told them that was his commission, and instantly broke them." To marry his soldiers with the natives was the plan of Albuquerque: his severity, therefore, seems unaccountable, unless we admit the 'perhaps' of Camoëns, ou de cioso, perhaps it was jealousy.—But, whatever incensed the general, the execution of the soldier was contrary to the laws of every nation;{*} and the honest indignation of Camoëns against one of the greatest of his countrymen, one who was the grand architect of the Portuguese empire in the East, affords a noble instance of that manly freedom of sentiment which knows no right by which king or peer may do injustice to the meanest subject. Nor can we omit the observation, that the above note of Castera is of a piece with the French devotion we have already seen him pay to the name of king, a devotion which breathes the true spirit of the blessed advice given by Father Paul to the republic of Venice: "When a nobleman commits an offence against a subject," says the Jesuit, "let every means be tried to justify him. But, if a subject has offended a nobleman, let him be punished with the utmost severity."

{*} *Osorius relates the affair of Diaz with some other circumstances; but with no difference that affects this assertion.*

[609] Not Ammon.—Campaspe, the most beautiful concubine of Alexander the Great, was given by that monarch to Apelles, whom he perceived in love with her. Araspas had strict charge of the fair captive, Panthea. His attempt on her virtue was forgiven by Cyrus.

[610] And Flandria's earldom on the knight bestow'd.—"Baldwin, surnamed Iron-arm, Grand Forester of Flanders, being in love with Judith, the daughter of Charles the Bald, and widow of Ethelwolf, king of England, obtained his desire by force. Charles, though at first he highly resented, afterwards pardoned his crime, and consented to his marriage with the princess."—CASTERA.

This digression in the song of the nymph bears, in manner, a striking resemblance to the histories which often, even in the heat of battle, the heroes of Homer relate to each other. That these little episodes have their beauty and propriety in an epic poem will strongly appear from a view of M. de la Motte's translation of the Iliad into French verse. The four and twenty books of Homer he has contracted into twelve, and these contain no more lines than about four books of the original. A thousand embellishments which the warm poetical feelings of Homer suggested to him are thus thrown out by the Frenchman. But what is the consequence of this improvement? The work of La Motte is unread, even by his own countrymen, and despised by every foreigner who has the least relish for poetry and Homer.

[611] And midnight horror shakes Medina's shrine.—Medina, the city where Mohammed is buried. About six years after GAMA'S discovery of India, the Sultan of Egypt sent Maurus, the abbot of the monks at Jerusalem, who inhabit Mount Sion, on an embassy to Pope Julius II. The sultan, with severe threats to the Christians of the East in case of refusal, entreated the Pope to desire Emmanuel, king of Portugal, to send no more fleets to the Indian seas. The Pope sent Maurus to Emmanuel, who returned a very spirited answer to his holiness, assuring him that no threats, no dangers, could make him alter his resolutions, and lamenting that it had not yet been in his power to fulfil his purpose of demolishing the sepulchre and erasing the memorials of Mohammed from the earth. This, he says was the first purpose of sending his fleets to India. It is with great art that Camoëns so often reminds us of the grand design of the expedition of his heroes to subvert Mohammedanism, and found a Christian empire in the East. But the dignity which this gives to his poem has already been observed in the preface.

[612] Where Sheba's sapient queen the sceptre bore.—The Abyssinians contend that their country is the Sheba mentioned in the Scripture, and that the queen who visited Solomon bore a son to that monarch, from whom their royal family, to the present time, is descended.

[613] Snatch'd from thy golden throne.—GAMA only reigned three months viceroy of India. During his second voyage, the third which the Portuguese made to India, he gave the zamorim some considerable defeats by sea, besides his victories over the Moors. These, however, are judiciously omitted by Camoëns, as the less striking part of his character.

The French translator is highly pleased with the prediction of GAMA'S death, delivered to himself at the feast. "The siren," says he, "persuaded that GAMA is a hero exempt from weakness, does not hesitate to mention the end of his life. GAMA listens without any mark of emotion; the feast and the song continue. If I am not deceived, this is truly great."

[614] Victorious Henry.—Don Henry de Menezes. He was only twenty-eight when appointed to the government of India. He died in his thirtieth year, a noble example of the most disinterested heroism.

[615] Great Mascarine.—Pedro de Mascarenhas. The injustice done to this brave officer, and the usurpation of his government by Lopez Vaz de Sampayo, afford one of the most interesting periods of the history of the Portuguese in India.

[616] Great Nunio.—Nunio de Cunha, one of the most worthy of the Portuguese governors.

[617] Awed by his fame.—That brave, generous spirit, which prompted Camoëns to condemn the great Albuquerque for injustice to a common soldier, has here deserted him. In place of poetical compliment, on the terrors of his name, Noronha deserved infamy. The siege of Dio, it is true, was raised on the report of his approach, but that report was the stratagem of Coje Zofar, one of the general officers of the assailants. The delays of Noronha were as highly blamable as his treatment of his predecessor, the excellent Nunio, was unworthy of a gentleman.

[618] A son of thine, O Gama.—Stephen de Gama.

[619] A vet'ran, fam'd on Brazil's shore.—Martin Alonzo de Souza. He was celebrated for clearing the coast of Brazil of several pirates, who were formidable to that infant colony.

[620] O'er blood-stain'd ground.—This is as near the original as elegance will allow—de sangue cheyo—which Fanshaw has thus punned:—

"With no little loss,
Sending him home again by Weeping-Cross"—

a place near Banbury in Oxfordshire.

[621] Cape Comorin, the southernmost point of India.—Ed.

[622] The Rumien fierce, who boasts the name of Rome.—When the victories of the Portuguese began to overspread the East, several Indian princes, by the counsels of the Moors, applied for assistance to the Sultan of Egypt, and the Grand Signior. The troops of these Mohammedan princes were in the highest reputation for bravery, and though, composed of many different nations, were known among the orientals by one common name. Ignorance delights in the marvellous. The history of ancient Rome made the same figure among the easterns, as that of the fabulous, or heroic, ages does with us, with this difference, it was better believed. The Turks of Roumania pretended to be the descendants of the Roman conquerors, and the Indians gave them and their auxiliaries the name of Rumēs, or Romans. In the same manner, the fame of Godfrey in the East conferred the name of Franks on all the western Christians, who, on their part, gave the name of Moors to all the Mohammedans of the East.

[623] No hope, bold Mascarene.—The commander of Diu, or Dio, during this siege, one of the most memorable in the Portuguese history.

[624] Fierce Hydal-Kan.—The title of the lords or princes of Decan, who in their wars with the Portuguese have sometimes brought 400,000 men into the field. The prince here mentioned, after many revolts, was at last finally subdued by Don John de Castro, the fourth viceroy of India, with whose reign our poet judiciously ends the prophetic song. Albuquerque laid the plan, and Castro completed the system of the Portuguese empire in the East. It is with propriety, therefore, that the prophecy given to GAMA is here summed up. Nor is the discretion of Camoëns in this instance inferior to his judgment. He is now within a few years of his own times, when he himself was upon the scene in India. But whatever he had said of his contemporaries would have been liable to misconstruction, and every sentence would have been branded with the epithets of flattery or malice. A little poet would have been happy in such an opportunity to resent his wrongs. But the silent contempt of Camoëns does him true honour. In this historical song, as already hinted, the translator has been attentive, as much as he could, to throw it into these universal languages, the picturesque and characteristic. To convey the sublimest instruction to princes, is, according to Aristotle, the peculiar province of the epic muse. The striking points of view in which the different characters of the governors of India are here placed, are in the most happy conformity to this ingenious canon of the Stagyrite.

[625]
In whirling circles now they fell, now rose,
Yet never rose nor fell.—

The motions of the heavenly bodies, in every system, bear at all times the same uniform relation to each other; these expressions, therefore, are strictly just. The first relates to the appearance, the second to the reality. Thus, while to us the sun appears to go down, to more western inhabitants of the globe he appears to rise, and while he rises to us, he is going down to the more eastern; the difference being entirely relative to the various parts of the earth. And in this the expressions of our poet are equally applicable to the Ptolemaic and Copernican systems. The ancient hypothesis which made our earth the centre of the universe, is the system adopted by Camoëns, a happiness, in the opinion of the translator, to the English Lusiad. The new system is so well known, that a poetical description of it would have been no novelty to the English reader. The other has not only that advantage in its favour: but this description is perhaps the finest and fullest that ever was given of it in poetry, that of Lucretius, l. v. being chiefly argumentative, and therefore less picturesque.

Our author studied at the university of Coimbra, where the ancient system and other doctrines of the Aristotelians then, and long afterward, prevailed.

[626] He holds His loftiest state.—Called by the old philosophers and school divines the sensorium of the Deity.

[627] These spheres behold.—According to the Peripatetics, the universe consisted of eleven spheres inclosed within each other; as Fanshaw has familiarly expressed it by a simile which he has lent our author. The first of these spheres, he says—

"Doth (as in a nest
Of boxes) all the other orbs comprise."

In their accounts of this first-mentioned, but eleventh, sphere, which they called the Empyrean, or heaven of the blest, the disciples of Aristotle, and the Arab Moors, gave loose to all the warmth of imagination. And several of the Christian fathers applied to it the descriptions of heaven which are found in the Holy Scripture.

[628] Hence motion darts its force.—This is the tenth sphere, the Primum Mobile of the ancient system. To account for the appearances of the heavens, the Peripatetics ascribed a double motion to it. While its influence drew the other orbs from east to west, they supposed it had a motion of its own from west to east. To effect this, the ponderous weight and interposition of the ninth sphere, or crystalline heaven, was necessary. The ancient astronomers observed that the stars shifted their places. This they called the motion of the crystalline heaven, expressed by our poet at the rate of one pace during two hundred solar years. The famous Arab astronomer, Abulhasan, in his Meadows of Gold, calculates the revolution of this sphere to consist of 49,000 of our years. But modern discoveries have not only corrected the calculation,{*} but have also ascertained the reason of the apparent motion of the fixed stars. The earth is not a perfect sphere; the quantity of matter is greater at the equator; hence the earth turns on her axis in a rocking motion, revolving round the axis of the ecliptic, which is called the procession of the equinoxes, and makes the stars seem to shift their places at about the rate of a degree in 72 years; according to which all the stars seem to perform one revolution in the space of 25,920 years, after which they return exactly to the same situation as at the beginning of this period. However imperfect in their calculations, the Chaldean astronomers perceived that the motions of the heavens composed one great revolution. This they called the annus magnus, which those who did not understand them mistook for a restoration of all things to their first originals.

{*} However deficient the astronomy of Abulhasan may be, it is nothing to the calculation of his prophet Mohammed, who tells his disciples, that the stars were each about the bigness of a house, and hung from the sky on chains of gold.

[629] And binds the starry sphere.—This was called the firmament, or eighth heaven. Saturn, Jupiter, Mars, Apollo, Venus, Mercury, and Diana, were the planets which gave name to, and whose orbits composed, the other spheres or heavens.

[630] In shining frost the Northern Chariot rides.—Commonly called Charles' Wain. Andromeda was the daughter of Cepheus, king of Ethiopia, and of Cassiope. Cassiope boasted that she and her daughter were more beautiful than Juno and the Nereids. Andromeda, to appease the goddess, was, at her father's command, chained to a rock to be devoured by a sea monster, but was saved by Perseus, who obtained of Jupiter that all the family should be placed among the stars. Orion was a hunter, who, for an attempt on Diana, was stung to death by a serpent. The star of his name portends tempests. The Dogs; fable gives this honour to those of different hunters. The faithful dog of Erigone, however, that died mad with grief for the death of his mistress, has the best title to preside over the dog-days. The Swan; whose form Jupiter borrowed to enjoy Leda. The Hare, when pursued by Orion, was saved by Mercury, and placed in heaven, to signify that Mercury presides over melancholy dispositions. The Lyre, with which Orpheus charmed Pluto. The Dragon which guarded the golden apples of the Hesperides, and the ship Argo complete the number of the constellations mentioned by Camoëns. If our author has blended the appearances of heaven with those of the painted artificial sphere, it is in the manner of the classics. Ovid, in particular, thus describes the heavens, in the second book of his Metamorphoses.

[631] Such are their laws impress'd by God's dread will.—Though a modern narrative of gallant adventures by no means requires the supposition of a particular Providence, that supposition, however, is absolutely necessary to the grandeur of an epic poem. The great examples of Homer and Virgil prove it; and Camoëns understood and felt its force. While his fleet combat all the horrors of unploughed

oceans, we do not view his heroes as idle wanderers; the care of heaven gives their voyage the greatest importance. When GAMA falls on his knees and spreads his hands to heaven on the discovery of India, we are presented with a figure infinitely more noble than that of the most successful conqueror who is supposed to act under the influence of fatalism or chance. The human mind is conscious of its own weakness. It expects an elevation in poetry, and demands a degree of importance superior to the caprices of unmeaning accident. The poetical reader cannot admire the hero who is subject to such blind fortuity. He appears to us with an abject, uninteresting littleness. Our poetical ideas of permanent greatness demand a GAMA, a hero whose enterprises and whose person interest the care of Heaven and the happiness of his people. Nor must this supposition be confined merely to the machinery. The reason why it pleases, also requires, that the supposition should be uniform throughout the whole poem. Virgil, by dismissing Eneas through the ivory gate of Elysium, has hinted that all his pictures of a future state were merely dreams, and has thus destroyed the highest merit of the compliment to his patron Augustus. But Camoëns has certainly been more happy. A fair opportunity offered itself to indulge the opinions of Lucretius and the Academic Grove; but Camoëns, in ascribing the government of the universe to the will of God, has not only preserved the philosophy of his poem perfectly uniform, but has also shown that the Peripatetic system is, in this instance, exactly conformable to the Newtonian.

Though the Author of nature has placed man in a state of moral agency, and made his happiness and misery to depend upon it, and though every page of human history is stained with the tears of injured innocence and the triumphs of guilt, with miseries which must affect a moral, or thinking being, yet we have been told, that God perceiveth it not, and that what mortals call moral evil vanishes from before His more perfect sight. Thus the appeal of injured innocence, and the tear of bleeding virtue fall unregarded, unworthy of the attention of the Deity.{*} Yet, with what raptures do these philosophers behold the infinite wisdom and care of Beelzebub, their god of flies, in the admirable and various provision he has made for the preservation of the eggs of vermin, and the generation of maggots.{**}

Much more might be said in proof that our poet's philosophy does not altogether deserve ridicule. And those who allow a general, but deny a particular providence, will, it is hoped, excuse Camoëns, on the consideration, that if we estimate a general moral providence by analogy of that providence which presides over vegetable and animal nature, a more particular one cannot possibly be wanted. If a particular providence, however, is still denied, another consideration obtrudes itself; if one pang of a moral agent is unregarded, one tear of injured innocence left to fall unpitied by the Deity, if Ludit in humanis Divina potentia rebus, the consequence is, that the human conception can form an idea of a much better God. And it may modestly be presumed we may hazard the laugh of the wisest philosopher, and without scruple assert, that it is impossible that a created mind should conceive an idea of perfection superior to that which is possessed by the Creator and Author of existence.

{*} Perhaps, like Lucretius, some philosophers think this would be too much trouble to the Deity. But the idea of trouble to the Divine Nature, is much the same as another argument of the same philosopher, who having asserted, that before the creation the gods could not know what seed would produce, from thence wisely concludes that the world was made by chance.

{**} Ray, in his Wisdom of God in the Creation (though he did not deny a Providence), has carried this extravagance to the highest pitch. "To give life," says he, "is the intention of the creation; and how wonderful does the goodness of God appear in this, that the death and putrefaction of one animal is the life of thousands." So, the misery of a family on the death of a parent is nothing, for ten thousand maggots are made happy by it.—O Philosophy, when wilt thou forget the dreams of thy slumbers in Bedlam!

[632] Here Christian Europe.—Vès Europa Christian.—As Europe is already described in the third Lusiad, this short account of it has as great propriety, as the manner of it contains dignity.

[633] Afric behold.—This just and strongly picturesque description of Africa is finely contrasted with the character of Europe. It contains also a masterly compliment to the expedition of GAMA, which is all along represented as the harbinger and diffuser of the blessings of civilization.

[634] Gonsalo's zeal shall glow.—Gonsalo de Sylveyra, a Portuguese Jesuit, in 1555, sailed from Lisbon on a mission to Monomotapa. His labours were at first successful; but ere he effected any regular establishment he was murdered by the barbarians.—CASTERA.

[635] Great Naya, too.—Don Pedro de Naya.... In 1505 he erected a fort in the kingdom of Sofala, which is subject to Monomotapa. Six thousand Moors and Caffres laid siege to this garrison, which he defended with only thirty-five men. After having several times suffered by unexpected sallies, the barbarians fled, exclaiming to their king that he had led them to fight against God.—CASTERA.

[636] In Abyssinia Heav'n's own altars blaze.—Christianity was planted here in the first century, but mixed with many Jewish rites unused by other Christians of the East. This appears to give some countenance to the pretensions of their emperors, who claim their descent from Solomon and the Queen of Sheba, and at least reminds us of Acts viii. 27, where we are told, that the treasurer of the Queen of Ethiopia came to worship at Jerusalem. Numerous monasteries, we are told, are in this country. But the clergy are very ignorant, and the laity gross barbarians. Much has been said of the hill Amara—

"Where Abyssin kings their issue guard ...
... by some suppos'd,
True Paradise, under the Ethiop line
By Nilus head, inclos'd with shining rock,
A whole day's journey high"—MILTON;

and where, according to Urreta (a Spanish Jesuit), is the library founded by the Queen of Sheba, and enriched with all those writings of which we have either possession or only the names. The works of Noah, and the lectures on the mathematics which Abraham read in the plains of Mamre, are here. And so many are the volumes, that 200 monks are employed as librarians. It is needless to add, that Father Urreta is a second Sir John Mandevylle.

[637] Thy son, brave Gama.—When Don Stephen de Gama was governor of India, the Christian Emperor and Empress-mother of Ethiopia solicited the assistance of the Portuguese against the usurpations of the pagan King of Zeyla. Don Stephen sent his brother, Don Christoval with 500 men. The prodigies of their valour astonished the Ethiopians. But after having twice defeated the tyrant, and reduced his great army to the last extremity, Don Christoval, urged too far by the impetuosity of his youthful valour, was taken prisoner. He was brought before the usurper, and put to death in the most cruel manner. Waxed threads were twisted with his beard and afterwards set on fire. He was then dipped in boiling wax, and at last beheaded by the hand of the tyrant. The Portuguese esteem him a martyr, and say that his torments and death were inflicted because he would not renounce the faith.—See Faria y Sousa.

[638] Infidel, pagan.

[639] Before the virgin-martyr's tomb.—He must be a dull reader indeed who cannot perceive and relish the amazing variety which prevails in our poet. In the historical narrative of wars, where it is most necessary, yet from the sameness of the subject, most difficult, to attain, our author always attains it with the most graceful ease. In the description of countries he not only follows the manner of Homer and Virgil, not only distinguishes each region by its most striking characteristic, but also diversifies his geography with other incidents introduced by the mention of the place. St. Catherine, virgin and martyr, according to Romish histories, was buried on Mount Sinai, and a chapel was erected over her grave. It is now the Monastery of St. Catherine.—Ed.

[640] The crescent, the sign of Turkish supremacy.—Ed.

[641] De Branco's sword.—Don Pedro de Castel-Branco. He obtained a great victory, near Ormuz, over the combined fleets of the Moors, Turks, and Persians.

[642] There Barem's isle.—The island of Bahrein is situated in the Persian Gulf. It is celebrated for the plenty, variety, and fineness of its diamonds.

[643] Her warrior sons disdain the arms of fire.—This was the character of the Persians when GAMA arrived in the East. Yet, though they thought it dishonourable to use the musket, they esteemed it no disgrace to rush from a thicket on an unarmed foe. This reminds one of the spirit of the old romance. Orlando having taken the first invented cannon from the King of Friza, throws it into the sea with the most heroic execrations. Yet the heroes of chivalry think it no disgrace to take every advantage afforded by invulnerable hides and enchanted armour.

[644]
There Gerum's isle the hoary ruin wears
Where Time has trod.—

Presuming on the ruins which are found on this island, the natives pretend that the Armuzia of Pliny and Strabo was here situated. But this is a mistake, for that city stood on the continent. The Moors, however, have built a city in this isle, which they call by the ancient name.

[645] He who first shall crown thy labours, Gama.—Pedro de Cabral, of whom see the preface.

[646] Ceylon.

[647] Some Macon's orgies.—Macon, a name of Mecca, the birthplace of Mohammed.

[648] The tomb where Thomas sleeps.—There is (to talk in the Indian style) a caste of gentlemen, whose hearts are all impartiality and candour to every religion, except one, the most moral which ever the world heard of. A tale of a Brahmin, or a priest of Jupiter, would to them appear worthy of poetry. But to introduce an apostle—Common sense, however, will prevail; and the episode of St. Thomas will appear to the true critic equal in dignity and propriety.

To renew and complete the labours of the apostle, the messenger of Heaven, is the great design of the hero of the poem, and of the future missions, in consequence of the discoveries which are the subject of it.

The Christians of St. Thomas, found in Malabar on the arrival of GAMA, we have already mentioned. The Jesuit missionaries have given most pompous accounts of the Christian antiquities of India and China. When the Portuguese arrived in India, the head of the Malabar Christians, named Jacob, styled himself Metropolitan of India and China. And a Syriac breviary{*} of the Indian Christians offers praise to God for sending St. Thomas to India and China. In 1625, in digging for a foundation near Sigansu, metropolis of the province of Xensi, was found a stone with a cross on it, full of Chinese, and some Syriac characters, containing the names of bishops, and an account of the Christian religion, "that it was brought from Judea; that having been weakened, it was renewed under the reign of the great Tam" (cir. A.D. 630). But the Christians, say the Jesuits, siding with the Tartars, cir. A.D. 1200, were extirpated by the Chinese. In 1543, Fernand Pinto, observing some ruins near Peking, was told by the people, that 200 years before, a holy man who worshipped Jesus Christ, born of a virgin, lived there; and being murdered, was thrown into a river, but his body would not sink; and soon after the city was destroyed by an earthquake. The same Jesuit found people at Caminam who knew the doctrines of Christianity, which they said were preached to their fathers, by John, the disciple of Thomas. In 1635, some heathens, by night passing through a village in the province of Fokien, saw some stones which emitted light, under which were found the figure of crosses. From China, St. Thomas returned to Meliapore in Malabar, at a time when a prodigious beam of timber floated on the sea near the coast. The king endeavoured to bring it ashore, but all the force of men and elephants was in vain. St. Thomas desired leave to build a church with it, and immediately dragged it to shore with a single thread. A church was built, and the king baptized. This enraged the Brahmins, the chief of whom killed his own son, and accused Thomas of the murder. But the saint, by restoring the youth to life, discovered the wickedness of his enemies. He was afterwards killed by a lance while kneeling at the altar; after, according to tradition, he had built 3300 stately churches, many of which were rebuilt, cir. 800, by an Armenian named Thomas Cananeus. In 1533, the body of the apostle, with the head of the lance beside him, was found in his church by D. Duarte de Meneses; and in 1558 was, by D. Constantine de Braganza, removed to Goa. To these accounts, selected from Faria y Sousa, let two from Osorius be added. When Martin Alonzo de Souza was viceroy, some brazen tables were brought to him, inscribed with unusual characters, which were explained by a learned Jew, and imported that St. Thomas had built a church at Meliapore. And by an account sent to Cardinal Henrico, by the Bishop of Cochin, in 1562, when the Portuguese repaired the ancient chapel of St. Thomas,{**} there was found a stone cross with several characters on it, which the best antiquarians could not interpret, till at last a Brahmin translated it, "That in the reign of Sagam, Thomas was sent by the Son of God, whose disciple he was, to teach the law of heaven in India; that he built a church, and was killed by a Brahmin at the altar."

{*} The existence of this breviary is a certain fact. These Christians had the Scripture also in the Syriac language.

{**} This was a very ancient building, in the very first style of Christian churches. The Portuguese have now disfigured it with their repairs and new buildings.

A view of Portuguese Asia, which must include the labours of the Jesuits, forms a necessary part in the comment on the Lusiad: this note, therefore, and some obvious reflections upon it, are in place. It is as easy to bury an inscription and find it again, as it is to invent a silly tale; but, though suspicion of fraud on the one hand, and silly absurdity on the other, lead us to despise the authority of the Jesuits, yet one fact remains indisputable. Christianity had been much better known in the East, several centuries before, than it was at the arrival of GAMA. Where the name was unknown, and where the Jesuits were unconcerned, crosses were found. The long existence of the Christians of St. Thomas in the midst of a vast pagan empire, proves that the learned of that kingdom must have some knowledge of their doctrines. And these facts give countenance to some material conjectures concerning the religion of the Brahmins.

[649] When now the chief who wore the triple thread.—Of this, thus Osorius: "Terna fila ab humero dextero in latus finistrum gerunt, ut designent trinam in natura divina rationem.—They (the Brahmins) wear three threads, which reach from the right shoulder to the left side, as significant of the trinal distinction in the Divine Nature." That some sects of the Brahmins wear a symbolical tessera of three threads is acknowledged on all hands; but, from whatever the custom arose, it is not to be supposed that the Brahmins, who have thousands of ridiculous contradictory legends, should agree in their accounts or explanations of it. They have various accounts of a Divine Person having assumed human nature. And the god Brahma, as observed by Cudworth, is generally mentioned as united in the government of the universe with two others, sometimes of different names. They have also images with three heads rising out of one body, which they say represent the Divine Nature.{*} But are there any traces of these opinions in the accounts which the Greek and Roman writers have given us of the Brahmins? And will the wise pay any credit to the authority of those books which the public never saw, and which, by the obligation of their keepers, they are never to see; and some of which, by the confession of their keepers, since the appearance of Mohammed, have been rejected? The Platonic idea of a trinity of divine attributes was well known to the ancients, yet perhaps the Athanasian controversy offers a fairer field to the conjecturist. That controversy for several ages engrossed the conversation of the East. All the subtilty of the Greeks was called forth, and no speculative contest was ever more universally or warmly disputed; so warmly, that it is a certain fact that Mohammed, by inserting into his Koran some declarations in favour of the Arians, gained innumerable proselytes to his new religion. Abyssinia, Egypt, Syria, Persia, and Armenia were perplexed with this unhappy dispute, and from the earliest times these countries have had a commercial intercourse with India. The number, blasphemy, and absurdity of the Jewish legends of the Talmud and Targums, bear a striking resemblance to the holy legends of the Brahmins. The Jews also assert the great antiquity of their Talmudical legends. Adam, Enoch, and Noah are named among their authors; but we know their date; Jerusalem, ere their birth, was destroyed by Titus. We also know, that the accounts which the Greek writers give of the Brahmins fall infinitely short of those extravagances which are confessed even by their modern admirers. And Mohammedanism does not differ from Christianity, more than the account which even these gentlemen give, does from that of Porphyry. That laborious philosopher, though possessed of all the knowledge of his age, though he mentions their metempsychosis and penances, has not a word of any of their idols, or the legends of Brahma or his brothers. On the contrary, he represents their worship as extremely pure and simple. Strabo's account of them is similar. And Eusebius has assured us they worshipped no images.{**} Yet, on the arrival of the modern Europeans in India, innumerable were their idols; and all the superstition of ancient Egypt, in the adoration of animals and vegetables, seemed more than revived by the Brahmins. Who that considers this striking alteration in their features, can withhold his contempt when he is told of the religious care with which these philosophers have these four thousand years preserved their sacred rites.

{*} To these undoubted facts the author will not add the authority of a Xavier, who tells us, that he prevailed upon a Brahmin to explain to him some part of their hidden religion; when to his surprise, the Indian, in a low voice, repeated the Ten Commandments.

{**} ... χιλιάδες πολλὰι τῶν λεγομένων Βραχμάνων, ὅιτινες κατὰ παραδισόν τῶν προγόνων καὶ νόμων, οὔτε φονεύουσιν, ΟΥΤΕ ΞΟΑΝΑ ΣΕΒΟΝΤΑΙ.—EUSEB. Prep. Evan. lib. 6, c. 10, p. 275. Ed. Paris, 1628.

[650] Thee, Thomas, thee, the plaintive Ganges mourn'd.—The versification of the original is here exceedingly fine. Even those who are unacquainted with the Portuguese may perceive it.

"Choraraóte Thomé, o Gange, o Indo,
Choroute toda a terra, que pizaste;
Mas mais te choráo as almas, que vestindo
Se hiáo dà Santa Fê, que lhe ensinaste;
Mas os anjos do ceo cantando, & rindo,
Te recebem na gloria que ganhaste."

[651] Like him, ye Lusians, simplest Truth pursue.—It is now time to sum up what has been said of the labours of the Jesuits. Diametrically opposite to this advice was their conduct in every Asiatic country where they pretended to propagate the gospel. Sometimes we find an individual sincere and pious, but the great principle which always actuated them as a united body was the lust of power and secular emolument, the possession of which they thought could not be better secured than by rendering themselves of the utmost importance to the see of Rome. In consequence of these principles, wherever they came their first care was to find what were the great objects of the fear and adoration of the people. If the sun was esteemed the giver of life, Jesus Christ was the Son of that luminary, and they were his younger brethren, sent to instruct the ignorant. If the barbarians were in dread of evil spirits, Jesus Christ came on purpose to banish them from the world, had driven them from Europe,{*} and the Jesuits were sent to the East to complete his unfinished mission. If the Indian converts still retained a veneration for the powder of burned cow-dung, the Jesuits made the sign of the cross over it, and the Indian besmeared himself with it as usual. Heaven, or universal matter, they told the Chinese, was the God of the Christians, and the sacrifices of Confucius were solemnized in the churches of the Jesuits. This worship of Confucius, Voltaire, with his wonted accuracy, denies. But he ought to have known that this, with the worship of tien, or heaven, had been long complained of at the court of Rome (see Dupin), and that after the strictest scrutiny the charge was fully proved, and Clement XI., in 1703, sent Cardinal Tournon to the small remains of the Jesuits in the East with a papal decree to reform these abuses. But the cardinal, soon after his arrival, was poisoned in Siam by the holy fathers. Xavier, and the other Jesuits who succeeded him, by the dexterous use of the great maxims of their master Loyola, Omnibus omnia, et omnia munda mundis, gained innumerable proselytes. They contradicted none of the favourite opinions of their converts, they only baptized, and gave them crucifixes to worship, and all was well. But their zeal in uniting to the see of Rome the Christians found in the East descended to the minutest particulars. And the native Christians of Malabar were so violently persecuted as heretics that the heathen princes took arms in their defence in 1570 (see Geddes, Hist. Malabar), and the Portuguese were almost driven from India. Abyssinia, by the same arts, was steeped in blood, and two or three Abyssinian emperors lost their lives in endeavouring to establish the pope's supremacy. An order at last was given from the throne to hang every missionary, without trial, wherever apprehended, the emperor himself complaining that he could not enjoy a day in quiet for the intrigues of the Romish friars. In China, also, they soon rendered themselves insufferable. Their skill in mathematics and the arts introduced them to great favour at court, but all their cunning could not conceal their villainy. Their unwillingness to ordain the natives raised suspicions against a profession thus monopolized by strangers; their earnest zeal in amassing riches, and their interference with, and deep designs on, secular power (the fatal rock on which they have so often been shipwrecked), appeared, and their churches were levelled with the ground. About 90,000 of the new converts, together with their teachers, were massacred, and their religion was prohibited. In Japan the rage of government even exceeded that of China, and in allusion to their chief object of adoration, the cross, several of the Jesuit fathers were crucified by the Japanese, and the revival of the Christian name was interdicted by the

severest laws. Thus, in a great measure, ended in the East the labours of the society of Ignatius Loyola, a society which might have diffused the greatest blessings to mankind, could honesty have been added to their great learning and abilities. Had that indefatigable zeal which laboured to promote the interests of their own brotherhood and the Roman see been employed in the real interests of humanity and civilization, the great design of diffusing the law of Heaven, challenged by its author as the purpose of the Lusiad, would have been amply completed, and the remotest hordes of Tartary and Africa ere now had been happily civilized. But though the Jesuits have failed, they have afforded a noble lesson to mankind.

"Though fortified with all the brazen mounds
That art can rear, and watch'd by eagle eyes,
Still will some rotten part betray the structure
That is not bas'd on simple honesty."

{*} This trick, it is said, has been played in America within these twenty years, where the notion of evil spirits gives the poor Indians their greatest misery. The French Jesuits told the Six Nations, that Jesus Christ was a Frenchman, and had driven all evil demons from France; that he had a great love for the Indians, whom he intended also to deliver, but taking England in his way, he was crucified by the wicked Londoners.

[652] The dying.—The innumerable superstitions performed on the banks of the river Ganges, afford a pitiable picture of the weakness of humanity. The circumstances here mentioned are literally true. It is no uncommon scene for the English ships to be surrounded with the corpses which come floating down this hallowed stream.

[653]
Pegu, whose sons (so held old faith) confess'd
A dog their sire.—

The tradition of this country boasted this infamous and impossible original. While other nations pretend to be descended of demi-gods, the Peguans were contented to trace their pedigree from a Chinese woman and a dog; the only living creatures which survived a shipwreck on their coast.—See Faria.

[654] A pious queen their horrid rage restrain'd.—Thus in the original:

"Aqui soante arame no instrumento
Da géraçáo costumáo, o que usaráo
Por manha da Raynha, que inventando
Tal uso, deitou fóra o error nefando."

[655] And 'mid white whirlpools down the ocean driven.—See the same account of Sicily, Virg. Æn. iii.

[656] Ophir its Tyrian name.—Sumatra has been by some esteemed the Ophir of the Holy Scriptures; but the superior fineness of the gold of Sofala, and its situation, favour the claim of that Ethiopian isle.—See Bochart. Geog. Sacr.

[657] And thousands more.—The extensive countries between India and China, where Ptolemy places his man-eaters, and where Mandevylle found "men without heads, who saw and spoke through holes in

their breasts," continues still very imperfectly known. The Jesuits have told many extravagant lies of the wealth of these provinces. By the most authentic accounts they seem to have been peopled by colonies from China. The religion and manufactures of the Siamese, in particular, confess the resemblance. In some districts, however, they have greatly degenerated from the civilization of the mother country.

[658] And gnaw the reeking limbs.—Much has been said on this subject, some denying and others asserting the existence of anthropophagi or man-eaters. Porphyry (de Abstin. i. 4 § 21{*}) says that the Massagetæ and Derbices (people of north-eastern Asia), esteeming those most miserable who died of sickness, when their parents and relations grew old, killed and ate them, holding it more honourable thus to consume them than that they should be destroyed by vermin. St. Jerome has adopted this word for word, and has added to it an authority of his own: "Quid loquar," says he, (Adv. Jov. l. 2, c. 6), "de cæteris nationibus; cum ipse adolescentulus in Gallia viderim Scotos, gentem Britannicam, humanis vesci carnibus, et cum per sylvas porcorum greges et armentorum, pecudumque reperiant, pastorum nates, et fæminarum papillas solere abscindere, et has solas ciborum delicias arbitrari?" Mandevylle ought next to be cited. "Aftirwarde men gon be many yles be see unto a yle that men clepen Milhe: there is a full cursed peple: thei delyten in ne thing more than to fighten and to fie men, and to drynken gladlyest mannes blood, which they clepen Dieu."—P. 235. Yet, whatever absurdity may appear on the face of these tales; and what can be more absurd than to suppose that a few wild Scots or Irish (for the name was then proper to Ireland), should so lord it in Gaul, as to eat the breasts of the women and the hips of the shepherds? Yet, whatever absurdities our Mandevylles may have obtruded on the public, the evidence of the fact is not thereby wholly destroyed. Though Dampier and other visitors of barbarous nations have assured us that they never met with any man-eaters, and though Voltaire has ridiculed the opinion, yet one may venture the assertion of their existence, without partaking of a credulity similar to that of those foreigners, who believed that the men of Kent were born with tails like sheep (see Lambert's Peramb.), the punishment inflicted upon them for the murder of Thomas à Becket. Many are the credible accounts, that different barbarous nations used to eat their prisoners of war. According to the authentic testimony of the best Portuguese writers, the natives of Brazil, on their high festivals, brought forth their captives, and after many barbarous ceremonies, at last roasted and greedily devoured their mangled limbs. During his torture the unhappy victim prided himself in his manly courage, upbraiding their want of skill in the art of tormenting, and telling his murderers that his belly had been the grave of many of their relations. Thus the fact was certain long before a late voyage discovered the horrid practice in New Zealand. To drink human blood has been more common. The Gauls and other ancient nations practised it. When Magalhaens proposed Christianity to the King of Subo, a north-eastern Asiatic island, and when Francis de Castro discovered Santigana and other islands, a hundred leagues north of the Moluccas, the conversion of their kings was confirmed by each party drinking of the blood of the other. Our poet Spenser tells us, in his View of the State of Ireland, that he has seen the Irish drink human blood, particularly, he adds, "at the execution of a notable traitor at Limerick, called Murrogh O'Brien, I saw an old woman, who was his foster-mother, take up his head whilst he was quartering and suck up all the blood that run thereout, saying, that the earth was not worthy to drink it, and therewith also steeped her face and breast and tore her hair, crying out and shrieking most terribly." It is worthy of regard that the custom of marking themselves with hot irons, and tattooing, is characteristic both of the Guios of Camoëns and of the present inhabitants of New Zealand. And if, as its animals indicate, the island of Otaheite was first peopled by a shipwreck, the friendship existing in a small society might easily obliterate the memory of one custom, while the less unfriendly one of tattooing was handed down, a memorial that they owed their origin to the north-eastern parts of Asia, where that custom particularly prevails.

{*} Ἰστοροῦνται γοῦν Μασσαγέται καὶ Δέρβυκες ἀθλιωτάτους ἡγεῖσθαι τῶν οἰκείων τοὺς αὐτομάτους τελευτήσαντας· διὸ καὶ φθάσαντες καταθύουσιν καὶ ἐστιῶνται τῶν φιλτάτων τοὺς γεγηρακότας.

[659] Other worlds the souls of beasts receive.—That Queen Elizabeth reigned in England, is not more certain than that the most ignorant nations in all ages have had the idea of a state after death. The same faculty which is conscious of existence whispers the wish for it; and, so little acquainted with the deductions of reasoning have some tribes been, that not only their animals, but even the ghosts of their domestic utensils have been believed to accompany them to the islands of the blessed. Long ere the voice of philosophy was heard, the opinion of an after state was popular in Greece. The works of Homer bear incontestable evidence of this. And there is not a feature in the history of the human mind better ascertained, than that no sooner did speculation seize upon the topic, than belief declined, and, as the great Bacon observes, the most learned, became the most atheistical ages. The reason of this is obvious. While the human mind is all simplicity, popular opinion is cordially received; but, when reasoning begins, proof is expected, and deficiency of demonstration being perceived, doubt and disbelief naturally follow. Yet, strange as it may appear, if the writer's memory does not greatly deceive him, these certain facts were denied by Hobbes. If he is not greatly mistaken, that gentleman, who gave a wretched, a most unpoetical translation of Homer, has so grossly misunderstood his author, as to assert that his mention of a future state was not in conformity to the popular opinion of his age, but only his own poetical fiction. He might as well have assured us, that the sacrifices of Homer had never any existence in Greece. But, as no absurdity is too gross for some geniuses, our murderer of Homer, our Hobbes, has likewise asserted, that the belief of the immortality of the human soul was the child of pride and speculation, unknown in Greece till long after the appearance of the Iliad.

[660] Oh gentle Mecon.—It was on the coast of Cochin-China, at the mouth of this river, the Maekhaun, or Camboja of modern writers, that Camoëns suffered the unhappy shipwreck which rendered him the sport of fortune during the remainder of his life. The literal rendering of the Portuguese, which Mickle claims the liberty of improving, is, "On his gentle, hospitable bosom shall he receive the song, wet from woful, unhappy shipwreck, escaped from destroying tempests, from ravenous dangers, the effect of the unjust sentence upon him whose lyre shall be more renowned than enriched."—Ed.

[661] Here ere the cannon's rage in Europe roar'd.—According to Le Comte's memoirs of China, and those of other travellers, the mariner's compass, fire-arms, and printing were known in that empire, long ere the invention of these arts in Europe. But the accounts of Du Halde, Le Comte, and the other Jesuits, are by no means to be depended on. It was their interest (in order to gain credit in Europe and at the court of Rome) to magnify the splendour of the empire where their mission lay, and they have magnified it into romance itself. It is pretended, that the Chinese used fire-arms in their wars with Zenghis Khan, and Tamerlane; but it is also said that the Sogdians used cannon against Alexander. The mention of any sulphurous composition in an old writer is, with some, immediately converted into a regular tire of artillery. The Chinese, indeed, on the first arrival of Europeans, had a kind of mortars, which they called fire-pans, but they were utter strangers to the smaller fire-arms. Verbiest, a Jesuit, was the first who taught them to make brass cannon, set upon wheels. And, even so late as the hostile menace which Anson gave them, they knew not how to level, or manage, their ordnance to any advantage. Their printing is, indeed, much more ancient than that of Europe, but it does not deserve the same name, the blocks of wood with which they stamp their sheets being as inferior to as they are different from the movable types of Europe. The Chinese have no idea of the graces of fine writing; here, most probably, the fault exists in their language; but the total want of nature in their painting, and of symmetry in their architecture, in both of which they have so long been experienced, afford a heavy accusation against their genius. But, in planning gardens, and in the art of beautifying the face of their

country, they are unequalled. Yet, even in their boasted gardening their genius stands accused. The art of ingrafting, so long known to Europe, is still unknown to them. And hence their fruits are vastly inferior in flavour to those of the western world. The amazing wall of defence against the Tartars, though 1500 miles in extent, is a labour inferior to the canals, lined on the sides with hewn stone, which everywhere enrich, and adorn their country; some of which reach 1000 miles, and are of depth to carry vessels of burthen. These grand remains of antiquity prove that there was a time when the Chinese were a much more accomplished people than at present. Though their princes for many centuries have discovered no such efforts of genius as these, the industry of the people still remains, in which they rival, and resemble, the Dutch. In every other respect they are the most unamiable of mankind. Amazingly uninventive, for, though possessed of them, the arts have made no progress among the Chinese these many centuries: even what they were taught by the Jesuits is almost lost. So false in their dealings, they boast that none but a Chinese can cheat a Chinese. The crime which disgraces human nature, is in this nation of atheists, and most stupid of all idolaters, common as that charter'd libertine, the air. Destitute, even in idea, of that elevation of soul which is expressed by the best sense of the word piety, in the time of calamity whole provinces are desolated by self-murder; an end, as Hume says, of some of the admired names of antiquity, not unworthy of so detestable a character. And, as it is always found congenial to baseness of heart, the most dastardly cowardice completes the description of that of the Chinese.

Unimproved as their arts is their learning. Though their language consists of few words, it is almost impossible for a stranger to attain the art of speaking it. And what a European learns ere he is seven years old, to read, is the labour of the life of a Chinese. In place of our 24 letters, they have more than 60,000 marks, which compose their writings: and their paucity of words, all of which may be attained in a few hours, requires such an infinite variety of tone and action, that the slightest mistake in modulation renders the speaker unintelligible. And in addressing a great man, in place of "my Lord," you may call him a beast, the word being the some, all the difference consisting in the tone of it. A language like this must ever be a bar to the progress and accomplishments of literature. Of medicine they are very ignorant. The ginseng, which they pretended was a universal remedy, is found to be a root of no singular virtue. Their books consist of odes without poetry, and of moral maxims, excellent in themselves, but without investigation or reasoning. For, to philosophical discussion and metaphysics they seem utterly strangers; and, when taught mathematics by the Jesuits, their greatest men were lost in astonishment. Whatever their political wisdom has been, at present it is narrow and barbarous. Jealous lest strangers should steal their arts—arts which are excelled at Dresden, and other parts of Europe—they preclude themselves from the great advantages which arise from an intercourse with civilized nations. Yet, in the laws which they impose on every foreign ship which enters their ports for traffic, they even exceed the cunning and avarice of the Dutch. In their internal policy the military government of Rome under the emperors is revived, with accumulated barbarism. In every city and province the military are the constables and peace officers. What a picture is this! Nothing but Chinese or Dutch industry could preserve the traffic and population of a country under the control of armed ruffians. But, hence the emperor has leisure to cultivate his gardens, and to write despicable odes to his concubines.

Whatever was their most ancient doctrine, certain it is that the legislators who formed the present system of China presented to their people no other object of worship than Tien Kamti, the material heavens and their influencing power; by which an intelligent principle is excluded. Yet, finding that the human mind in the rudest breasts is conscious of its weakness, and prone to believe the occurrences of life under the power of lucky or unlucky observances, they permitted their people the use of sacrifices to those Lucretian gods of superstitious fear. Nor was the principle of devotion, imprinted by Heaven in the human heart, alone perverted; another unextinguishable passion was also misled. On tablets, in every family, are written the names of the last three of their ancestors, added to each, "Here rests his soul:" and before these tablets they burn incense, and pay adoration. Confucius, who, according to their histories, had been in the West about 500 years before the Christian era, appears to be only the confirmer of their old opinions; but the accounts of him and his doctrine are involved in uncertainty. In their places of worship, however, boards are act up, inscribed, "This is the seat of the soul of Confucius," and to these, and their ancestors, they celebrate solemn sacrifices, without seeming to possess any idea of the intellectual existence of the departed soul. The Jesuit Ricci, and his brethren of the Chinese mission, very honestly told their converts, that Tien was the God of the Christians, and that the label of Confucius was the term by which they expressed His divine majesty. But, after a long and severe scrutiny at the court of Rome, Tien was found to signify nothing more than heavenly or universal matter, and the Jesuits of China were ordered to renounce this heresy. Among all the sects who worship different idols in China, there is only one which has any tolerable idea of the immortality of the soul; and among these, says Leland, Christianity at present obtains some footing. But the most interesting particular of China yet remains to be mentioned. Conscious of the obvious tendency, Voltaire and others have triumphed in the great antiquity of the Chinese, and in the distant period they ascribe to the creation. But the bubble cannot bear the touch. If some Chinese accounts fix the era of creation 40000 years ago, others are contented with no less than 884953. But who knows not that every nation has its Geoffry of Monmouth? And we have already observed the legends which took their rise from the Annus Magnus of the Chaldean and Egyptian astronomers, an apparent revolution of the stars, which in reality has no existence. To the fanciful who held this Annus Magnus, it seemed hard to suppose that our world was in its first revolution of the great year, and to suppose that many were past was easy. And, that this was the case, we have absolute proof in the doctrines of the Brahmins, who, though they talk of hundreds of thousands of years which are past, yet confess, that this, the fourth world, has not yet attained its 6000th year. And much within this compass are all the credible proofs of Chinese antiquity comprehended. To three heads all three proofs are reduceable—their form of government, which, till the conquest of the Tartars in 1644, bore the marks of the highest antiquity; their astronomical observations; and their history.

Simply and purely patriarchal, every father was the magistrate in his own family; and the emperor, who acted by his substitutes, the Mandarins, was venerated and obeyed as the father of all. The most passive submission to authority thus branched out was inculcated by Confucius, and their other philosophers, as the greatest duty of morality. But, if there is an age in sacred or profane history where the manners of mankind are thus delineated, no superior antiquity is proved by the form of Chinese government. Their ignorance of the very ancient art of ingrafting fruit-trees, and the state of their language (like the Hebrew in its paucity of words), a paucity characteristic of the ages when the ideas of men required few syllables to clothe them, prove nothing farther than the early separation of the Chinese colony{*} from the rest of mankind; nothing farther, except that they have continued till very lately without any material intercourse with the other nations of the world.

{} The Chinese colony! Yes, let philosophy smile; let her talk of the different species of men which are found in every country; let her brand as absurd the opinion of Montesquieu, which derives all the human race from one family. Let her enjoy her triumph. Peace to her insolence, peace to her dreams and her reveries. But let common sense be contented with the demonstration (See Whiston, Bentley, etc.) that a creation in every country is not wanted, and that one family is sufficient in every respect for the purpose. If philosophy will talk of black and white men as different in species, let common sense ask her for a demonstration, that climate and manner of life cannot produce this difference; and let her add, that there is the strongest presumptive experimental proof that the difference thus happens. If philosophy draw her inferences from the different passions of different tribes; let common sense reply, that stripped*

of every accident of brutalization and urbanity, the human mind in all its faculties, all its motives, hopes and fears, is most wonderfully the same in every age and country. If philosophy talk of the impossibility of peopling distant islands and continents from one family, let common sense tell her to read Bryant's Mythology. If philosophy asserts that the Kelts wherever they came found aborigines, let common sense reply, there were tyrants enough almost 2000 years before their emigrations, to drive the wretched survivors of slaughtered hosts to the remotest wilds. She may also add, that many islands have been found which bore not one trace of mankind, and that even Otaheite bears the evident marks of receiving its inhabitants from a shipwreck, its only animals being the hog, the dog, and the rat. In a word, let common sense say to philosophy, "I open my egg with a pen-knife, but you open yours with the blow of a sledge hammer."

A continued succession of astronomical observations, for 4000 years, was claimed by the Chinese, when they were first visited by the Europeans. Voltaire, that son of truth, has often with great triumph mentioned the indubitable proofs of Chinese antiquity; but at these times he must have received his information from the same dream which told him that Camoëns accompanied his friend GAMA in the voyage which discovered the East Indies. If Voltaire and his disciples will talk of Chinese astronomy, and the 4000 years antiquity of its perfection, let them enjoy every consequence which may possibly result from it. But let them allow the same liberty to others. Let them allow others to draw their inferences from a few stubborn facts, facts which demonstrate the ignorance of the Chinese in astronomy. The earth, they imagined, was a great plain, of which their country was the midst; and so ignorant were they of the cause of eclipses, that they believed the sun and moon were assaulted, and in danger of being devoured by a huge dragon. The stars were considered as the directors of human affairs, and thus their boasted astronomy ends in that silly imposition, judicial astrology. Though they had made some observations on the revolutions of the planets, and though in the emperor's palace there was an observatory, the first apparatus of proper instruments ever known in China was introduced by Father Verbiest. After this it need scarcely be added, that their astronomical observations which pretend an antiquity of 4000 years, are as false as a Welch genealogy, and that the Chinese themselves, when instructed by the Jesuits, were obliged to own that their calculations were erroneous and impossible. The great credit and admiration which their astronomical and mathematical knowledge procured to the Jesuits, afford an indubitable confirmation of these facts.

Ridiculous as their astronomical, are their historical antiquities. After all Voltaire has said of it, the oldest date to which their history pretends is not much above 4000 years. During this period 236 kings have reigned, of 22 different families. The first king reigned 100 years, then we have the names of some others, but without any detail of actions, or that concatenation of events which distinguishes authentic history. That mark of truth does not begin to appear for upwards of 2000 years of the Chinese legends. Little more than the names of kings, and these often interrupted with wide chasms, compose all the annals of China, till about the period of the Christian era. Something like a history then commences, but that is again interrupted by a wide chasm, which the Chinese know not how to fill up otherwise, than by asserting that a century or two elapsed in the time, and that at such a period a new family mounted the throne. Such is the history of China, full brother in every family feature to those Monkish tales, which sent a daughter of Pharoah to be queen of Scotland, which sent Brutus to England, and a grandson of Noah to teach school among the mountains in Wales.

[662] Immense the northern wastes their horrors spread.—Tartary, Siberia, Samoyada, Kamtchatka, etc. A short account of the Grand Lama of Thibet Tartary shall complete our view of the superstitions of the East. While the other pagans of Asia worship the most ugly monstrous idols, the Tartars of Thibet adore a real living god. He sits cross-legged on his throne, in the great temple, adorned with gold and

diamonds. He never speaks, but sometimes elevates his hand in token that he approves of the prayers of his worshippers. He is a ruddy well-looking young man, about 25 or 27, and is the most miserable wretch on earth, being the mere puppet of his priests, who dispatch him whenever age or sickness make any alteration in his features; and another, instructed to act his part, is put in his place. Princes of very distant provinces send tribute to this deity and implore his blessing, and, as Voltaire has merrily told us, think themselves secure of benediction if favoured with something from his godship, esteemed more sacred than the hallowed cow-dung of the Brahmins.

[663] How bright a silver mine.—By this beautiful metaphor (omitted by Castera) Camoëns alludes to the great success, which in his time attended the Jesuit missionaries in Japan. James I. sent an embassy to the sovereign, and opened a trade with this country, but it was soon suffered to decline. The Dutch are the only Europeans who now traffic with the Japanese, which it is said they obtain by trampling on the cross and by abjuring the Christian name. In religion the Japanese are much the same as their neighbours of China. And in the frequency of self-murder, says Voltaire, they vie with their brother islanders of England.

[664] The ground they touch not.—These are commonly called the birds of Paradise. It was the old erroneous opinion that they always soared in the air, and that the female hatched her young on the back of the male. Their feathers bear a mixture of the most beautiful azure, purple, and golden colours, which have a fine effect in the rays of the sun.

[665] From hence the pilgrim brings the wondrous tale.—Streams of this kind are common in many countries. Castera attributes this quality to the excessive coldness of the waters, but this is a mistake. The waters of some springs are impregnated with sparry particles, which adhering to the herbage, or the clay, on the banks of their channel, harden into stone, and incrust the original retainers.

[666] Here from the trees the gum.—Benzoin, a species of frankincense. The oil mentioned in the next line, is that called the rock oil, petroleum, a black fetid mineral oil, good for bruises and sprains.

[667] Wide forests there beneath Maldivia's tide.—A sea plant, resembling the palm, grows in great abundance in the bays about the Maldivian islands. The boughs rise to the top of the water, and bear a kind of apple, called the coco of Maldivia, which is esteemed an antidote against poison.

[668] The tread of sainted footstep.—The imprint of a human foot is found on the high mountain, called the Pic of Adam. Legendary tradition says, that Adam, after he was expelled from Paradise, did penance 300 years on this hill, on which he left the print of his footstep. This tale seems to be Jewish, or Mohammedan; for the natives, according to Captain Knox (who was twenty years a captive in Ceylon), pretend the impression was made by the god Budha, when he ascended to heaven, after having, for the salvation of mankind, appeared on the earth. His priests beg charity for the sake of Budha, whose worship they perform among groves of the Bogahah-tree, under which, when on earth, they say he usually sat and taught.

[669] And lo, the Island of the Moon.—Madagascar is thus named by the natives.

[670] The kingfishers.

[671] Now to the West, by thee, great chief, is given.—The sublimity of this eulogy on the expedition of the Lusiad has been already observed. What follows is a natural completion of the whole; and, the

digressive exclamation at the end excepted, is exactly similar to the manner in which Homer has concluded the Iliad.

[672] Near either pole.—We are now presented with a beautiful view of the American world. Columbus discovered the West Indies before, but not the continent till 1498—the year after GAMA sailed from Lisbon.

[673] The first bold hero.—Cabral, the first after GAMA who sailed to India, was driven by tempest to the Brazils, a proof that more ancient voyagers might have met with the same fate. He named the country Santa Cruz, or Holy Cross; it was afterwards named Brazil, from the colour of the wood with which it abounds. It is one of the finest countries in the new world.

[674] To match thy deeds shall Magalhaens aspire.—Camoëns, though he boasts of the actions of Magalhaens as an honour to Portugal, yet condemns his defection to the King of Spain, and calls him—

O Magalhaens, no feito com verdade
Portuguez, porèm naó na lealdade.

"In deeds truly a Portuguese, but not in loyalty." And others have bestowed upon him the name of traitor, but perhaps undeservedly. Justice to the name of this great man requires an examination of the charge. Ere he entered into the service of the King of Spain by a solemn act, he unnaturalized himself. Osorius is very severe against this unavailing rite, and argues that no injury which a prince may possibly give, can authorize a subject to act the part of a traitor against his native country. This is certainly true, but it is not strictly applicable to the case of Magalhaens. Many eminent services performed in Africa and India entitled him to a certain allowance, which, though inconsiderable in itself, was esteemed as the reward of distinguished merit, and therefore highly valued. For this Magalhaens petitioned in vain. He found, says Faria, that the malicious accusations of some men had more weight with his sovereign than all his services. After this unworthy repulse, what patronage at the Court of Lisbon could he hope? And though no injury can vindicate the man who draws his sword against his native country, yet no moral duty requires that he who has some important discovery in meditation should stifle his design, if uncountenanced by his native prince. It has been alleged, that he embroiled his country in disputes with Spain. But neither is this strictly applicable to the neglected Magalhaens. The courts of Spain and Portugal had solemnly settled the limits within which they were to make discoveries and settlements, and within these did Magalhaens and the court of Spain propose that his discoveries should terminate. And allowing that his calculations might mislead him beyond the bounds prescribed to the Spaniards, still his apology is clear, for it would have been injurious to each court, had he supposed that the faith of the boundary treaty would be trampled upon by either power. If it is said that he aggrandized the enemies of his country, the Spaniards, and introduced them to a dangerous rivalship with the Portuguese settlements; let the sentence of Faria on this subject be remembered: "Let princes beware," says he, "how by neglect or injustice they force into desperate actions the men who have merited rewards."

In the end of the 15th and beginning of the 16th centuries, the spirit of discovery broke forth in its greatest vigour. The East and the West had been visited by GAMA and Columbus; and the bold idea of sailing to the East by the West was revived by Magalhaens. Revived, for misled by Strabo and Pliny, who place India near to the west of Spain, Columbus expecting to find the India of the ancients when he landed on Hispaniola, thought he had discovered the Ophir of Solomon. And hence the name of Indies was given to that and the neighbouring islands. Though America and the Moluccas were now found to be at a great distance, the genius of Magalhaens still suggested the possibility of a western passage. And accordingly, possessed of his great design, and neglected with contempt at home, he offered his service to the court of Spain, and was accepted. With five ships and 250 men he sailed from Spain in September, 1519, and after many difficulties, occasioned by mutiny and the extreme cold, he entered the great Pacific Ocean or South Seas by those straits which bear his Spanish name Magellan. From these straits, in the 52-1/2 degree of southern latitude, he traversed that great ocean, till in the 10th degree of north latitude he landed on the island of Subo or Marten. The king of this country was then at war with a neighbouring prince, and Magalhaens, on condition of his conversion to Christianity, became his auxiliary. In two battles the Spaniards were victorious, but in the third, Magalhaens, together with one Martinho, a judicial astrologer, whom he usually consulted, was unfortunately killed. Chagrined with the disappointment of promised victory, the new baptised king of Subo made peace with his enemies, and having invited to an entertainment the Spaniards on shore, he treacherously poisoned them all. The wretched remains of the fleet arrived at the Portuguese settlements in the isles of Banda and Ternate, where they were received, says Faria, as friends, and not as intruding strangers; a proof that the boundary treaty was esteemed sufficiently sacred. Several of the adventurers were sent to India, and from thence to Spain, in Portuguese ships, one ship only being in a condition to return to Europe by the Cape of Good Hope. This vessel, named the Victoria, however, had the honour to be the first which ever surrounded the globe; an honour by some ignorantly attributed to the ship of Sir Francis Drake. Thus unhappily ended, says Osorius, the expedition of Magalhaens. But the good bishop was mistaken, for a few years after he wrote, and somewhat upwards of fifty after the return of the Victoria, Philip II. of Spain availed himself of the discoveries of Magalhaens. And the navigation of the South Seas between Spanish America and the Asian Archipelago, at this day forms the basis of the power of Spain: a basis, however, which is at the mercy of Great Britain, while her ministers are wise enough to preserve her great naval superiority. A Gibraltar in the South Seas is only wanting. But when this is mentioned, who can withhold his eyes from the isthmus of Darien—the rendezvous appointed by nature for the fleets which may one day give law to the Pacific and Atlantic Oceans: a settlement which to-day might have owned subjection to Great Britain, if justice and honour had always presided in the cabinet of William the Third?

[675] A land of giants.—The Patagonians. Various are the fables of navigators concerning these people. The Spaniards who went with Magalhaens affirmed they were about ten feet in height, since which voyage they have risen and fallen in their stature, according to the different humours of our sea wits.

[676] The goddess spake.—We are now come to the conclusion of the fiction of the island of Venus, a fiction which is divided into three principal parts. In each of these the poetical merit is obvious, nor need we fear to assert, that the happiness of our author, in uniting all these parts together in one great episode, would have excited the admiration of Longinus. The heroes of the Lusiad receive their reward in the Island of Love. They are led to the palace of Thetis, where, during a divine feast, they hear the glorious victories and conquests of the heroes who are to succeed them in their Indian expedition, sung by a siren; and the face of the globe itself, described by the goddess, discovers the universe, and particularly the extent of the eastern world, now given to Europe by the success of GAMA. Neither in grandeur, nor in happiness of completion, may the Æneid or Odyssey be mentioned in comparison. The Iliad alone, in epic conduct (as already observed) bears a strong resemblance. But however great in other views of poetical merit, the games at the funeral of Patroclus, and the redemption of the body of Hector, considered as the interesting conclusion of a great whole, can never in propriety and grandeur be brought into competition with the admirable episode which concludes the poem on the discovery of India.

Soon after the appearance of the Lusiad, the language of Spain was also enriched with an heroic poem, the author of which has often imitated the Portuguese poet, particularly in the fiction of the globe of the world, which is shown to GAMA. In the Araucana, a globe, surrounded with a radiant sphere, is also miraculously supported in the air; and on this an enchanter shows to the Spaniards the extent of their dominions in the new world. But Don Alonzo d'Arcilla is in this, as in every other part of his poem, greatly inferior to the poetical spirit of Camoëns. Milton, whose poetical conduct in concluding the action of his Paradise Lost, as already pointed out, seems formed upon the Lusiad, appears to have had this passage particularly in his eye. For, though the machinery of a visionary sphere was rather improper for the situation of his personages, he has, nevertheless, though at the expense of an impossible supposition, given Adam a view of the terrestrial globe. Michael sets the father of mankind on a mountain—

"From whose top
The hemisphere of earth in clearest ken
Stretch'd out to th' amplest reach of prospect lay....
His eye might there command wherever stood
City of old or modern fame, the seat
Of mightiest empire, from the destin'd walls
Of Cambalu ...
On Europe thence and where Rome was to sway
The world."

And even the mention of America seems copied by Milton:—

"In spirit perhaps he also saw
Rich Mexico, the seat of Montezume,
And Cusco in Peru, the richer seat
Of Atabalipa, and yet unspoil'd
Guiana, whose great city Geryon's sons
Call El Dorado."

It must also be owned by the warmest admirer of the Paradise Lost, that the description of America in Camoëns—

"Vedes a grande terra, que contina
Vai de Calisto ao sen contrario polo—

To farthest north that world enormous bends,
And cold beneath the southern pole-star ends,"

conveys a bolder and a grander idea than all the names enumerated by Milton.

Some short account of the writers whose authorities have been adduced in the course of these notes may not now be improper. Fernando Lopez de Castagneda went to India on purpose to do honour to his countrymen, by enabling himself to record their actions and conquests in the East. As he was one of the first writers on that subject, his geography is often imperfect. This defect is remedied in the writings of John de Barros, who was particularly attentive to this head. But the two most eminent, as well as fullest, writers on the transaction of the Portuguese in the East, are Manuel de Faria y Sousa, knight of the

Order of Christ, and Hieronimus Osorius, bishop of Sylves. Faria, who wrote in Spanish, was a laborious inquirer, and is very full and circumstantial. With honest indignation he rebukes the rapine of commanders and the errors and unworthy resentments of kings. But he is often so drily particular, that he may rather be called a journalist than an historian. And by this uninteresting minuteness, his style, for the greatest part, is rendered inelegant. The Bishop of Sylves, however, claims a different character. His Latin is elegant, and his manly and sentimental manner entitles him to the name of historian, even where a Livy or a Tacitus are mentioned. But a sentence from himself, unexpected in a father of the communion of Rome, will characterize the liberality of his mind. Talking of the edict of King Emmanuel, which compelled the Jews to embrace Christianity under severe persecution: "Nec ex lege, nec ex religione factum ... tibi assumas," says he, "ut libertatem voluntatis impedias, et vincula mentibus effrenatis injicias? At id neque fleri potest, neque Christi sanctissimum numen approbat. Voluntarium enim sacrificium non vi malo coactum ab hominibus expetit: neque vim mentibus inferri, sed voluntates ad studium veræ religionis allici et invitari jubet."

It is said, in the preface to Osorius, that his writings were highly esteemed by Queen Mary of England, wife of Philip II. What a pity is it, that this manly indignation of the good bishop against the impiety of religious persecution, made no impression on the mind of that bigoted princess!

[677] *And the wide East is doom'd to Lusian sway.*—Thus, in all the force of ancient simplicity, and the true sublime, ends the poem of Camoëns. What follows is one of those exuberances we have already endeavoured to defend in our author, nor in the strictest sense is this concluding one without propriety. A part of the proposition of the poem is artfully addressed to King Sebastian, and he is now called upon in an address (which is an artful second part to the former), to behold and preserve the glories of his throne.

[678] *And John's bold path and Pedro's course pursue.*—John I. and Pedro the Just, two of the greatest of the Portuguese monarchs.

[679] *Reviv'd, unenvied.*—Thus imitated, or rather translated into Italian by Guarini:—

"Con si sublime stil' forse cantato
Havrei del mio Signor l'armi e l'honori,
Ch' or non havria de la Meonia tromba
Da invidiar Achille."

Similarity of condition, we have already observed, produced similarity of complaint and sentiment in Spenser and Camoëns. Each was unworthily neglected by the grandees of his age, yet both their names will live, when the remembrance of the courtiers who spurned them shall sink beneath their mountain tombs. These beautiful stanzas from Phinehas Fletcher on the memory of Spenser, may also serve as an epitaph for Camoëns. The unworthy neglect, which was the lot of the Portuguese bard, but too well appropriates to him the elegy of Spenser. And every reader of taste, who has perused the Lusiad, will think of the Cardinal Henrico, and feel the indignation of these manly lines:—

"Witness our Colin{*}, whom tho' all the Graces
And all the Muses nurst; whose well-taught song
Parnassus' self and Glorian{**} embraces,
And all the learn'd and all the shepherds throng;
Yet all his hopes were crost, all suits denied;

Discouraged, scorn'd, his writings vilified:
Poorly (poor man) he liv'd; poorly (poor man) he died.

"And had not that great hart (whose honoured head{***}
All lies full low) pitied thy woful plight,
There hadst thou lien unwept, unburied,
Unblest, nor graced with any common rite;
Yet shalt thou live, when thy great foe{****} shall sink
Beneath his mountain tombe, whose fame shall stink;
And time his blacker name shall blurre with blackest ink."

{} Colin Clout, Spenser.*

*{**} Glorian, Elizabeth in the Faerie Queen.*

*{***} The Earl of Essex.*

*{****} Lord Burleigh.*

[680] Achilles, son of Peleus.